Strategic Supply Management

The Chartered Institute of Purchasing and Supply is the centre of excellence in all matters relating to procurement and supply chain management. It is the central reference point worldwide for this significant management process – a process with an annual 'spend' in excess of £750bn in the UK alone.

The Chartered Institute's range of services reflects the professional requirements of individuals and their employers – public or private, large or small.

For a free information pack please contact:

The Chartered Institute of Purchasing and Supply
Easton House
Easton on the Hill
Stamford
Lincolnshire
PE9 3NZ

Tel: 01780 56777
Fax: 01780 51610

Strategic Supply Management

An implementation toolkit

Tom Chadwick and Shan Rajagopal

Butterworth-Heinemann
Linacre House, Jordan Hill, Oxford OX2 8DP
225 Wildwood Avenue, Woburn, MA 01801-2041
A division of Reed Educational and Professional Publishing Ltd

-R A member of the Reed Elsevier plc group

OXFORD   BOSTON   JOHANNESBURG
MELBOURNE   NEW DELHI   SINGAPORE

First published 1995
Paperback edition 1998

© Tom Chadwick and Shan Rajagopal 1995

British Library Cataloguing in Publication Data
Chadwick, Tom
    Strategic Supply Management:
    An Implementation Toolkit
    I. Title II. Rajagopal, Shan
    658.7

ISBN 0 7506 3680 7

Printed and bound in Great Britain by
MPG Books Ltd, Bodmin, Cornwall

Contents

Preface

One of the most interesting aspects of a career in supply management is the very large number of personal contacts made throughout the world, and across a wide range of industries. These are the people who with enthusiasm and commitment make the business world go round, and make purchasing and supply so full of opportunity, challenge and fun, and not the dreary, boring and frustrating life it could so easily be.

All the ideas in this book have either come from these enthusiastic people, or have certainly been modified and developed with the help of their input. Hopefully none of the boring and frustrating aspects have come through. This is designed to be a very practical book, a toolkit of ideas and techniques for strategic supply management that is straightforward to apply. Toolkits are all very well in their own right, but they don't really come into their own until someone takes them out and starts to use the tools with care, but most of all with enthusiasm.

The toolkit is designed to help you to contribute much more to your organization by developing the supply management function to play the major role necessary to work towards future success. Used in its entirety, it can assist in stimulating strategic change throughout all types of organization. Used individually, there are tools for all men and women working away diligently in purchasing tasks, and contributing by their good performance to the advancement of the supply management function.

Supply management provides the almost unique opportunity to look at supplier organizations as a whole in the process of external resource management. As closer relationships develop, they provide the fascinating prospect of a mirror in which a rare image of our own organization appears.

Speaking at the dinner of the first UK conference of the Purchasing and Supply Education and Research Group in 1992, Professor David Farmer concluded a speech which spawned around a dozen suggestions for purchasing and supply research, with the words:

> Finally, one thing I have always tried to keep in mind, that is that nobody is in business simply to buy things. We buy things to add value to them in some way and then to sell. Thus effective purchasing is, as it were, an 'enabler' for effective marketing. Indeed I would argue that many Western companies which were seemingly effective in marketing their products, failed because their purchasing was not good enough to give

their products competitive advantage in their end markets. However, as I am sure everyone here will agree, the marketing–production–purchasing relationship is not simply linear, it is iterative. Further, purchasing can provide the source of marketing advantage, as well as identifying benefits for production.

Tom Chadwick
Shan Rajagopal

Part One

The Need for Revolutionary Change

1 The increasing importance of strategic supply management

Introduction

The supply management function is at last emerging from the doldrums. For so long it has suffered as the poor, unglamorous relation to sales and marketing. Considering the fact that strategy and strategic planning are by definition concepts related to the external environment of the organization, it seems mysterious that the supply side has been so neglected while the marketing side has gained so much attention.

In fact not only has marketing been so thoroughly studied, researched and written about relative to supplies, but complete subspecialities have developed like market research, consumer behaviour, advertising, merchandising and sales management to name only a few. While this development of specialized and sophisticated planning techniques for the output side has been going on, so little has been considered concerning the input side. The accepted standard texts on strategy and planning, Ackoff (1970), Hofer and Schendell (1978), Higgins (1980), Hussey (1982), Jauch and Glueck (1988), Wheelen and Hunger (1989), give very brief, if any, mention of procurement strategy. Reasons for this major omission have been postulated by Farmer (1974), Aggarwal (1982) and Doyle (1989) as among the following:

- Following the Second World War, productivity outstripped demand, resulting in more marketing problems than buying problems.
- Marketing and other disciplines give a more strategic focus versus the perceived tactical focus of purchasing.
- Purchasing has been an isolated function in the organization, consequently not attracting much attention.

Purchasing does not appear to have the glamour associated with marketing. Purchasing personnel have been passive due to the fact that they haven't controlled many of the strategic decisions (or perhaps didn't realize they did). Many purchasing decisions include judgmental considerations, making them resistant to the creation of quantitative decision models.

In addition, a study of multinational firms by Adamson in 1980 yielded the following arguments for not including procurement in long-range planning:

- Marketing and finance are tough enough to include; firms shouldn't make it more difficult by including supply factors.
- Most purchasing activities involve frequent short-term problems making long-range planning ineffective.
- Supply matters are rarely strategic, and therefore don't require top quality managers, decision techniques or long-range planning.

These myopic opinions were reported by top management in the same survey that reported problems. Despite the lack of attention that has been given to materials supply in the literature, there are important features of procurement that have all the elements requiring strategic consideration. Risk is involved. The organization's external environment is being considered. Opportunities exist and an important proportion of resources is being expended. Accordingly it seems logical to assume that there should be as many purchasing strategies as marketing strategies, for buying is in a sense the mirror image of selling. Strategic supply management is a vital component in the corporate planning process. All the requirements, such as environmental scanning, strategy formulation, strategy implementation and evaluation cited in the standard texts, are present in purchasing. In more recent publications, Michael Porter, the 'competitive strategy guru', considers the element of strategic purchasing as a vital component in the corporate planning process aimed at gaining competitive advantage. Slowly but surely the importance of strategic supply management is coming out of its closet.

Purchasing personnel, for a long time relegated to positions of paper pushers, are gaining the chance to become strategic supply managers. Companies are starting to move purchasing managers to the executive suite and increasingly they are reaching director and vice-president level. Supply management is at last beginning to gain the respect that it deserves.

The need for a toolkit

While many firms have yet to include the supply management function in their strategy, others are increasingly becoming converts to the new religion of sophisticated procurement policy. Business education has for so long been limited in relation to purchasing and supply, that the need is now urgent for sound practical texts that can satisfy both practitioners and academics alike. Globalization, developments in technology, shortened product life cycles and process advances are altering the way in which organizations compete. The ability to be strategically oriented, remaining focused on long-term objectives while being flexible enough to react quickly to these rapidly changing environmental forces, has become a key to corporate success (Hamel and Prahaled 1989). This strategic focus has necessitated major shifts in the traditional modes of operation of both organizations and the purchasing functions within them (Wriston 1990). Only purchasing departments that provide a value added service will be maintained (Kanter 1989a).

New flexible organizational forms are evolving, with increasingly blurred functional and corporate boundaries. Network organizations are becoming commonplace. Priority now lies in identifying the most efficient methods for supplying services and obtaining desired objectives (Miles 1989). Some of the results have been the purchasing from outside of services formerly provided within the firm, the development of joint ventures and partnerships, and improved collaboration between customers and suppliers at all levels of the organization (Kanter 1989b, Peters 1988, Wriston 1990). All these changes are altering the expectations of the supply management function. Global sourcing is becoming a necessity in many sectors of business in order to remain cost, price, and quality competitive. Shortened product development cycles have made purchasing participation necessary in the design team. Innovations in the marketplace and technological product advances have increased the degree of outsourcing being performed to secure the objective of enhanced value. The introduction of quality programmes and just-in-time philosophies have enlarged the scope of purchasing with added responsibility for supply chain management, inventory control, and evaluation as well as selection of supply sources. As organizations potentially become suppliers, customers and competitors at the same time, the need for relationship management has become very important. Cost containment has become a strategic tool for both procurement efficiency and marketing effectiveness.

There is a need for empowerment change within the supply management function. The toolkit is necessary to construct the framework of interacting forces which promote change in the purchasing orientation, in order to improve the performance of the whole business. The toolkit works by aligning the supply function in strategic orientation to improve the business's competitive position in the marketplace.

The need for empowerment to create changes

'We need to change. We're in trouble. Business as usual is out' claimed James Belasco in 1990. He argued that many companies are hide-bound by earlier conditional constraints and successes. 'We've always done it this way' imposes a limit on an organization's progress especially in circumstances of rapid environmental change.

Several well known companies can be cited as examples of having become prisoners of their own success. Two examples are Xerox (*Business Week* February 1986) and still more dramatically IBM (Carroll 1993). In both instances the companies spent lavishly on research and development, had proficient marketing organizations and dominated their markets, to the point where they appeared to refuse to take new competitors as serious threats, until they had actually lost significant market share.

Another example is Courtaulds, the £3 billion plus UK textile manufacturer. When Sir Christopher Hogg arrived in 1980, the outlook was extremely poor for both Courtaulds and the rest of the UK textile business. Managers were trapped in a vicious circle of poor results and management which became even more conservative, leading directly on to even poorer results. Hogg realized that he had to break the mould. He reorganized the company into six business sectors. He insisted on meeting or beating the standards set by the best world class competitors. Those operations that did not meet the test were closed or sold, a thing hitherto unheard of in the UK textile business. Since 1982, Courtaulds' pre-tax profit rose an average of 37 per cent per year (Kirkland 1988).

Previous success and past practices have tended to root American and European companies firmly in old habits. It has gradually become recognized that the old way of doing business will not necessarily succeed in the future. Markets continually change. Customers continually change. Technology continually changes. Competitors continually change. Each change triggers the need to create flexibility to meet future challenges.

Leaders at any level in the organization should identify this need and move quickly to develop a new strategic approach. This new strategic approach can contain three elements, according to Belasco (1990), the management of which can help an organization to determine the 'right' new directions:

1 Repositioned products and services to build a competitive advantage;
2 Talented people to execute the new strategies;
3 Organizational resources that tightly focus on the new strategies.

Handsome and Norman in 1989 identified significant marketing developments which have taken place and which are taking place that highlight the need to form strategic relationships and understandings with both key customers and key suppliers. These major developments enforce change in the ways that companies do business:

- The shortening of product life cycles, coupled with a significant specification upgrading, mean that change in product design can only be harnessed by close strategic relations between customer and supplier.
- The global development of marketing key product areas in which only the best international products are winners.
- A focus on the total quality of the product or service as a key international marketing priority. Here Japan has understood this problem from the point of view of the product but, it is suggested, can in the longer-term only remain successful by strategic integration of priorities and objectives with suppliers, as well as focusing on customers' needs.
- The increasing number of strategically minded customers who are looking for strategic relationships with suppliers who have the desire and the capability to match their strategic interactions.
- Dealing with the competitive pressures of over-capacity in Western industry. The UK and USA had to face these problems in the 1980s, but the emergence of the single European market in 1992, and continued global recession ensured that this issue extended throughout Europe in the 1990s. Only the best prepared and co-ordinated businesses will survive to prosper from this rationalization. Close strategic relationships between customer and supplier will be crucial to both parties.
- The emergence of new trade blocks represents a challenge to many industries with global consciousness.

Drucker in 1992 identified five important areas which he believes will bring far-reaching changes in the social and economic environment, and in the strategies and management of business. These are:

1 International economic integration and reciprocity (economic relations);
2 Alliances (customer and supplier partnerships);
3 Radical restructure of corporate organizations (reshaping companies);
4 Governance of companies (challenge to management);
5 Rapid changes (international politics and policies).

Change can be implemented or enforced by various means. Interactions between internal forces which are notionally controllable, and external forces which may be much less controllable, play major roles in the evolution of competitive industry as well as of individual purchasing scenarios (Hakansson 1983). Standing between customer and supplier marketplaces, individual firms have to recognize and manage the complex inter-relationships simultaneously in both environments, if they are to develop optimal strategies for short- and long-run benefits. As supply management develops into a recognizably strategic function, it becomes increasingly capable of contributing proactively to improvement in company performance. Thus supply market forces and management can act as catalysts for the purchasing function to change in order to gain and exploit competitive advantage.

The role of supply market forces in the creation of strategic purchasing orientations

The influence of supply markets on many aspects of change in today's commercial environment necessitates careful consideration by planners. No organization is an island, and to achieve change we need to pay close attention to planned developments with key sources. The corporate problems faced by Rolls-Royce as the result of its involvement in the development of new technology engines for the Lockheed L1011 aircraft illustrates the interrelationships of change patterns in technological industries. Similar patterns may be observed in many other situations. The external competitive strength of a company may be considerably affected by its relationships with its supply sources and their technological capability, research and development activities, and financial management. Thus, in attempting to analyse a company's performance we should also consider its strengths in establishing and developing external relationships. These relationships may well have considerable bearing on future product direction and mix. For example ICI and Courtaulds man-made fibre developments were key factors in the planning of many clothing and carpet manufacturers in the UK in the early 1960s. Chemicals developed by Shell had a similar effect on plastic bottle manufacturers at about the same time (Farmer 1972).

In their current planning, car manufacturers must take note of potential developments by outside sources regarding for instance, the questions of electric battery developments. Oil companies must consider their source planning in a different light as activities among the Gulf States develop.

A study by Farmer in 1970 in the construction industry indicated that the product mix and basic policy of a company was at least partially changed as a result of external stimulus from its raw material supply market. Many companies have to react to these changes rather than plan to take advantage of the new circumstances, yet in retrospect, there were many economic pointers in the supply market which would have suggested that changes were developing. Effective supply data generated as part of the company's corporate plan would have proved extremely beneficial. Increasingly aggressive global and domestic competition and improved mass communications are key forces which promote the need for reduced product development time. The strategic implications of compressing time are clearly significant, and it becomes readily apparent that speed to market creates opportunities in market share, market leadership and profits. For example, as Fortune reported in 1990: 'By introducing six all-new vehicles within 14 months, Toyota has captured a crushing 43 per cent share of car sales in Japan. In the 1990 model year, it sold more than one million cars and trucks in the US for the first time – strengthening its position as number four to the hard pressed Big Three'. A study by Clark in 1987, indicated that the Japanese could, on average, complete a new car development project about 18 months faster than either their US or Western European competitors, with a cost of about half a billion dollars in lost profits to the lagging firms. According to a McKinsey study, a product that was six months late to market would miss out on one third of the potential profit over the product's lifetime. (Schonberger 1986) These are only a few examples of many that point out a clear set of economic and operational reasons to reduce the time to market part of the cycle. In 1992, Mendez and Pearson identified clearly that in a well structured organization a multi-discipline team can reduce the time to market and at the same time increase a product's adaptability. They state that purchasing personnel should be primarily responsible for providing advice on availability of materials and components, quality and costs. The feasibility of outsourcing by the development of strategic alliances or partnerships should be considered where potential exists to increase service or to reduce cost and risk.

A framework of supply market forces affecting a change in purchasing orientation to improve performance

The world market is progressively becoming more challenging for marketers, producers and their suppliers with increased availability of world class, high quality products at costs which are low in both relative and absolute terms. With purchased content accounting in many organizations, of up to 70 per cent and more of the total cost of manufactured goods, the strategic significance of the supply management function has become recognized as a major determinant both of competitiveness in the market, and corporate profitability (Baily and Farmer 1990, Rajagopal and Bernard 1992, 1993). Supply managers must therefore be proactive in the conduct of their activities in order not just to make supplier choices, but to ensure that the best available solutions are sought in the first instance.

A framework can be developed to demonstrate the interaction of forces which can give rise to the necessary changes in supply management orientation. The framework reflects changes in the environment and in the purchasing function itself, in the need for improved performance to sustain the overall competitive advantage of the firm through optimized costs, improved quality, rapidity of response to market demands and opportunities, and technological superiority.

The framework was developed from a forced collision between models proposed by Farmer in 1972, Knox and Denison in 1989, and Burt and Doyle in 1991. It may not be all inclusive and does not purport to be managerially prescriptive, but it attempts to isolate the interacting forces which can promote the emergence of a strategic approach to purchasing. The linkages can then be analysed to see how their operation and interactions can give rise to a change in focus of the strategies available.

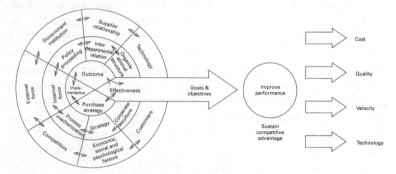

Figure 1.1 *A framework of supply market forces affecting purchasing's performance*

Figure 1.1 depicts the forces in the form of two concentric circles revolving around a conventional decision making model. The output is a set of goals and objectives, expressed in terms identified by Burt and Doyle (1991) as comprising the principal competitive drivers open to direct influence by the procurement function: cost, quality, velocity or time to market, and technology of product and process.

The outer ring depicts what are perceived as the principal external forces which influence the determination of procurement objectives, and thus impinge upon the strategies which may be adopted. Several of these external factors have been subject to change in recent years, and their impact on procurement operations has been consequently reappraised. The inner core depicts the managerial functions of strategy derivation, implementation and control of outcomes. These outcomes depend on the interactions between the external environmental factors and the intra-corporate structures and processes which may act as barriers or facilitators to the conduct of an effective procurement strategy.

Between the outer ring and the inner operational core, lies the middle range of internal forces operating on the conduct of the purchasing process. Once again it is possible to identify changes in practice and emphasis which have arisen as the competitive environment has altered the established position. Ways can be postulated in which strategically planned and implemented change can permit and facilitate the attainment of competitive edge by improving purchasing effectiveness.

Analytically the elements identified in the three rings may be seen as similar to the structural factors and process forces postulated by Knox and Denison in 1989 in the context of intra-corporate transfers of technology. Knox and Denison suggested the depiction of the transfer and adoption of new technologies in a matrix format in which structural elements could perhaps be seen as impediments or barriers. Environmental, organizational and human individual elements are set against the change facilitators of information, authority and enthusiasm. The elements in the new model represent an expansion of the ingredients of Knox and Denison, illustrating not only that change processes are complex, but also that the recipes for effective change are flexible combinations which despite having common foundations are capable of being highly individualized.

The external force elements can be identified and summarized as follows:

- *Governments and institutions:* Government actions and interventions play major roles in the operation of most major national economies. In the purchasing area the government may attempt to enact social policy through public sector procurement legislation.
- *Supplier relationships:* The way in which buyers are beginning to regard their suppliers may represent the biggest change in the purchasing function for a long time. Suppliers are increasingly looked upon as partners rather than adversaries, and purchasing managers as managers of outside manufacturing facilities (Hutt and Spell 1992).

- *Technology:* Changing technology has had an impact on all functions and supply management has certainly not been left out. This is particularly true in the area of information processing where electronic data interchange and decision support systems have changed the way of doing work for many buyers. Developments in manufacturing and process technology and philosophy such as just-in-time and flexible manufacturing systems have also had a major influence on purchasing strategy.
- *Customers:* Organizations are focusing more on the necessity to ensure they satisfy customer needs. This involves purchasing in the integration of customer input to design, production and supply to optimize the deliverable benefits.
- *Competitors:* It is important for purchasing to keep up to date on the movements and developments of competitors. New technological developments or product innovations of competitors must be matched and exceeded if the purchasing firm is to hold its position. Better still, competitive advantage should be sought proactively rather than being perceived as a defensive necessity.
- *Economic, social and psychological environments:* The economic environment refers to the organization's business cycle, inflation, exchange rates and interest rates, all of which affect both ends of the supply market. Social and psychological forces relate to value systems, human attitudes and behavioural patterns. These forces can have a major influence on establishing supplier relationships and upon willingness and ability to forge new alliances or change established patterns.

Within the organization, the forces impinging on purchasing embrace the procedures, structures, strategies and culture which act as the channel between the external environment and the desired actions and outcomes. The main elements are identifiable as follows:

- *Interdepartmental relations:* Changes in management and manufacturing philosophies and customer demands have necessitated closer relations between departments.
- *Organization structure:* As organizations change their structure to adapt to changes in their environment and their strategy, so must the purchasing department change the way in which it is organized.
- *Organization strategy:* When the strategy of the organization changes so must the strategy of the purchasing function, and vice versa.
- *Organization policies and procedures:* As changes occur in both the external and internal environment, so the policies and procedures

that guide behaviour should alter in response to these changes. A good example of this in the purchasing area might be the changing relationship between buyers and sellers towards partnering, which requires mutually beneficial agreements with a smaller number of suppliers. This change should result in a new policy controlling how an organization deals with its suppliers, such as longer term contracts with less reliance on continual competitive bidding.

- *Corporate culture:* Corporate culture has been defined by Baker in 1980 as the 'interrelated set of beliefs, shared by most of an organization's members, about how people should behave at work and what tasks and goals are important'. While an organization's corporate culture can be derived from its development over a long period of time, the current emphasis of top management may also go a long way in determining what things are important or stressed by the organization. A key element in the development of corporate culture may be the backgrounds of key executives in the organization. The task for the supply manager in changing purchasing's role from one which focuses on tactics to one which emphasizes strategy, entails a clear understanding of the culture of the organization in which he or she works. For example, gearing purchasing's role to a cost reduction strategy with careful monitoring and control may increase the chances of purchasing being viewed as a strategic corporate function.
- *Process mechanism:* This refers to control mechanisms such as resource allocation systems, evaluation, rewards and sanctions. These might include internal staff appraisal, procurement audit or other measures of evaluation of purchasing effectiveness.
- *The managerial functions:* The inner core of the model embraces the overall outcomes of the interactions between external and internal environments, and has four components:

  - purchasing strategy derivation;
  - implementation;
  - resulting outcomes; and
  - controlled, effective contribution to corporate strategy and competitive success.

The successful implementation of a purchasing strategy will be reflected in the outcome. Hence the outcome of an effective purchasing strategy will satisfy the goals and objectives set by the procurement function. This in turn will be compatible with the organization's overall goals and objectives and thus give rise to improved performance and differential advantage. The contribution of effective purchasing strategy to sustained competitive advantage can be achieved through cost, quality, efficiency and breakthroughs in technology, because of the significant influence that suppliers have on these.

Change and challenge to gain opportunity for the future

As discussed in the previous sections, the world is very turbulent. As Gersick (1991) claims, to guide firms through chaos towards renewed competitiveness, managers are increasingly compelled to conceive and execute metamorphic transformation of their organization's strategic posture and internal features. To put this into context for the purchasing function, it becomes essential for supply managers themselves to identify the need to change towards the strategic orientation that will contribute towards their organization's overall competitiveness. Figure 1.2 proposes the change to strategic orientation of purchasing as a set of processes, described by Ginsberg in 1988 in the context of 'mechanical analogy', as 'movements that can result from an imbalance between forces that stimulate or retard change'. However in reality, managers and employees experience these forces subjectively. They often succumb to individual bias that clouds their interpretation of events.

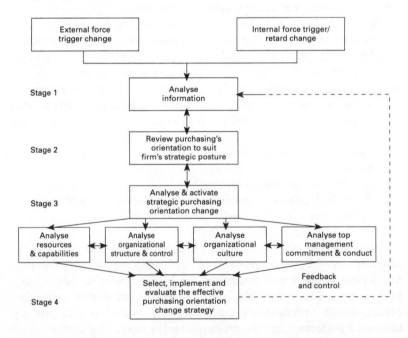

Figure 1.2 *Model for strategic purchasing orientation change strategy*

The strategic directions on which organizations embark depend heavily therefore on how managers think about their environments, about their firm's capabilities, and about themselves. If particular managers select different strategic trajectories when faced with seemingly identical circumstances, they must evidently be interpreting those circumstances differently (Fombrun 1992).

Analytically, the model in Figure 1.2 proposes that strategic purchasing change orientation involves four distinct stages. During Stage 1, supply managers have to make sense of the environmental forces that surround their organizations. They can actively search for information, through their suppliers and other sources, to see how rival forces are changing the prospects for their industry or sector at large. Developing threats and probable outcomes can be speculated upon. But environments are difficult to interpret. Technological changes can hamper as well as facilitate planning. Many questions about environmental impact are difficult to answer primarily because they are cloudy and difficult to read. It is also interesting to note that they often operate in paradoxical, contradictory ways. For instance: efficiency versus innovation; competitiveness versus institutional effectiveness; globalization versus nationalism (Fombrun 1992).

An interesting example is Whirlpool, the world's largest manufacturer of major domestic appliances. In the search for global economies of scale, the US based company acquired the European appliance business of Philips. Yet many uncertainties emerged. There was no certainty that the fragmented European market could be supplied in the long run from centralized manufacturing facilities like those in the USA. Companies have limited brand awareness abroad. Multiple national standards hamper the use of common parts, and patriotic sentiments prevail (*Business Week* 3 June 1991). So seemingly simple changes in environment require considerable interpretation of how economic, social and political forces will or may combine. To conceive a strategic supply management change is a deeply subjective process. Internally, organizational features create a degree of inertia either resistant to, or heavily influencing the direction of change. Astute purchasing managers need to decipher how both external and internal environments are likely to impede the correct reorientation of purchasing strategy.

Stage 2 involves assessing how these internal and external conditions affect an organization's strategic posture. Radically changing environments demand attention to the ways in which organizations compete. For example, changes in technology and globalization of markets tend to increase rivalry and so demand efficiency. To keep up, the managers tend to contemplate changes in business, corporate or collective strategies. Supply managers must review their orientation to suit the change in the organization's strategic posture. In some cases, managers opt for conservative responses. They try to accommodate turbulence by making peripheral modifications that allow their organizations to continue orbiting around the same old historical trajectories. They deny that the system is broken, so they just don't try to fix it.

In some vanguard organizations, however, supply managers accept that their internal systems are indeed beyond repair and require a complete overhaul. So they call for strategic change. Strategic change modifies both the speed and path of the organization's trajectory through time and space. It involves a redeployment of the organization's resources to a new configuration, and entails the rebuilding of corporate momentum in a new direction (Griener and Bhambri 1989). There are three types of key strategic changes: Business level changes in the organization's competitive position; corporate level changes; collective level changes in the organization's external posture towards regulators and competitors. The three modes of strategic change are also achievable through a change in the orientation of the supply management function. At the business level the objective is to increase competitive advantage. Many firms seek to improve their competitive position by investing aggressively in the development of a more differentiated market presence. Some firms throw money behind the idea that they can improve their ability to compete through new product introductions. Others try to differentiate their products and services by cutting costs or improving product quality. A further approach is to target products and services more carefully at narrower market segments.

From a supply management perspective, business level strategic change will put pressure on purchasing managers to think like executive management. They will have to examine what their companies are producing and ask: 'What do we need, by product, to become more competitive in generating more return on investment, more profit, more market share and more volume?' They have to consider how suppliers can contribute better to gain mutual competitive advantage in terms of quality, cost, delivery, technology, cycle time, responsiveness, as well as materials management factors of transportation and inventory. It is important for supply management's focus to be on optimizing the use of information to gain a competitive advantage from the supplier. It can create business level strategic net changes by collection, analysis and application of information relevant to a business situation. For example, purchasing will have to determine the cost of producing a product, understand the costs involved in producing the product at their suppliers, and comprehend what can be done to change the product cost structure, especially driving out non-value-added cost. Further, supply management as a function needs to provide for integration across other functions and also work with suppliers to provide a window on the commercial supply base in order to gain a source of differential advantage (Monczka 1989).

In corporate level strategy, firms aim to extend their core capability. This can be observed where some firms have rapidly divested assets to reduce their firm's exposure to environmental forces. This change has been predominant in successful corporations in Europe who have pursued a strategy of cutting back marginal and unrelated business areas in order to concentrate more effectively on the core business. Ernest Saunders excised the 'nightmare jungle' of the 280 businesses within the Guinness Group to concentrate on the core business of brewing (Weir 1992). Another more dramatic example is Honeywell, which since 1986 has systematically sold off its computer, semiconductor, and defence businesses and has made acquisitions designed to consolidate its operations around its original business in automated controls. The restructuring has enabled increased global co-ordination of parts purchasing, marketing and distribution, giving it a strategic edge (*Business Week* 3 June 1991).

Since the mid 1980s there has been a pronounced evolution within core business strategy. The threat from Japan has obviously been highly significant in this evolution. Large companies which are able to pursue efficiencies of scale have had to adjust their perception of production realities by adding quality to low cost as competitive weapons. Introduction of new production technologies has permitted successful manufacturers to add flexibility to efficiency and quality. Although there are many different ways and correspondingly diverse technological underpinnings to this process, the route to success lies in driving costs down, being able to guarantee predictable high quality to the consumer, out-pacing competition by speed of adjustment to changing customer requirements flexible low cost quality production.

Earlier writers have identified the crucial change in the philosophy of manufacturing planning as being a recognition that quality and quality assurance are not costs of production, but investments in the improvement of production. This internally driven change has been matched by a change in the nature of the product market particularly for products such as colour television, video recorders, cameras and even cars. Emphasis on internal efficiencies, rigorous attention to quality, continuous product updating and the commercial imperative to stay close to the customer have combined to reinforce the pressure on companies to attend to their core business above all else. This has led to a vast increase in out-sourcing. The major contribution of supply management to core business strategy will come in the form of being able to be a key participant in analysis, evaluation, development and management of the supply base and over time being able to establish some distinctive competency in that supply base over and above the competition. Corporate level strategy change will focus on purchasing to develop distinctive core competency in their supply base to gain competitive advantage in their end market.

Collective level strategy focuses on the need to broaden networks of alliances. The strategy at the collective level involves developing network partners. Strategic alliances with rivals have proved increasingly vital to firms striving to maintain their competitiveness in industries such as telecommunications and financial services sectors bombarded by burst of technological innovation and deregulation. The agreement between Apple and IBM to share technology shocked the computer world (*Business Week* 22 July 1991). It also highlighted the power of joint ventures and partnership as a vehicle for improving firms' competitive postures without taxing scarce resources, and showed how increasingly competition is no longer simply between individual firms, but between networks of firms. Monczka (1989) identified that firms who plot long-term competitive strategies expect to be moving farther and farther upstream in responding to customer demands for quality and low cost and also expect to utilize new technology faster. This requires that waste be driven out early in the design process and elimination of non-value added cost in manufacturing. The result is more value engineering at the design stage. To achieve greater awareness of value benefits between firms, formation of strategic alliances is growing in importance in strategic thinking as companies reach further into the 1990s. Such alliances take a number of forms including joint ventures, technology sharing agreements with supply firms, use of distribution channels on a shared basis, and a wide range of partnering agreements with prime suppliers.

Stage 3 analyses and dissects the crucial roles in activating strategic supply management orientation change. Planning a change is not enough: much is required to get there. It is suggested that strategic supply management orientation change requires a new mind set, a new way of organizing. Resistance to change results because history and lack of market appreciation constrain the conduct of firms and institutions. To carry out change entails coming to grips with the emotional implications of living through revolutionary circumstances. Transformations that disrupt the established order invariably create uncertainty and threaten vested interests, and so may generate panic. Coping with the personal sentiments of employees is therefore one of the key challenges facing managers attempting to effect strategic change. To reinvent their firms, managers need to understand, identify, analyse and manipulate four key internal features:

- resources and capabilities;
- organizational structure and control;
- organizational culture;
- top management commitment and conduct.

In analysing resources and capabilities, managers need to know whether resources can be reallocated in ways that enhanced firms' competitive capabilities. In understanding organizational structure and control, it is fundamental for managers to know the underlying structural controls needed to support the new strategic direction. When analysing organizational culture, careful attention must be paid to the implications of the strategic change for the firm's internal culture. Finally, in analysing top management commitment and conduct, it is important to know whether the top managers show visionary leadership and an ability to mobilize employees as they seek to redefine their firm's strategic conduct. These four internal features tend to have an interactive link which is depicted in Figure 1.3. The essence of the link is enhanced by top management commitment.

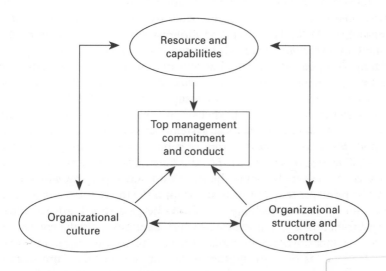

Figure 1.3 *Interactive links in activating strategic orientation change*

In analysing resources and capabilities, organizations th[...] involve themselves in reallocating resources to projects mo[...] assist in coping with changing environments. Managers in[...] by purchasing equipment and hiring employees. The basi[...]

ties even of large companies like Exxon or Ford are built up from their core technological and human skills; the factories, offices, and laboratories they own; their capital equipment base; the skills of their labour force; and their strengths in research communication, transportation, purchasing and distribution. In so far as firms' resources and capabilities provide them with an advantage in the marketplace, potential for improved performance exists. From a purchasing perspective, it is logical to suggest that the procurement function should develop its own capabilities before it can become a competitive weapon in the battle for markets. Supply managers need to understand the essential components of the chosen competitive strategy and set their orientation priorities accordingly. As the supply management function gains expertise and experience, focusing on decision areas such as suppliers, personnel, and information, it can then begin to make positive contributions toward improving the firm's competitive effectiveness. Over time, the purchasing function can thus become an integral part of the firm's competitive success. Company managers and supply managers must surmount many obstacles based on traditions, attitudes, and outdated behaviour patterns in order to reorientate the function at a strategic level.

To realize this potential and to capitalize on their firms' capabilities, managers will frequently need to design an organizational structure and control system for administering and co-ordinating the many transactions involved in producing products and services. Many companies still rely heavily on bureaucratic hierarchies to control activities. They also devise overly complex systems for recruiting, evaluating, and compensating employees; and administrative systems for monitoring expenses, making decisions and assigning tasks. When well crafted, these systems serve to channel interactions between employees and so produce good job performance (Fombrun 1992, Tichy and Devanna 1986, and Galbraith and Kazanjian 1986). It should however be noted that this 'traditional' pattern, which rests on the principle that authority stems from the top of the company and that therefore responsibility can always be passed upwards, is under significant attack in organizations which have espoused the concept of lean production and lean management. The essence of the principle of leanness is not solely that of group or 'cellular' production operations, but also entails the acceptance of responsibility for initiating and implementing change at the lowest possible level in the company. Womack, Jones and Roos (1990) point out that this philosophy enhances operational flexibility, personnel involvement with the quality of the output and enhanced job satisfaction, but at the potential risk of increased levels of individual stress and perceived personal risk, as well as diminishing significantly the traditional importance of predictable ladders of promotional or career path development.

Employees are also heavily influenced by many beliefs and norms that are part of their company's culture. Over time, employees acquire a shared understanding of a firm's competitors, their products and strategies. A company-wide culture, often made evident in 'corporate credos' and codes of conduct, delimits the action deemed legitimate for everyone to pursue, including the social and ethical postures taken in dealing with clients, suppliers and other stakeholders. Like controls, cultures require people to act in ways consistent with shared beliefs and company norms about, for instance, punctuality, product quality, customer service or social responsibility. Corporate culture has significant impact on changing the supply management role from one which focuses on tactics to one which emphasizes strategy. Different corporate cultures will stress different values or beliefs about what is important for a particular company. For example, in a company with manufacturing or production culture, the normal strategy is lower cost with a focus on internal efficiencies. A manufacturing dominated company uses budgets extensively to monitor and control operations. As competition increases, cost cutting often becomes the most likely response by the company. Due to supply management's influence and, to some extent, control over costs, purchasing and manufacturing personnel may have much in common regarding operating efficiencies. Gearing supply's role to a cost reduction strategy with careful monitoring and control may increase the profile of purchasing towards being viewed as a strategic corporate function.

On the other hand, in technology or research and development driven companies, a research strategy is pushed with a focus on increasing product performance. The desire to have a 'new' or at least an 'improved' product may take precedence over other decisions. This type of company tends to make extensive use of product performance tests in order to meet the competition by improving the product offering. The purchasing department in this type of organization may be expected to be ever on the alert for new materials, components, and parts and hence sources of supply which may aid overall product performance improvement. A study and understanding of the company's corporate culture should enable purchasing personnel to respond and adapt to changes and emphasis in the company so as to be compatible with the overall strategy.

In practical terms and in the short run at least, management of such cultural issues takes place within the extant 'technological' context of the company; this is its existing markets and core functions. In the longer term, a change in corporate culture may very well prove to be a necessary precursor to real change in technological and market environment.

The top management's commitment and conduct reflects the strategies through which the firm competes. The firm's commitment and conduct can be constrained by underlying resource and capabilities, structure and control and corporate culture. For example, firms lacking research and development capability will find it difficult to pursue a strategy of market development or innovation which rests on significant departures from previous practice or familiar technology applications. Firms relying on low-wage labour tend to reduce production techniques to basic routines and develop authoritarian hierarchies, making it difficult for managers to improve the commitment and involvement of employees.

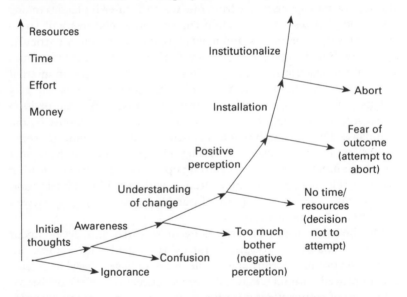

Figure 1.4 *Implementation of effective purchasing orientation change strategy*

Finally, Stage 4 of the change process illustrated in Figure 1.2 comprises selecting, implementing and evaluating an effective purchasing orientation change strategy. The set of effective change strategy steps can be depicted as in Figure 1.4. The diagram identifies the characteristics of selecting and implementing change. The characteristics of change are influenced by resources, time, effort and money, progressing from initial thoughts, to awareness and understanding the change. As the people begin to develop positive perception the installation and institutionalization of the change can be accomplished. During the process of change there can be feelings and doubts generated of ignorance, confusion, negative perception (too much bother), no time available, and worst of all, fear of outcome. These all make change difficult. External extraneous factors like economic recession and unemployment weigh heavily, especially in countries like the UK where the fear of redundancy is a potentially crippling factor in the change process.

Thus, empowering a purchasing department to play its full strategic role in the survival, profitability, and expansion of a business requires more than just an enlightened executive decision. Supply management is a profession, but it is also a functional necessity, and nearly all its practitioners are fully occupied in the day-to-day problems and factors of placing orders and hastening deliveries. To make a change really effective it is vital to allocate considerable resources and time to the needs of everyone employed in the purchasing department. The strategic role of farming and managing the external resources of the supplier base to identify new product developments and to work together to eliminate cost drivers, can only work when opportunities are created and not squandered by 'upstream' decisions and commitments.

Conclusion

Top management who undervalue supply management in the scheme of today's corporate and product strategy commit an error in sound business management. No longer can firms create, design, launch, and provide viable products throughout their life cycles without regard to the supply aspects of the material and components that go into them. The cost, value and time contributions of supply elements are too great, and when they are ignored, the penalty can be too much for the survival of today's organization.

Functions like supply management need to be aware of its external and internal interacting forces which may trigger or retard the change process. An incremental planned approach should be used for changing operations, management structures, and evaluation systems.

The supply management function affects corporate and product strategies in many ways. In an increasing number of firms it is seen as adding value through creative product enhancement through external resource management. As organizations evolve towards a strategic orientation which is more sharply focused, it is imperative that the supply management function supports the overall system with the full range of acquisition and supply management skills.

Part Two

Supply Management's New Power Tools

2 Designing organizational structure for supply management

Introduction

It is the organizational structure which most affects the co-ordination of activities, delegation of authority, communication flows and task responsibilities, both within the purchasing function and between purchasing and other departments. The choice of structure also influences supply management's scope and priorities in goal setting, planning, problem solving and decision making. The objective in designing a structure is to incorporate competitive effectiveness into the organizational system, rather than concentrate solely on narrow operational efficiency (Scheuing 1989).

The most suitable structure will always be governed by the extent to which the business or organization is dependent on effective management of external resources. If the percentage of non-pay expenditure and input is high, then a suitable proportion of management effort with appropriately positioned authority will be needed for optimum results.

Supply management can be a board level appointment in its own right, and play a full role in the strategic management of the business, or it can be tucked away under another department like production as a 'place and chase' junior activity. Procurement is a necessary function which will have to happen in some form, consuming some level of resource however badly it is placed or organized. But just how much does a lowly ranked fortuitous mode of acquisition actually cost? How much expensive time is being diverted and frustrated as designers buy instead of designing, and professors negotiate instead of teaching? The choice is to decide where supply management's strategic importance lies and whether the organization's future is inherently bound up with good management of outside suppliers. If it is, and there can be few examples these days where this is not the case, then supply management clearly ought to be professionally staffed and its organizational structure and reporting level suitably appropriate.

Even when supply management is given a top level role, it can rapidly become bogged down in the day-to-day dealings in nuts and bolts, and the acquisition of humdrum but necessary services like window cleaning. The effectiveness of supply management as a strategic contributor can so easily be lost in the welter of fire fighting and defence building as divisional management or product teams cast doubts on the value of what can be seen as an intrusive and unnecessary layer of interference. Proposing the 'lean enterprise' in the *Harvard Business Review* of February 1994, James Womack and Dan Jones show that supply management should define the principles of purchasing, form links with suppliers and work to improve their performance continuously. Supply management has a very important role as the 'architect of the value stream'; in orchestrating the uninterrupted flow down the stream; and creating the principles which underpin the relationships. However the traditional role of actually buying goods and services can often be left to each product development team or devolved budget holder.

So how can the optimum structure for strategic supply management be achieved?

In *The Practice of Management* (1955) Peter Drucker describes the relationship analysis required to start us thinking in the right direction:

> 'Traditionally we tend to define the job of a manager only in terms of the activity he heads, that is only downward...Indeed the first thing to consider in defining a manager's job is the contribution his activity has to make to the larger unit of which it is a part. In other words the upward relationship must be analysed first and must be established first.

Procurement is not confined to simply shopping around and the management information system necessary to support it must be more comprehensive than the usual print order and record expenditure files. There must be scope for supplier appraisal and performance measurement; quality assurance and control; project monitoring and management; contract drafting and implementation; as well as inventory control and expediting facilities. An adequate information system will provide management reports to support decision making, and be a ready mechanism for improved productivity, performance monitoring and comprehensive financial control.

Requirements and relationships analysis: the vision of the structure needed

What is the extent of dependence on the provision of resources from external agencies in terms of :

Expenditure: What percentage of cost of operations is non-salary?

Risk: Does the provision of supplies from outside represent an area of major risk?
Innovation: How many of our new ideas, development starts come from outside?
Marketing: Do/Can suppliers contribute marketing leads?

Does the business and its overall size best suit a centralized or decentralized philosophy?

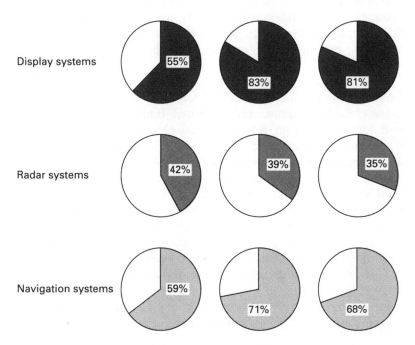

Figure 2.1 *The procurement element in a range of strategic bids. (Defence contractor, 1992)*

Figure 2.1 shows an analysis of the procurement element in a number of strategic bids by one of Europe's leading manufacturers of military radar and avionics defence equipment in 1992. The lowest percentage of works cost made up by expenditure with external suppliers turned out to be in airborne radar projects. Here there was still a very large involvement in vertically- integrated assembly from basic components, and considerable in-house machining of the sophisticated miniature microwave parts. Even in airborne radar bought out content exceeded 35 per cent. In state of the art mission planning systems and integrated helmet displays, the dependence on external resources was found to be as high as 83 per cent. It almost seemed like the more advanced and innovative the system was, the higher the contribution of the procurement element became.

To survive at all with such a significant dependence on external resources, the supply management function needs to be able to provide very strong upwards flowing communications channels which are recognized and listened to by top management. But as Drucker again points out, the sideways relationship is also critical. Supplies must bring a very strong influence to bear across the other major functions. If it cannot be independent, it is better to be allied to the commercial or finance directorates. As described in Chapters 3 and 7, this enables supplies to play a full role in current and future business, making major contributions both to design and to marketing.

The University of Edinburgh was founded in 1583 as the fourth of Scotland's ancient universities. Today it has over 18 000 students and is one of the largest universities in Britain. It has a world-wide reputation for excellence in research and teaching in a wide range of traditional, high-tech and professional disciplines. It also spends almost one third of its income with external suppliers. Its continued success is heavily dependent on its ability to work effectively with these external resources within the public sector constraints of the European Community Procurement Directives and the Higher Education Funding Council requirements for 'value for money'. The University of Edinburgh operates a structure of devolved budgetary control, but in 1993 it became the first university in Britain to appoint a Director of Procurement on the top professorial grade. The sideways relationship in this case ensures strategic management of common supplies, developing common sources and providing performance monitors and goals for continuous improvement.

Influence, trust, control and doughnuts

Charles Handy in *The Empty Raincoat* (1994) describes the inside-out doughnut. The filled-in centre is the solid core of things in any job or role that has to be done as basic essential duties. 'All the things', in Handy's words, 'which have to be done in that job or role if you are not to fail'. These are the basic tasks, the job procedures, the work instruction manuals, the necessary chores of day-to-day operation. Beyond that filled-in centre there is the annular ring of space, the area for creativity, contribution and empowerment – 'This space is our opportunity to make a difference, to go beyond the bounds of duty, to live up to our full potential'. An old adage describes taking any group of employees and looking what they do outside working hours: winning golf championships, growing prize cucumbers, running Scout troops, and asks how it is that we turn them into morons from

8.30 to 5 each working day? Management structures have a huge part to play in determining just how much of the critically important 'outer ring' of the doughnut we can stimulate, support and farm contributions from.

Formal, rigid structures are there to give lines of command, to define responsibility and to provide a system of control and accountability. This only addresses the core of the doughnut. The more productive space around the core requires flexibility. Influence, mutual respect and trust can build, feed and develop relationships which are much more capable, more resilient yet more open to change than those ruled by the crude force of control alone. At one extreme there is the constrictive reins and petty bureaucracy of an overly-centralized and often founder-dominated monolith. The other is typified by a battlefield of bickering chieftains squabbling and posturing, and too dazzled by the particulars of their local division to view the 'big picture' and to contribute properly to the management and investment decisions for survival and growth. There is a sensible and comfortable middle ground. Sir Denys Henderson was chairman of Imperial Chemical Industries through the period of the giant's successful demerger of drugs division Zeneca in 1993. He has described the culture before the change as baronial, with the chiefs less concerned with the corporate good than of showing how well their section was doing. The suppression of sectoral interests following the change has made for a much better interaction with the centre (Jackson 1994).

Charles Handy goes on to describe the 'Twin Citizenship' of the local part and corporate whole. Supply management is a business function which it may make sense to manage centrally. This steals power and decisions from the independent divisions and provokes resentment. Divisions and parts of a greater whole need to be helped to realize that in order to get most value out of their independence it often pays to sacrifice some of that independence to a central function. But that central function must inspire and sustain confidence. No customers need to be actively and continuously delighted more than internal customers.

The prospects for supply management to make an effective contribution are inextricably bound up in the nature of the total organization structure and the philosophy from which it is derived.

Don't start from here! The assessment of present position

Just like the traveller in Ireland who asked for the best way to Dublin, and supposedly received the reply: 'If I was going, I would not start from here!', the present position in most organizations is hardly the best place to start building a new and better structure from. However there is usually no choice. All organizational structures exist because of strategic decisions made or not made in the past. Personalities, power base struggles, whims, pet theories and quid pro quo reactions to shocks and crises, can batter, bruise and rip asunder functions and groupings perceived as non-strategic fringe activities. The vital importance of the purchasing and supply function is still not widely understood. Many chief executives who have skilfully managed change in other areas still give scant regard to the significance of supply management, and many subscribe to the adage expressed by Chaucer in *The Canterbury Tales:*

> So great a purchasour was nowhere none ...
> Nowhere so busy a man as he there was,
> And yet he seemed busier than he was.

And many buyers and supplies managers don't give them very good reason to vary their opinion. Supply management can so often be accused of confusing activity with action. Even experienced professionals can escape into the welter and petty excitement of day-to-day routines and interactions. Strategic supply management requires brains to be applied to the issues and purposes of the business. Systems must be developed to handle the everyday tactical activities.

Scenarios 1 to 4 encapsulate four versions of how the supply management function might find itself today, and how it might be changed to meet the challenges of tomorrow. The scenarios have been inspired by, and developed and adapted from many sources including the four cameos projected in the Ernst and Young document Good Management of Purchasing (1993).

> 'Would you tell me please, which way I ought to go from here?' she asked.
> 'That depends a good deal on where you want to get to,' said the cat.
>
> Lewis Carroll, *Alice's Adventures in Wonderland.*

Scenario 1: The clerical supply management function

- Supply management is a sub-section of another support department, usually production for manufacturing requirements and/or accounts for stationery and consumables.
- No overall head of supply management. No contribution to planning.
- Internal initiators of requirements decide needs, choose supplier, agree price, then pass to purchasing to raise the order and sort out the invoice, not always in that order.

- Few if any written procedures except some reference in the finance manual. Performance measures, if any, limited to the time it takes to raise orders.
- Staff are on low grades and have had little or no training. Usually the junior becomes the assistant then the buyer. No authority to question demands or suggest standard alternatives.
- Purchase orders are placed mainly informally by telephone, letter or fax with no discussion of terms and conditions or regard to contractual risk.
- No purchasing or commodity strategy. Large numbers of suppliers used. Poor, if any, recognition of repeat requirement history or trends.
- Little, if any, aggregation of demand. No standardization policy, user specifiers dominate. Very few bulk purchasing agreements.
- No real understanding or measure of supplier performance. Individual user perceptions and memories of the last disaster cloud rational thinking.

Scenario 2: The commercial supply management function

- Supply management is recognized as a distinct function with a head of department at junior management level. Individual departments with more senior management heads retain the most 'interesting' commodities under their own control.
- Supply management staff are not involved in the specification process, and the supplier is often pre-determined by the initiator's choice of a single source brand.
- Requirements arrive at the last minute with no time properly to assess the market and examine competition.
- Supply management lacks the ability in terms of time and authority to implement a sourcing strategy, so the available expenditure cake crumbles into tiny portions making any negotiation a tactical skirmish at best.
- No real difference in the way large important orders and small trivial demands are met.
- Strategy and commitment are impossible because of dominance in user preference and upstream decision making.
- Standard terms and conditions go backwards and forwards on purchase order forms, acknowledgements and invoices in the classical 'battle of the forms' routine.
- Performance monitoring includes claims of 'savings'. Supplier rating is subjective and largely complaints based.

Scenario 3: The supportive supply management function

- The supply management function is recognized in policy planning and expected to return a contribution to the overall aims and objectives of the organization.
- Functional head reports to the board of directors through an intermediary.
- A supply management manual exists with properly documented procedures. Standard terms and conditions are used for goods and services. Introductory training is provided for all new recruits to the supply management team.
- Supply management is recognized throughout the organization as a department whose support is available on request. Better managed projects will be involving supply management staff at a reasonably early stage.
- Specifications are sufficiently broad to allow competitive quotations to be obtained.
- No common commodity coding system exists, hence analysis of expenditure tends to be reactive and retrospective using data trawled from suppliers.
- Lead buyers are established for particular commodities where usage is high and common to a number of departments. Efforts are made to aggregate expenditure in these areas whenever possible.
- Performance monitoring includes price variation compared to indices. Quality checks are made on incoming goods, and adherence to promised delivery schedule is monitored. Delinquent suppliers are provided with data on their performance.

Scenario 4: The strategic supply management function

- Supply management is a core business activity, staffed by qualified professionals and with its functional head a board level appointment.
- Supply management is recognized throughout the organization as the centre of expertise and the starting point for information on all aspects of external resource management.
- Partnership agreements exist with strategic suppliers with agreed goals and regular performance review meetings.
- Cost of acquisition and cost of ownership are both well understood, controlled using monitors, and targets are set for continuous improvement.
- Comprehensive coding system used for commodities and suppliers with access to databases for pricing history and comparison with indices.

- Supply management is a total quality management operation with all staff working to agreed and documented work procedures and committed to understanding and meeting customer requirements.
- Suppliers are rated and recognized for excellence in all aspects of performance including conformance with specification, delivery, cost reduction, contributions to innovation, and responsiveness.
- There is an ongoing process of supplier development to work with suppliers to better achieve our goals. Suppliers regularly take part in value analysis and value engineering activities.

Figure 2.2 summarizes the four scenarios in a form which may be useful for self-assessment. The backward looking dimension will help to see whether momentum already exists for change and if so how much this needs to be accelerated. Time may not be on your side.

Manufacturing environment

Nowhere has the supplies function seen a greater change in significance than in the manufacturing industry. Evolution has taken place from a preponderance of vertically integrated juggernauts where the only input from external suppliers was crude raw material and basic components, worth less than 15 per cent of the works cost. With the rapid growth in technology which dominates today's reality, it is simply not possible for any company to be master of all the technology required to produce the products and services necessary for a competitive market. The 15 per cent has become 50 per cent, and for some individual products it can be as high as 90 per cent. Today's top manufacturers harness the intelligence of marketing, design and management to make margins. It is no longer possible to survive solely on margins gained by the work and method study of soldering or production-line assembly. Supply management has inherited the new role of managing the largest proportion of the company's resources, costs, risks and potential for profit. Supply management must be a top level strategic function, part of the top management team, with a board member at its head, reporting directly to the chief executive.

There is a 'Catch-22' problem in many organizations even when the importance of purchasing and supplies is recognized and reasonably well understood. There may well be no senior enough supply management professional available, or one who is perceived to be experienced enough for appointment at the top level.

Responsibility for supply management is then placed with the head of production or operations. Unless this is an exceptional individual, the supply management function will steadily progress to being used

	Three years ago	One year ago	Current position	One year hence	Three years hence
STRATEGIC					
Core business activity					
Reporting to Chief Executive					
Professionally staffed centre of expertise					
Partnerships with strategic suppliers					
Total quality management organization					
SUPPORTIVE					
Recognized in policy planning					
Purchasing manual with documented procedures					
Specifications being challenged					
Performance monitoring of suppliers					
COMMERCIAL					
Purchasing department as part of another function					
Standard terms and conditions					
No involvement in specification					
Claims of savings					
CLERICAL					
Very limited responsibilities					
Few, if any, written procedures					
No standardization or aggregation of demand					
Supplier performance rated by user perception					

Figure 2.2 *The assessment of present position*

almost exclusively on production-related logistical problems. This policy will obstruct the crucial sideways contribution to design, marketing and competitiveness available from the involvement of suppliers in value analysis and bidders' conferences. Supply management becomes a busy, valuable, but purely tactical function with ever-lessening opportunity for strategic input. Designers will continue to escape from the difficult responsibilities of defining critical parameters. Salesmen will continue their successful upstream influence on component selection. A glass ceiling will form in the structure, frustrating the development of future top flight directors of supply management.

In other circumstances it may be the head of finance who is handed responsibility for supply management when the requirements analysis comes up with a significant pound or dollar number against external expenditure. *Relevance Lost*, a Harvard Business School book by Thomas Johnson and Robert Kaplan (1987) gives a lucid explanation of how management accountancy has lost its way over the years, and why the finance department is seldom the most popular of central functions to be allied to. Accountants are usually thought of as controllers rather than creators. Responsibility for purchasing expenditure and the management of supplier credit can be used as a very crude short-term braking mechanism with serious damage to long-term goals.

However heads of finance can also prove to be very effective supporters of supply management initiatives. The recession of the early 1970s pushed many UK household names in manufacturing to the very edge of survival. Ferranti, a technology leader in military avionics, computer and industrial control systems, hit severe cash flow problems in 1974, and was forced into the National Enterprise Board set up by the government of Harold Wilson as a sanctuary for lame ducks. The high interest rates and low levels of business activity made hand-to-mouth supply management a prerequisite. Placing responsibility for supply management under finance seemed an appropriate strategic move. This proved to be effective and Ferranti went on to flourish successfully for almost a further two decades. The company was fully back on the stock market by 1981 and went on to bring many innovative products to markets throughout the world before falling victim to one of the most spectacular corporate frauds in 1989, after the ill-judged merger with Jim Guerin's International Signal and Control.

Just as under production or operations, there is always the danger that the real contribution of supply management both upwards and sideways is lost or minimized by placing responsibility for it in an area likely to have a biased and blinkered view of its potential input.

If supply management is definitely not to be allowed to speak for itself in the manufacturing sector, then the very best alternative is usually as a direct report to the commercial director. Here it is important to define the commercial director as the individual responsible for the approval of proposals and quotations for new and existing products. There will be a formal set of procedures and checklists to examine the appropriateness of the bid to corporate strategy, and to ensure that sufficient resources exist in financial and manufacturing terms to carry the work through successfully. There will be some value limitations below which the approval can be delegated to a divisional level, and at the other extreme there will be a top limit where the potential business would be so significant that full corporate approval will be necessary.

The important point is that the commercial director will be directly in touch with what it takes to win or lose business. If the works cost estimates in the approval checklist contain a substantial proportion of bought out expenditure, it will not be difficult to demonstrate the potential win/lose contribution from supply management. Pre-bid involvement by supply management will become mandatory and bidders' conferences and value analysis programmes will cement the sideways relationships and fuel the successes to make supply management fully recognized in, if not an actual occupant of, mahogany row.

Service and public sector organizations

Traditionally here supply management has played at best a supporting role. Indeed the report Good Management of Purchasing by Ernst & Young published in 1993 for the Higher Education Funding Council for England specifically concludes that the 'Supportive' level of purchasing capability is the one required, though in fairness the same report goes on to say that an individual at policy-making level (e.g. Pro-Vice Chancellor or Assistant Director) should take responsibility for purchasing in the institution. But will he or she be suitably qualified and experienced?

There is also the seeming dilemma of devolved responsibility for budget autonomy. What was it Robert Townsend said in his book *Up the Organization*? (1970)?

> So let's be sensible. Fire the whole purchasing department. The company will benefit from having each department dealing in the free market outside instead of being victimized by internal socialism. And don't underestimate the morale value of letting your people *waste* some money. If you must, have a one-person *buying department* for those who want help in the purchasing area and ask for it.

In his 1984 revised volume entitled *Further up the Organization* Townsend added the footnote 'I'm told that the Federal Government, with all its joint-use purchasing economies, really pays 20 per cent more for a pencil than you do at the Five-and-Ten.'

Devolved and local responsibility for purchasing depend very heavily on three major issues: good information systems, good working practice guidelines and excellent training. The structure for a devolved organization should have a strong strategic centre. If felt necessary, this can be backed by a top-level purchasing committee with representation from the heads of the semi-autonomous subsidiary groups. The committee will ensure that the authority of the centre carries due weight throughout the operating levels. It can also serve to bridge the inevitable barrier between centre and distributed power bases. It can be very useful to have active contributions from outside the organization, perhaps a supply director from a local commercial operation. If such a committee is put in place, it should be used not to drive policy but rather to act as a sounding board for the head of supply management, and to provide backing and authority from the highest level for initiatives and directives which otherwise might be seen as cutting across the remit of local management.

The centre retains ultimate responsibility for all aspects of supply management but activities are distributed after analysis using a form of the procurement positioning tool. This device is covered in more detail in Chapter 3 where various applications are described, but for the purposes of designing a balanced structure in a devolved organization, products and services can be analysed on the criteria of value and commonality. Without the need for more than order of magnitude calculations, a simple four cell matrix can be drawn up as shown in Figure 2.3.

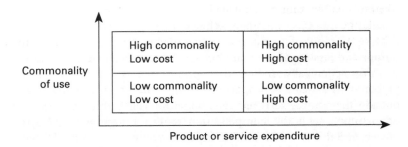

Figure 2.3 *Cost and commonality matrix*

The most workable structure must mirror the optimum arrangement in the matrix with strong leadership from the centre on the areas of high commonality, particularly in the high commonality/high cost sector. Any initial analysis can clearly only display the status quo so it is important that the structure is tuned towards the strategic goals of the organization, and not be just a reflection of the current less satisfactory position. For instance there should be enough resources at the centre to examine the low commonality areas where it is likely that ownership costs like cost of acquisition and the stockholding of minimum order quantities may yield substantial savings if these commodities can be moved vertically up the commonality axis.

Supply management should concentrate very clearly on three main areas: defining the principles of purchasing; forming links with suppliers; working with them to establish monitors and continuously to improve performance levels.

Product buyers, project buyers, lead buyers

Rigidly, controlled centralized procurement systems will often have specialist commodity buyers dedicated to a single product or narrow range of related items. These experts develop knowledge and experience and act to cross-fertilize ideas between project teams in large organizations. The hindsight benefits of one application can prevent the same mistakes being suffered in another. The problem with product buyers is that they are never really part of the project team. They have difficulties splitting up their time and enthusiasm, and can easily be resented as meddling outsiders.

Decentralized structures will have buyers who belong lock, stock and barrel to the project team they are working with at present. They will be dedicated and enthusiastic, for their future is directly linked to the project. However, the narrow confines of their operation will cut them off from seeing the bigger picture, and can easily lead to wasteful 'reinventing of the wheel'.

Lead buyers can potentially achieve the best of both worlds. They achieve the clout of greater purchasing power and the exposure to the bumps and lessons of the marketplace, without being seen as a threat to those specifically dedicated to project teams. They need to be prepared to allocate a proportion of their time and thinking power outside their home territory, but hopefully relish this as a learning opportunity, with the compensation that it brings greater buying power, and that in other commodity areas someone is doing the same for them.

In the ideal organization, the function will have a small, highly professional centre. There will be just three or four permanent members with the rest seconded for periods of six months to learn and develop the art of project work or a with small number of product specialists. They will then be recycled through the organization as lead buyers or just part time buyers in smaller departments. Where high levels of supply management skills exist, the professional core will be a centre of excellence. Procurement research projects will be ongoing, driven by the vision and umbrella goals of continuous improvement for the people within the supply management function, the performance of supplier base, and the quality of service to internal customers. There will be consultative and working relationship with professionals in similar markets with bench marking, and joint development of best practice.

Network sourcing: as many suppliers as you can manage

The other principal relationship which the strategic structure must be designed to address is the interface with the supplier base. Traditionally organizations deal with a few thousand individual external sources. Purchasing and supply research by Carlisle and Parker (1989), Lamming (1993), Hines (1994), and others examining best sourcing practices in the global automotive and Japanese electronics sectors highlight the great advantages gained by drastically reducing the supplier base to one or two hundred at a maximum. Suppliers are essentially formed into pyramidal tiers with the much smaller number of first-tier companies each taking delivery from and managing groups of second tier suppliers, and so on. Touch is not lost with companies in lower tiers, and indeed a great strength of Japanese manufacturing is the *kyoryoku kai*. This has been translated as 'co-operative circle' or 'supplier association'. These provide the regular forum for all communications from business trends to social activities. Rather than contact being lost, it is strengthened and broadened by well developed network sourcing. The steps towards achieving this and the full implications of it are explored in detail in subsequent chapters. But it has a very important bearing on the shape and style of the ultimate structure for strategic supply management, and for the people who will operate in it and harness its optimum contribution.

The accent must be on high level management of fewer, more powerful external resources. The driver will be understanding, co-operation and trust rather than confrontation and control. It will be a culture of the common purpose but there will still need to be pressure, excitement and the competition of market forces to stimulate mutual advantage and gain. Womack and Jones (1994) liken the central purchasing function to a 'university' where specialists learn and develop supplies management techniques then go out to practise them either as part of or in support of a sub-division's project team. The structure must be strong with expertise at the centre with active leaders alert to and if possible participating in professional research, to keep abreast of best practice. It must be even stronger in self confidence and not be afraid to release the day-to-day tactical decision making to local management, and to first and second tier suppliers once network sourcing begins to become established. Functions which allow themselves to be bogged down entirely in reactive tactics can never be a strategic force in any organization, no matter how clever their structure.

The people: qualifications and ongoing learning

What sort of people do you have staffing supply management? They are probably honest, reliable and hard-working. They will usually have mixed backgrounds, from Production, Drawing office or Estimating if you are a manufacturer; from Administration, Accounts or Services if you are in the public sector. They will be reasonably self-confident and rugged individuals, able to stand up to the test of tough negotiations. They will have a wide range of contacts and knowledge, and will be used to getting through a variety of tasks, jumping from one to the next and back again as information arrives or suffers last minute changes. Like Chaucer's 'purchasour' they may seem busier than they are, at least as far as effectiveness is concerned. But it certainly won't be their fault. A busy buying office is demanding of time and people. It can frequently be a reactive fire fighting arena giving fun and satisfaction as well as frustration in the resolution of exciting tactical problems. But it also provides a refuge for escapism away from the real responsibilities of strategic supplies management.

Crosfield Electronics Limited is a leading UK based supplier of electronic colour and communications systems to the graphic design, printing and publishing industries. During a major transformation of the purchasing function, Paul Briggs (1994) found that with the changing role of the buyer came a barrier in the form of the limited core skills of some personnel. The new role required a different set of skills at a much higher competence level. While some skills may be developed through training, Crossfield felt that others had to be bought in anew. Changes occurred in the personnel, including the recruitment of new buyers with a much higher level of education. P. D. Cousins (1993) of the School of Management at the University of Bath, has noted a trend of up to a threefold increase in the percentage of graduates entering the purchasing profession. Professor Douglas Macbeth (1994) of the Supply Chain Management Group, University of Glasgow, reasons that the purchasing person's character must develop to that of a team player. This will involve some degree of apparent inefficiency when the buyer is seen from the singular viewpoint, but of increased system effectiveness when seen from this wider perspective. Contribution to team effort becomes the basis for reward. From being the enemy in the win–lose negotiation, the purchasing person's role becomes one of friend to the partner. As such the buyer will have to act as the champion of the supplier partner, supporting involvement in new product opportunities as well as protector against any attempt to obtain short-term benefit through opportunistic behaviour.

Professional stage

Compulsory	Optional	Elective
1 PSCM I: Strategy	1 Purchasing	1 A project
2 PSCM II: Tactics and Operations	2 Stores and Inventory Management	2 Operations Management
3 Legal Aspects of Supply Chain Management	3 Distribution	3 Marketing
4 Case study	4 Commercial Relationships	4 Project and Contract Management
		5 Retail Merchandise Management
		6 International Purchasing

Recommended Sequence of Study
(including 'Foundation Stage' subjects)

Foundation stage	Professional stage	
1 Introduction to Purchasing and Supply Chain Management	1 PSCM I: Strategy	A total of **FOUR** subjects to be taken: at least one Optional plus the balance from the list of Optional or Elective subjects.
2 Management Principles and Practice	2 PSCM II: Tactics and Operations	
3 Economics	3 Legal Aspects of Supply Chain Management	+
4 Quantitative Studies		Case study
5 Business Accounting		

Figure 2.4 *The revised professional education scheme. (PSCM, Purchasing and Supply Chain Management)*

As supply management moves steadily away from getting and spending and becomes more and more concerned with the management of external resources of increasing significance, it needs also to attract, and be attractive to, staff of the very highest calibre. It will become a normal and seemingly natural route to general management, bringing forward executives who have true management experience with the almost unique asset of having looked at their organization from the outside. In some organizations there will be much to do to expand and develop the buyer's role, and create a proper foundation on which effective supply management can be built.

The Chartered Institute of Purchasing and Supply provides a professional education scheme leading to full membership. Courses are provided at two levels, foundation and professional. These are designed to cover the full range of responsibilities faced in supply management, including the strategic role. Universities and colleges throughout the UK offer modules of the institute's scheme in a variety of evening class, day release, block release, and correspondence methods.

The scheme of study is comprehensive and has been regularly updated to keep abreast of developments and research in supply management matters. The revised structure introduced in 1995 is shown as Figure 2.4. As the Institute has grown both in size and recognition, participation in the education route to membership has increased. Classes have attracted students from a much wider range of business and public sector organizations, bringing much improved interchange of ideas and experience among participants.

Several UK universities offer first degree, or postgraduate courses in purchasing and supply of one form or another. Degree level qualifications in supply management, or with purchasing and supply as a major theme, will inevitably promote improved awareness and recognition of the importance of the function in general management circles. The research work by academics associated with teaching these courses is a further dimension of this on top of the direct result of improved understanding.

Another route towards relevant qualification is provided by the National Vocational Qualifications (NVQ) process (Scottish Vocational Qualifications in Scotland). This is a programme of training and assessment carried out at the workplace using nationally set competence standards and controlled validation and approval of each scheme. There are benefits in that it provides a mechanism for coaching staff who might not otherwise readily participate in development. There are four levels of increasing complexity of required competence, with links across to the Chartered Institute of

Purchasing and Supply's educational scheme.

The UK Government became very conscious that a significant gap in qualifications and skills had developed in the 1970s and 1980s between the British workforce and its major economic competitors, particularly Germany, USA, France and Japan, over a wide range of occupations. The National Standards Development Programme which ensued defined a range of competences including sets of units for the purchasing profession. The concept is based on personal development of the employee following assessment and training to close the identified competence gap. This can be done by the line manager backed by a training team from the professional core. Even staff whose buying duties occupy just part of their day-to-day responsibilities, can gain a start on a ladder of qualifications leading up to full professional status.

The National Standards Development Programme for purchasing competences was carried out at the University of Ulster. Authors Andrew Erridge and Shayne Perry (1993) see NVQs as a route to making substantial improvements to staff in the purchasing function, as measured by qualifications obtained:

> bringing into the network of available qualifications a large section of the workforce previously excluded, namely the large proportion of early school leavers with no or few formal qualifications. The link between that and international competitiveness, however that may be defined, is more tenuous. However, the circumstantial evidence from countries such as Japan and Germany is that education and training, and particularly vocational training, has a crucial role to play.

Management information systems

Only the most rudimentary clerical purchasing function can operate without a comprehensive management information system. Although this is well-understood at surface level, there remains a vast difference between the standard purchasing software module and the sophisticated set of tools necessary to properly manage the interface with external suppliers. Supply management information systems often have a purchase order create and print module which is quite separate from the commodity and production schedule data necessary to ensure sensible decision making. Information on suppliers themselves is very often a part of the Accounts Department's payment ledger package. Vital data on commodities and suppliers is entered and controlled by staff with quite different priorities from purchasing.

A very comprehensive exercise in analysis and specification of supply management information system requirements was carried out for the UK Government's PURSUIT project. The requirements

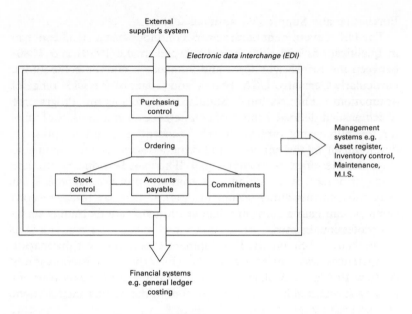

Figure 2.5 *The overall scope of PURSUIT*

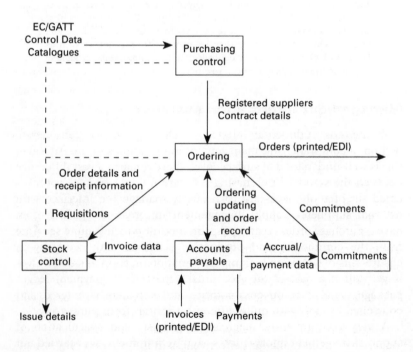

Figure 2.6 *The primary inter-relationship between components*

specification was published by HMSO in 1992. There is no attempt to include the sophisticated manufacturing techniques of materials requirements planning, and manufacturing resource planning, which are well covered elsewhere, but the detail of the functional purchasing process is impressive. The overall scope of PURSUIT and the primary inter-relationship between components are illustrated in Figures 2.5 and 2.6.

Information management

The purpose of an information system is to support decision making and play a key role in the process of innovation (Porter 1990). If a proactive approach to planning is adopted then the success of the strategy will depend on the availability of concise and accurate up-to-date information which is relevant to the buying organization and its supply environment. By actively monitoring the supply market, purchasing management should be able to spot any threats and opportunities as they emerge. The emphasis in the development of a purchasing information system should be on data which assists buyers in making decisions in line with the organization's competitive strategy. Information gathering and processing systems are a vital part of any strategic approach to management.

Purchasing decisions which are recurring as part of ongoing routine need continuing and regular information updates with data that is routinely collected and systematically analysed. On the other hand decisions which are made only infrequently have information needs which are more erratic. The requirements may be less precisely defined in generalizable terms, but that does not mean that the needs are less significant. Major purchases of capital equipment may for example be relatively rare, but the need for access to short- and long-range information can scarcely be dismissed merely because the demand is not a regular event.

Information capture

Classification and coding of all goods and services bought externally is a primary supply management function. Not only does it focus attention immediately on the fact that external sourcing is a major issue, but it also involves professional supply staff right at the initial conception where there is maximum potential for influence, cost reduction and standardization.

Availability of the right information from a variety of sources with rapid access will normally require a relational database system. The strategic aims of 'zero delay, zero defects, zero stock and zero paperwork' need maximum effectiveness in information processing.

To carry out the day-to-day function of provisioning goods and materials, the following tools are needed: requisition and enquiry analysis to establish and define the need; identification of potential suppliers, their status, history and track record; survey of market and evaluation of responses; establishment of contractual agreements and performance monitors; receipt of supplies and confirmation that acceptance criteria are met, and finally, clearing of payment obligations in the correct timescale.

Buyers' tools

Active and busy buyers need a computer system which is both fast and easy to use. Screen division into windows is essential. Interruptions from external telephone calls and internal consultations with specifiers and users form a large part of the daily life in most purchasing departments. Computer systems must be sympathetic to this environment, providing the simplest of routes between the many screens which may have to be consulted.

There are basically four necessary tools:

- information retrieval and analysis;
- decision making and authorization;
- execution and performance monitoring;
- payment and recording.

The first of these is by far the most important and the most complex. At the same time it is often least understood or catered for in standard purchasing packages. This is the principal point for differentiating between the actual procurement execution at the lowest cost of acquisition in different circumstances such as: local placing of low-value, high-frequency call-offs, by a large number of users with appropriate levels of delegated authority and negotiation of technically complex, high value orders by professionally qualified supplies staff.

Price indexing

Strategic supply management is most concerned with long-term partnership relationships with suppliers, but for the successful survival of all parties it is very important to keep in touch with market forces. Fortunately there is an alternative to the daily scramble for three quotations so typifying clerical buying. Several price indexing systems now exist giving regular comparisons for real prices for a moderate annual subscription to a central database. With careful selection, a 'shopping basket' of frequently used and representative commodities can be set against the highest, lowest and average prices being obtained by other subscribers to the same database. In the better agencies close attention is given to specification parameters, annual usage and quantities being purchased, to ensure that like is being compared to like. It is a relatively crude tool, but the monthly graphical output can indicate very quickly where things are going astray if the partner supplier is slow to reflect significant market trends. This simple performance monitor is particularly valuable in devolved structures where commodities are being called off from longish-term, centrally negotiated supply agreements.

The PI Price Management Service provides a confidential exchange of pricing information, and has considerable experience across a broad range of sectors including health service, higher education and financial sectors. The sort of monitoring available from them is shown in Figure 2.7.

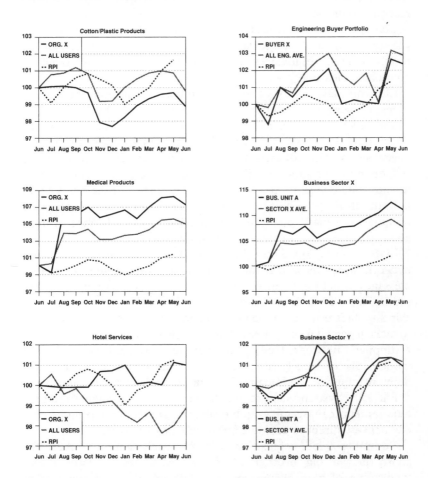

Figure 2.7 *Three types of shopping basket applications: affinity products and services, a buyer portfolio and business units (Purchasing Index (UK) Ltd)*

Electronic data interchange

Electronic data interchange or EDI is more than just a panacea for paperwork and postal delays. It is an important structural component of a well-managed supply policy. Effective use pre-necessitates the best aspects of partnership relationships including shared awareness and understanding of logistics and agreement on terms and conditions of trading.

Electronic data interchange interfaces between buyer and seller in the areas of purchase ordering and accounts payable, and when implemented carefully, can speed and clarify: The exchange of information between departments, e.g. requisition raising; receipt of specifications from requisitioners and transmission to suppliers; receipt and distribution of catalogue information; issue of requests for quotations and tenders; issue and amendment of purchase orders and call-off demands; receipt and monitoring of delivery schedules; receipt and issue of invoices, and transfer of payments using bankers' automated clearing service.

EDI can make a very significant improvement in order processing times, reducing the traditional purchase order raising to receipt and confirmation of supplier acknowledgement cycle from as long as fifteen days down to less than a fifth of this. Once database protocols have been established, the system is virtually error free. The resulting reduction in lead-times possible paves the way for implementation of just-in- time deliveries in manufacturing industry. In the retail world a form of EDI combined with electronic point-of-sale checkout terminals has made practicable the service levels and range of fresh goods that we have come to expect in our supermarkets.

In its fully developed form EDI works via a third party value-added network which is a sort of electronic clearing house to receive messages and pass them on to their correct destination. In a less sophisticated form paperless trading can be carried out with partner-ship suppliers using a simple modem and terminal emulating software to make a personal computer behave exactly like a remote terminal on a supplier's network. Good emulation software packages include a modem dialler usually holding around ten telephone numbers for different suppliers. Although this cannot provide all the advantages of a full EDI system, its use for frequent demands like stationery requirements can free up valuable purchasing effort and facilitate next day delivery direct to customers throughout your organization.

Computer-aided acquisition and logistical support, CALS for short, is the big brother of EDI. CALS encompasses direct monitoring of performance and progress on the most complex of projects. Often several sub-contractors will be linked together to share technical databases, support documentation generation and even specialist computer-aided design and manufacturing facilities.

CALS began as an initiative to support military projects. To support the deployment of a main battle tank like the UK Challenger requires over 20 000 pages of text in instruction and service manuals. By organizing new projects to start with a common computer database shared by all contractors, this complexity and the waste in costs associated with it can be substantially reduced. From the bidding stage onwards, weighty piles of paper will be replaced by machine readable data files. Information transfer between contractors and with the defence procurement authority will ultimately provide a much more manageable system for field support and logistics units.

3 Applying tools and techniques to implement strategic supply management

Review the organization's business plan

It is important to work out just where supply management fits in the organization, and what is the best role for it to play.

Just like the production department in Eli Goldratt's book *The Goal*, an effective supply management function must first carefully align itself with the strategic aims and corporate plan of its parent organization. Differing supply requirements need methods and techniques specifically tailored to provide the best results with an appropriate level of committed resource. Targeting strategic goals is fairly straightforward at first sight in a manufacturing business, where supply management's influence and control over costs appears to link directly to operating efficiency.

Concentrating too much on costs however can divert attention away from vital contributions to other corporate objectives. Then there are the 'not for profit' organizations like universities and hospitals where the potential for other than basic price reduction is certainly not immediately obvious. A much closer look is necessary in these areas with the conviction that while savings are certainly a consequence of good external resource management, they must not be seen as its solitary purpose.

Searching out the business plan, and putting it under close scrutiny, immediately stimulates thinking and discussion. Challenge its relevance, and then check out your relevance to it. Selection and effective application of power tools needs a clear understanding of the context culture and climate prevailing if the result is to be positive and as planned. There can never be a substitute for doing your own thinking. Progress forward can only be built on a foundation of facts, not on some vague aim to do things better.

Empowering the team

Many brains are better than one. The great tragedy of many organizations is that people arriving for work hang up their thinking power with their raincoats, content to spend the day carrying out the routine daily tasks, doing what they are told to do without putting much of themselves into it. Many books have been written on team building and motivational techniques, however one method which definitely works is to operate a formally structured quality improvement process. Again there are many available, but personal experience favours a system like that provided by the Quality Improvement Company of Cupertino in California. This is broadly a Philip Crosby style approach, much developed and refined by managing partners Chuck Harwood and Gerald Pieters.

The system is based on the cycle of quality improvement, a perpetual wheel of identification of problems, monitoring, analysis and corrective action. The wheel is driven round by eight managing elements: commitment, awareness, results, organization, planning, accountability, recognition and renewal. All of this is centred on the core concepts defining: the meaning of quality; its true impact on customers; who is responsible for it; how it can be measured; the importance of prevention; and just what standards can be achieved. There is a top level quality improvement team which is usually the manager and his direct reports. These are each given one of the managing elements to lead. Training then cascades down through the organization to establish weekly meeting units at all levels.

The supply management team will have to carry out a comprehensive assessment of needs and of resources. This will involve conducting surveys of the internal customers of our service, the principal external suppliers, and the people within the supply management organization itself. Operational measures will be established and registered. Sufficient time should be allocated so that this process can be carried out properly. The use of questionnaires and structured interviews is the normal means of conducting the surveys. Even just deciding who your customers are and where they are located can be an illuminating experience. The way forward must have a well-defined start point and signs and milestones which are clear and recognizable, not vague and questionable.

Vision and umbrella goals

From the clear understanding of requirements won from examination and questioning of the business plan, and from the benchmarking of present position gained from the assessment surveys, it should be possible to brainstorm a vision of the optimum scenario for the future. This will be different for every organization, but it is possible that you will come up with something like the following.

There will probably be three main elements to the vision:

1 People within supply management. People will have total commitment to continuous improvement, and will feel happy and
   fulfilled, working comfortably to clear published procedures.
   People will be fully trained and active in weekly meeting units
   searching out and correcting root causes of problems and working
   to prevent their recurrence.
2 Suppliers. The supplier base will be the right size with a very high
   proportion having the top 'A' class vendor rating for quality,
   delivery, service, responsiveness, contribution to innovation and
   value for money. Supply management will work with these
   vendors as partners not adversaries, with the emphasis clearly
   placed on ensuring that our requirements and their capabilities are
   clearly communicated and understood.
3 Internal customers. The users of the services of the supply
   management function will be in a position to provide the information and authorization necessary to enable us to provide a right
   first-time service. Supply management will be highly rated in
   terms of capability, contribution, accuracy and speed of response.
   Supply management will play a full role in the strategic planning,
   and be consulted at the earliest opportunity on all matters of
   external resource management. Supply management will make a
   recognized and measurably cost-effective contribution to the
   success of the overall organization.

Umbrella goals will clarify, amplify and develop the aims in the
vision. Short- and medium-term goals will use the quantified
measures registered during the assessment survey to target improvements in performance and monitor progress towards full achievement. There will be short- and medium-term goals in each of the
three elements of the vision. Existing resources will need to be
developed, and strategic changes made. Professor David Farmer, the
inspirational Welsh father of much of the current research into
purchasing in the UK, likes to talk about 'Gap analysis'. If you know
where you are and where you want to get to, then all you have to do
is take steps to narrow the gap. There may be a substantial cost in the
realignment of resources but an even greater return in the increased
empowerment and focused efforts that the review, assessment, vision
and goals will bring.

The vision and umbrella goals are shared and discussed and a series
of detail goals established in the context of the main objectives but
within the scope of the local groups. Techniques like brainstorming,

defect logs, impact and trend ranking, monitor charts, requirements analysis and flowcharting, cause and effect analysis and corrective action planning are easy to teach, readily acceptable and fun to use with people who may never have been asked to contribute before, and who have certainly never had the chance to put their ideas into action. Identifying issues, defects and problems and using the 'ask why five times' principle made famous at Toyota by Taiichi Ohno, not only effectively search out the real root cause, but in a way that brings everyone involved a richer, deeper understanding of each process and the theory and planning behind it.

Progress against goals is monitored and recognition awarded, but only when the progress is real and some physical change has been made. Be careful of the 'Hawthorne' effect named after experiments at the American Western Electric Company in the early 1920s, where it was found that any process which is subject to management scrutiny improves for a time no matter what change is made. Some critics have called the quality improvement process 'constant Hawthorne'. Permanent improvement can be achieved however when the corrective action is a physical change in working practice or procedure. Often this means writing a new procedure as the requirements are studied and understood for the first time. Quality means meeting the agreed requirements of the customer, and this is clearly impossible if the requirements are undefined.

Monitoring is a process best done as closely as possible to the point of action creation. It is one thing for a manager to look at a weekly printout of say purchase order amendments and send down instructions that the number should be reduced. But so much more effective if the staff creating the amendments are keeping the tab and hence understanding why each one was made and how and where unnecessary actions can be prevented. Only once local monitoring starts do people including managers begin to really understand what is actually being measured, often quite a different thing from the age-old assumptions. Only when activities are understood and accurately measured can they be controlled, and who better to do the controlling than the people carrying out the activity.

Figures 3.1 and 3.2 illustrate the principles of total quality management and extensive kit of tools developed by Analog Devices Inc., one of the world leaders in electronic component manufacture. Inspired originally by Art Schneiderman, Vice President for Quality and Productivity Improvement, Analog have successfully established a quality improvement culture throughout every function and aspect of their business world-wide. Just like any other business process, total quality management itself needs to be developed and improved to

---

Focus on customers
Focus on customers – customer satisfaction and even delight is the best and only means of achieving business success.

Continuous improvement
Management by fact – the discovery and analysis of facts is the basis of systematic problem solving, continuous improvement and decision making.

Management by process – focus on process improvement to achieve results. A process is a series of actions, operations or motions involved in accomplishing an end, in other words, it is the way we do our jobs. Management by process requires that managers consciously define the method they will use to make decisions.

Continuous improvement – a never-ending step-by-step improvement of business processes is required to achieve customer satisfaction and business success.

Focus on the vital few – focus on those activities which make a big difference in the company's quality and performance.

Total company involvement
We each have the responsibility to do our jobs daily without error, but, in addition, all employees are expected to continuously improve the processes by which they do their jobs.

Management leadership of TQM – management must be committed to TQM and must lead by example.

Respect for people – we must listen to, trust and serve each other.

Mutual learning – TQM begins and ends with education. Most of us can learn faster by learning from each other, individuals, teams and organizations.

Teamwork – there are many problems which cannot be solved by individuals but require a team effort.

Figure 3.1 *Principles of total quality management at Analog Devices Inc. (reproduced with permission).*

gain the maximum from recent advances. Analog Devices have developed a nine-step process which is based on positive opportunities, in contrast to a weakness-based approach, with the technique of participants writing out labels instead of brainstorming:

1   Select the opportunity. Write a positive sentence.
2.1   Explore the essentials

1 Ask why the objective is necessary.
2 Each team member writes labels answering the question.
3 Group similar labels together.
4 Title the groups of labels.
5 As a group, vote for top priority.

2.2 Examine constraints. Generate a list of constraints against the selected opportunity.

3.1 Determine objectives. Convert the essence of the prioritized 'why' answers from Step 2.1 into an action statement.

3.2 Set up a metric. Determine how to measure results and output.

4.1 Identify possible alternatives.
1 Start with the objective.
2 Ask how to achieve it.
3 Write one label per person.
4 Group similar labels.
5 Use a tree diagram.
6 Pick one alternative.

4.2 Select a solution. Carry forward the most important alternative from Step 4.1.

5.1 Develop plan. Develop an optimistic plan to achieve the objective using the selected alternative from Step 4.2.

5.2 Forecast obstacles to solution. For each stage of the optimistic plan, pessimistically develop potential obstacles to achievement.

5.3 Countermeasures. For each obstacle identified, develop countermeasures.

6 Plan and implement schedule. Use a PERT chart and time network to plan high level schedule and implementation.

7 Evaluate effects. Results and data from the implementation step are collected and analysed. Comparison with prior results, clearly understood, provide the basis for the next step.

8 Standardize. Once improvements have been implemented, they are standardized.

9 Reflect on the process. This is the opportunity to step back and ask whether the right process or problem was chosen for improvement and whether the improvement method itself was executed fully, or could be improved.

On a lower but very much simpler to apply level, the ship diagram in Figure 3.3 shows how the problems influencing any supply management operation can be thought of as jagged rocks, above which the ship is sailing happily, and probably ignorant of the dangers below. Not only do the rocks signify the risk of catastrophic failure, but they also force up the level of water required if safe navigation is to continue. This high water level represents high costs in terms of

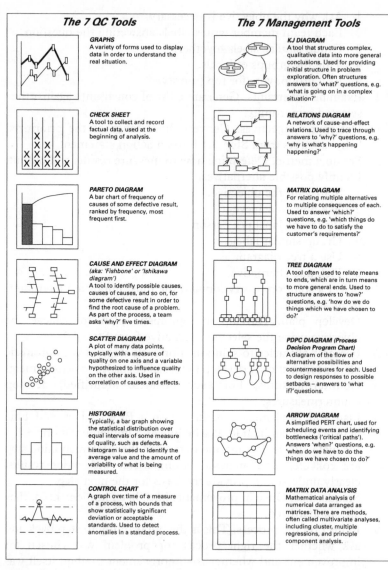

Figure 3.2 *Quality and management tools used by Analog Devices Inc. (reproduced with permission)*

having extra stock just in case we run out, or extra suppliers in case the usual one cannot cope. It represents the resources required because we need to do things more than once to get them right, and the waste because our specifications are not clear enough.

The example in Figure 3.3 shows the successful changes made by the staff of a small central supplies office in the purchase and

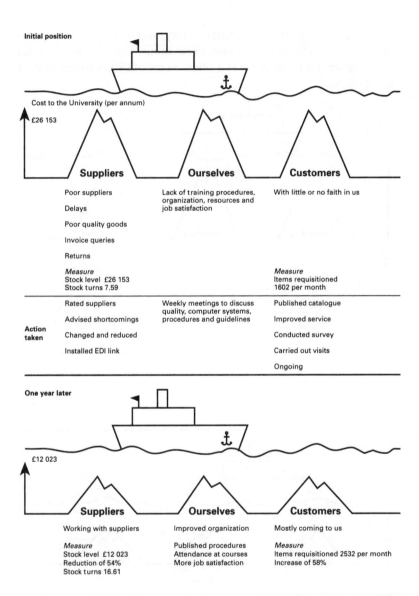

Initial position

Cost to the University (per annum)

£26 153

Suppliers	Ourselves	Customers
Poor suppliers	Lack of training procedures, organization, resources and job satisfaction	With little or no faith in us
Delays		
Poor quality goods		
Invoice queries		
Returns		
Measure Stock level £26 153 Stock turns 7.59		*Measure* Items requisitioned 1602 per month

Action taken

Suppliers	Ourselves	Customers
Rated suppliers	Weekly meetings to discuss quality, computer systems, procedures and guidelines	Published catalogue
Advised shortcomings		Improved service
Changed and reduced		Conducted survey
Installed EDI link		Carried out visits
		Ongoing

One year later

£12 023

Suppliers	Ourselves	Customers
Working with suppliers	Improved organization	Mostly coming to us
Measure Stock level £12 023 Reduction of 54% Stock turns 16.61	Published procedures Attendance at courses More job satisfaction	*Measure* Items requisitioned 2532 per month Increase of 58%

Figure 3.3   *The ship now sails on safer seas*

distribution of a wide range of common consumables for the University of Edinburgh. At the outset people were working very hard but getting little recognition or job satisfaction. The university has sites and faculties dispersed over a wide area in and around Edinburgh. Many departments had lost faith in the central service and were doing their own purchasing and stockholding, duplicating effort and using up valuable resources. By setting aside one hour per week to study the principles of total quality, and by making the transition from suspicion to enthusiasm, great things were achieved within a year. Figure 3.4 is included as a blank to try out somewhere in your organization.

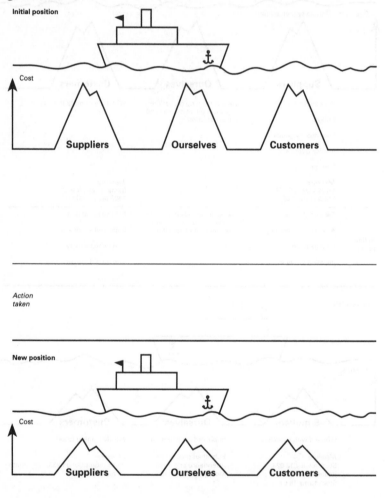

Figure 3.4   *Chart your progress*

Procurement manual and work instructions

The procurement manual will follow naturally from the vision and umbrella goals outlined above. It will normally start with a short, unequivocal statement of policy, followed by a description of the assessment, vision and umbrella goals being used to drive the organization forward.

The rest of the manual and the detailed sets of work and process instructions can be derived from quality meeting groups of the people who actually carry out the various tasks. Requirements will be analysed and defined. Output requirements will be clarified with customers. Input requirements will be clarified and agreed with suppliers. Process requirements will be clarified and agreed with the people carrying out the process. Documented procedures and work instructions should not become a restrictive web of dictated bureaucracy. Provided the people involved in the processes are responsible for raising and reviewing the manuals, there will be comfortable security that the essential tasks in the centre of Charles Handy's doughnut are sensible and practicable and being done without stress. In a culture of continuous improvement this will free up more energy for the creative outer ring of each person to flourish.

Classification and coding

Classification is the organization of knowledge into groups or classes. These are then coded according to some convenient reference system. Coding is the allocation of a unique code number to an item which has itself become unique by the precise nature of its description and specification of parameters. These techniques will ensure that distinct identification permeates through management information systems and logistical databases. Classification into families ensures that items of like kind are coded into groups. This provides an easy route to standardization and selection from like alternatives. Aggregation into shopping baskets for purchasing agreements is simplified. Supplier approvals and subsequent vendor rating analysis can be done neatly according to commodity groupings.

It would be good to report on world-wide coding systems which could easily be adopted. However, except in certain specialist areas mainly in consumer goods, no one system has proved capable of general adoption. Relational databases are normally capable of coping with dual identities so it is possible to combine an organization's unique requirements with code numbers used by customers and suppliers.

Classification and coding must never be seen as a clerical activity. Situated very close to design conception, the allocation of identification codes provides the difficult-to-repeat opportunity of questioning selection criteria and avoiding single source commitment. It is a job for a person with a good understanding of sourcing and supply management, with previous experience as an operational buyer.

Pareto analysis: beautifully simple, or dangerously simplistic?

The principle that the top 20 per cent of almost anything accounts for 80 per cent of the significance is one of the most commonly applied, and most useful tools in supply management. However, is the rule, normally credited to nineteenth-century Italian sociologist Vilfredo Pareto, rather too simple? So often buyers are encouraged to do a Pareto analysis of their purchase orders by value. 'Concentrate on the top 20 per cent, that's where the savings are to be made!' Similarly with expenditure by supplier, 'Don't bother with the trivial 80 per cent of companies with low spend figures!'

The problem is not Pareto's but rather the failure to understand that order value, and expenditure with a supplier are both only parts of the real cost of acquisition. In most cases it costs significantly more in time and resources to deal with the trivial many than with the significant few. Many buying offices would do better to allocate more time to sorting out the trivial many and getting them firmly under control. The savings in actual resources applied within and outside supply departments can be very significant indeed. Once things are properly organized and true costs are being measured, then use Pareto analysis.

Cost analysis can be done at all levels, business, department, product or project. The straightforward sorting in descending order quickly identifies the most important areas. Risk analysis is equally important but tends to receive less attention because it is more difficult to quantify. Risk management is fully covered in Chapter 8, and to ensure that the correct tools are being applied to the correct task, it is fairly simple to make a risk exposure rating for Pareto ranking purposes.

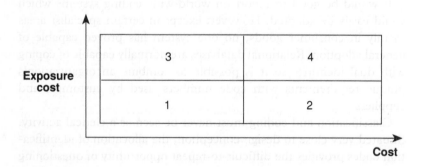

Figure 3.5 *The positioning tool matrix*

The positioning tool matrix

Figure 3.5 shows a four-sector positioning tool matrix which provides a useful means of sorting commodities or suppliers into separate compartments for different methods of attack. Sector 1 contains the low cost, low risk, 'trivial' many, and is so often allocated scant attention.

The importance of Sector 1

This is the sector that consumes so much of the tactical resources because insufficient strategic thinking is applied to it. The sum total of the costs of acquisition of all the items in sector one is very high indeed. So rather than being ignored as the trivial many, considerable attention should be paid to the items in this sector with the aims of simplification and standardization into product ranges. This can be a fairly complex engineering exercise or something as simple as highlighting a restricted range of preferred items in stock catalogues and databases.

George Stewart and Co., a leading Scottish supplier of stationery, has cut the stock range demands of some of its customers to a fifth by simply publishing a pre-printed requisition with the fifty of its most popular items already filled in, needing just a quantity and an authorization signature. There is a space on the requisition headed 'other items' but nearly everyone is content to choose from those already entered for them. This subtle customer conditioning works much better than restrictions imposed in a heavy handed manner. Caring about and delighting customers can legitimately include a little gentle manipulation towards a mutually beneficial realignment of requirements.

Sector 1 suppliers usually gain a very low annual income in return for a few of the crumbs of the supply cake. It is not surprising that their service and responsiveness sometimes slip up a little, as they concentrate attention on more important customers. This means that even more time and resources have to be expended in chasing and expediting. A much better approach is to combine as many items together into a decent shopping basket, and to go out to tender once a year or so with a more attractively sized portion of cake which the chosen supplier will pay much more careful attention to because of the larger annual income it brings in. Call-off arrangements and fax or EDI links can then be employed to automate the whole interface. The price indexing tool referred to in Chapter 2 can be employed to ensure that all contact is not lost with competitive market forces. However, again it must be remembered to take account of the total cost of acquisition in all comparisons if occasional spot buying opportunities seem very tempting.

Sector 1 commodities are extremely important. Traditional approaches call for 'low attention' and for procurement to be 'delegated'. Jumping straight to Sectors 2 and 4 where the high-profile big people are supposed to play, can result in brief glory followed by a spectacular fall as the organization collapses due to the absence of nuts and bolts. Alternatively and much worse is the permanent diversion of scarce and expensive non-supplies resources in a daily struggle to just keep things going. Neither result encourages the perception of supply management as being positive or strategic. The positioning tool matrix can also be seen as one of Charles Handy's inside-out doughnuts. Sector 1 is the core and unless it is properly, comprehensively and comfortably understood and organized, then there will be no time, space and creative energy for any of the other three areas. Don't skimp in your attention to Sector 1 or it will slowly, but steadily overwhelm and destroy you.

Sectors 2, 3, and 4 are important too

The prime drive here is to spend the time and space generated by successful management of Sector 1 to attack the high levels of cost and risk in a relatively small number of items and suppliers. These are the big issues which our main power tools can be deployed against.

Examine the supplier base

The principal purpose of the supply management function is the management of external resources. Does the existing supplier base meet the requirements in an optimum way? Good products and services come in easily once good suppliers are well managed. Supplier appraisal and ongoing performance rating and supplier development are areas of major responsibility and potential contribution. We are in this business with and because of our suppliers, not against them or in spite of them. Our interests and aims are to our mutual advantage and progress is a continuous process of identification and discussion of issues and problems. Targets for improvement must be the subject of agreements, and be realistic and measurable.

When suppliers are examined closely, they may well fail to meet all of our requirements or expectations. They probably don't fully understand what it is that we want from them. The measurements of performance must be made, but there is little to be gained from beating the supplier about the head with poor results. Much better to look together to see if, and where, improvements can be made.

Peter Stanack and Joy Batchelor of Coventry Business School (1994) have looked at partnership sourcing under two hypotheses:

- That customers and suppliers are involved in a teaching and learning process.
- That the effectiveness of teaching and learning strategies within the customer–supplier relationship will be affected by the nature of the relationship and the strategies used.

In the sample of organizations covered by them they found that adversarial models of purchasing seemed to predominate. Extensive use is made of normative or rule making strategies to protect the organization. This involves the implementation of tight contracts and specifications and rigorous quality controls. Since power is jealously guarded, the minimum information possible is given to the supplier leaving them blindfolded, slow to respond and seemingly inflexible. This leads to a vicious circle of increased quality controls.

The way we treat our suppliers in the teaching and learning process will have a significant effect on the prospects of achieving successful results. In Chapters 5 and 6 the progress which can be made in developing close relationships with the best suppliers will be developed fully. Unless the traditional adversarial approach can be laid to rest, there is no prospect for winning the real benefits. This is not to recommend a subservient approach or suggest that the supplier is always right. The supplier is sometimes about as likely to be right as the purchaser, and until they both get together to understand the actual requirements, and the progress made so far in meeting them, neither party has much chance of doing a particularly good job. The supplier base should be developed like any other vitally important resource, with lots of cultivation, but also careful pruning where necessary.

Vendor rating – simple and done with the supplier

The examination can be at many levels of detail and rigour. It does not need to involve complex analysis and exponential smoothing techniques. Fully computerized integrated and objective systems are great if you have them and are confident that you understand the logic behind their results. But don't despair if you have no such level of sophistication, and don't neglect vendor rating through perceived lack of time and resources. This is the classic fire fighting trap. In its very simplest form the review can be a very easy checklist:

	Supplier A	Supplier B	Supplier C	Supplier D
Good quality products	3	4	5	5
Good prices	4	5	5	5
Good deliveries	3	5	5	3
Good communication	3	5	5	3
Work with us	3	4	5	3
Leads on new products	1	4	3	4
Advance warning of problems	1	5	3	2

The score ranges from one for very poor to five for very good. It is subjective and some of the criteria may need weighting according to their relative importance. However it is the sort of result that a small meeting unit of supplies or cross functional personnel can come up with in about fifteen minutes. It quickly shows that a lot of work will have to be done with Supplier A, and that Supplier C who is not far from a perfect rating will probably quickly react to a request for more attention to the last two categories to improve the areas where a low score of three has been awarded. This sort of simple survey can either be done in a brainstorming session involving a group of at least five purchasers and users, or by a questionnaire circulated among the most interested parties.

Vendor rating should be as fair and objective as possible and its results shared openly with the supplier involved. It is much simpler to carry out in a centralized system with the classic incoming inspection department providing a standard set of quality criteria such as functional features, physical features, freedom from damage, identification etc. Service requirements such as sending the correct item; packaging; documentation, etc., and conformance to a defined delivery schedule window can also be measured mechanistically and objectively at a central goods inwards facility. Responsiveness and contribution to innovation are not so straightforward and usually have at least an element of subjectivity. In a totally decentralized operation, objective data becomes much more difficult to collect. Major suppliers themselves should be required to monitor their own performance and present it for review on a regular, say quarterly, basis with plots of trends, targets for improvement and explanations of root cause and corrective action where things have gone wrong.

When this is done successfully, simple surveys like the illustration above, are a ready check on current status and a quick way of indicating areas for further improvement.

Finally be sure to communicate your findings to the supplier concerned, and especially make sure not to neglect the ones that you rate as having performed well. A positive customer rating is always an encouraging spur to keep up the good work, and go on to even greater things. Letters tend to get onto notice boards, or copied up to senior executives. Even better if you are prepared to produce a nice certificate of satisfaction rating. In many North American suppliers there is a special notice board in reception for vendor rating certificates with positive results. Once these plaudits are in place for all to see, there is a powerful self-induced pressure to make sure that ongoing performance is good enough to win another one next year.

More sophisticated supplier appraisal and development

At the other end of the scale the McDonnell Douglas Corporation supplier certification process deploys a team of six senior personnel to spend a week examining seventy-three areas of management and control, each subdivided into around six separate aspects. The visit comes about six weeks after completion of a self-assessment questionnaire listing the areas to be surveyed, and required to be returned with a self-marked score against each question. The major categories examined are: management, quality, delivery, cost, technology and customer support. Sectors within the categories include topics like communication, career development, health and safety, pricing procedures, as well as more usual criteria like change control procedures, process control strategy and problem correction.

The McDonnell Douglas process distils the individual scores into award categories up to gold standard. Each area has an assessment summary detailing the expectations in this particular section, the strengths observed and a comment on any areas where improvement is required. Actions and timescales for this are agreed for subsequent follow-up review in an ongoing process of supplier development.

Hewlett Packard is another successful corporation which sets great store by examination and development of the supplier base. Their common procurement objective is to:

> Maintain a competitive advantage by providing materials of the highest quality and lowest cost, with the best delivery, responsiveness and technology available by selecting fewer but better suppliers.

Key aspects of Hewlett Packard's 'Mutual working relationship strategies' include: 'active supplier management program'; 'consider suppliers an extension of HP's process'; and 'forecast sharing'. Hewlett Packard's TQRDCE matrices cover technology, quality, responsiveness, delivery dependability, cost and environmental management. Scoring is on a basis of zero when none of the criteria are met, to four when all of the criteria are achieved. There are between four and sixteen questions in each category. Reviews are ongoing and regular.

Hewlett Packard is well aware that the results that it seeks will not occur from random sourcing or selecting suppliers solely on competitive quotations. It will result from making the correct selection of suppliers and then working closely with them in specific areas to improve quality and productivity. To accomplish the objectives of its supplier performance expectations, the need is to establish and maintain long-term commitments; promote effective communications; obtain mutual agreement on expectations and goals; treat a supplier's process as an extension of Hewlett Packard's processes; and utilize a team approach to achieve performance improvements.

Hewlett Packard will share the success of this programme with suppliers who specifically contribute to their commitment to excellence. Successful supplier performance in the areas of TQRDCE can look forward to repeat business, increased sales, and profitable growth.

The Centre for Advanced Purchasing Studies (CAPS) at Arizona State University has carried out extensive research into cross-functional sourcing team effectiveness, summarized in a report by Robert Monczka and Robert Trent in 1993. The implementation plan in Figure 3.6 shows just how complex a task the selection process is.

The CAPS report sees the critical relationship between cross-functional sourcing team authority and increased team effectiveness as an important research finding.

> If the reason to use a team is to improve the quality of organizational decision making and goal achievement, then a group of competent professionals should have internal and external decision making authority.

A separate local study of Japanese-owned companies in South Wales found that sourcing change decisions had to be fed back to Japan for approval (Davies 1994) The three to six months that this took had a negative effect on the 'objectivity' of the local sourcing teams.

Progression from a start with a few thousand direct suppliers to a network sourcing status with every supplier chosen by a cross-functional team is certainly not likely to happen overnight. Many good supplier relationships will have formed naturally already and can be developed further to mutual benefit. As discussed under

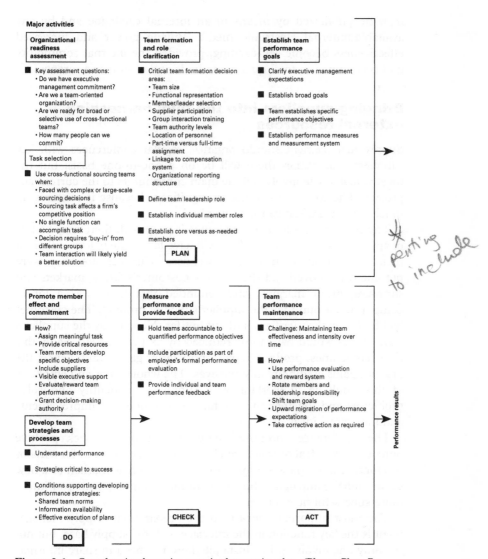

Figure 3.6 *Cross-functional sourcing team implementation plan. (Phases: Plan, Do, Check, Act.)*

Sector 1 in the positioning tool matrix, there is no substitute for careful attention to standardization and combining like-products into shopping baskets. One initial version of a first-tier supplier might be an internal commodity store which may later be completely replaced by a distribution agency. In a totally decentralized organization with devolved purchasing powers, the first move towards more strategic procurement may well be a drive to improve the efficiency of any internal commodity arrangements already in existence. These can then be publicized by means of an internal catalogue and by any available internal electronic media. Buying power and increased effectiveness become self-exciting, provided the internal commodity group is trained in total quality methods and customer awareness.

Bringing suppliers into the fold: harnessing external resources

Supply management should organize regular conferences with key suppliers. Sometimes these will be on a one-to-one basis, but the most valuable will involve all the main contributors to the current key project. The word 'conference' is significant because it conjures up much more significance than 'meeting'.

The first time a supplier conference is proposed, there may be lots of apprehension. Many suppliers will have faced one before, either on their own or at a customer's premises. Chances are they were presented with overhead slides of the customer's fading markets and shrinking profit margins, and reminded that there was a lot of competition around for the supplier's type of product. The customer had had to make sacrifices and cut out fat. Now it was the supplier's turn. Prices would have to be reduced by xx per cent etc. Sadly this does sometimes produce small short-term gains, and hence the practice gains credibility in some eyes. The whole ethos and emphasis of this book lie in working with suppliers to identify and solve problems, and together to look for opportunities for improvements and innovative ideas.

The conferences proposed here are set out to seek positive outcomes. An ideal occasion can be in the run-up to a bid for a major product, or in preparation for the launch into a new market, or a new promotional campaign. The aim is to take suppliers with you into a more successful new future.

The most important work is in the preparation. Supply management is the key function in the interface with the supply base, but not the only one involved. For instance there is a need to share information about future market prospects. Marketing should be represented to give as much data as possible on projected sales, volumes and timescales, a few pictures and some of the bullish charts that all marketeers have and love. Most of all marketing should be present to sell the positive nature of the new requirement and to hear and react to suggestions from suppliers.

It is important to include the specifiers, be they engineers, architects or whatever. Latest versions of plans drawings and specifications should be freely available, together with if possible, a mock-up model, or an early prototype. Hardware of any form is stimulating.

Suppliers are too often left to concentrate on just their little corner of the detail, with very little chance to see it as a vital part of a greater whole. Operations, users, quality, safety, and anyone with a significant input can be included. Supply management needs to be able to cover the practical logistical aspects, including payment and contractual terms, but their main thrust is to chair and manage the whole thing, to set it up properly and see it through to its successful conclusion.

Work needs to be done to make sure that it happens at all. Verbal promises of support a few weeks in advance need to be turned into physical reality on the day. It is obvious to the supply management function that interaction with suppliers is important, but it might not be perceived in such sharp focus all round. Other functions have pressing priorities of their own. Visits need to be made prior to the meeting to extract details of the key issues marketing intend to bring on the day.

Time can be spent with the specifiers familiarizing yourself with the important broad aspects. Seeking help to identify and list the cardinal points which are vital to the function of the project, also sows the seeds of thinking that other less important parameters should not be set in concrete. Make sure that models or prototype hardware are available. Arrange to collect them personally if necessary. Produce a formal agenda for circulation in advance with a list of the names and functions of participants. These points may seem trivial, but can do so much to establish teamwork and set the significance of the event in its proper context. Especially if the holding of supplier conferences is a new idea, it is worth making every effort to attract the best teams from all the participating organizations. Preparing an agenda and listing participants is a discipline which enforces thought about the best sequence of events and about who should be there. Only a few people can take in the names of a room full of new faces. Phone numbers, particularly of the representatives from other functions in your own organization immediately signal openness to communicate.

Preparing a half-decent cover and putting the papers together in a folder speaks volumes more than a few photocopied sheets stapled at one corner. Arrange parking spaces and pre-prepared visitors' badges. Put up some signposts to the conference room. Be there early yourself to check arrangements and to meet and greet people. It will work if you put work into it (Chadwick, 1993).

Requirements analysis: examining requirements and processes

Requirements analysis is a simple but productive way to unearth any problems, waste and gaps in understanding that may exist in the relationships with key suppliers. It is often said that purchasing is very easy if you know what it is you want to buy. Unfortunately buyers and suppliers have become skilled at making do with only part of the information. A surprising number of important goods and services are defined more by a series of assumptions rather than a carefully drawn up and agreed specification.

Requirements analysis is often used as part of a total quality approach. In the customer–supplier relationship there are really just three sets of factors:

- *Output:* The agreed requirements of the customer.
- *Input:* All the information and materials needed to do the job.
- *Process:* The major operations to be carried out to produce the output.

Once a few sheets of a flipchart have been filled with lists, it is beneficial to draw up a flowchart or series of related flowcharts. It always works out to be much more complicated than at first sight. The value comes from the greater understanding gained from questioning the various linkages and assumptions. Flowcharts which are complicated beg to be simplified. It is an excellent forum for 'what-if'? questioning and debate. It is particularly useful for establishing dependencies and making clear the implications of being late, meeting a critical design review, or failing to approve a proof.

Statistical process control

The collection and application of data can be used to bring any process under control. Statistical process control provides an objective means of monitoring any process where transformation takes place, be it in manufacturing, the provision of a service, or the communication of information. A principal feature of this tool is the creation and display of simple charts and graphs.

Processes are studied and their variabilities and inconsistencies recognized and recorded. Why do they vary so much? Do we understand fully what is happening in the process under investigation? Whether the process is a critical part of the manufacturing cycle at a supplier's works, or the time it takes to process a purchasing requisition in our own buying office, there will be control data which can be captured relatively easily. Variability and inconsistency are the causes of most quality problems. By first measuring just how far the divergence from the norm is, many clues are uncovered as to what is really going on. There can be variation in the way people do things, perhaps through lack of agreed requirements, (Is more training required?); variation in materials, (Is there ambiguity in the specification?); variation in machine operation, (Is it the right machine for the application?, Does it need more regular maintenance?).

Because it looks specifically at variation, statistical process control can be much more powerful than other total quality tools. It is not just concerned with problems and deviations. It is a tool which can be applied to processes which are within specification and believed to be satisfactory. Statistical process control can be a vital part in the ongoing search for improvement and brings powerful diagnostic pressures from the display of relatively simple data.

Value engineering and value analysis

Value engineering and value analysis are techniques which date back to around 1950 when Lawrence Miles of General Electric in the USA defined the process as 'an organized creative approach which has for its purpose the efficient identification of unnecessary cost; i.e. cost which contributes neither quality, nor use, nor life, nor appearance, nor customer features'. Value analysis is used where an existing product is picked apart and examined. Value engineering is the process of taking all of the considerations into mind while designing a new product.

Value analysis is the ideal tool to stimulate thinking and suggestions, and to identify aspects of a product or service which can be usefully modified or omitted.

The stages are as follows:

- Identify and list the major cost elements.
- Arrange in descending order.
- Examine each principal cost driver with the questions:
  What are its basic functions?
  Are they all necessary?
  Can they be simplified?
  Can they be performed in some other way?
  Can unnecessary display features be eliminated?
  Can the physical parameters be reduced?
  Are tolerances too stringent?
  Are specifications too tight?
  Can manufacturing methods be simplified?
  Can operations be combined?
  Can standard methods, tools etc. be used?
  Can prefabricated parts be used?
  Can alternative materials be used?
  Can materials be standardized?
  Where can waste be reduced?

The whole process needs to be as interactive as possible and no suggestion, however obscure, should be ruled out of court without proper consideration.

An excellent opportunity to put this process into practice occurs at the proposal preparation stage of any project which contains a significant proportion of bought-in material and parts. Rather than simply obtaining quotations and discussing the major cost drivers at an internal cross-functional meeting, much better results can be gained by inviting the suppliers to be present to play a full part. This makes sure that suppliers or potential suppliers understand the requirements as clearly as possible, and that the buyer's organization, including the specifiers, the operations people and marketing, is party to all the assumptions that have been made. Even more importantly, it is a means of creating a forum where everyone can work together to identify real cost and risk reductions.

Life cycle costing – terotechnology or 'womb to tomb'

The true cost of ownership of any supply or service includes events which take place before and after the delivery date. In some circumstances the purchase price can be a minor factor in the total expenditure necessary to plan for, own and use, and finally to dispose safely of a piece of equipment or service provided by an external agency.

- Pre-acquisition costs   Investigation; Specification; Design; Budget allocation; Preparation for receipt.
- Acquisition costs   Purchase price including delivery, insurance and taxes; Installation; Commissioning; Training.
- Operating costs   Labour; Material; Consumables; Energy supply.
- Maintenance costs   Specialist labour; Specialist tooling; Spare and replacement parts; Reduced output with age.
- Downtime costs   Lost profits; Extra costs of overtime or sub-contracting charges.
- Disposal costs   Safe disposal by resale including any ongoing liabilities; Cost of removal for sale or scrap; Re-instatement of land or buildings for alternative use.

From nuclear power stations to humble photocopiers, owners have discovered that no procurement decision should be taken on purchase price alone. Once a cash-flow plan is established, costs should be brought forward to a common point in time using a present value calculation. Only then can the real cost of ownership be seen clearly and in a way which can be readily compared with alternative investment proposals.

Use of consortium agreements

Aggregating purchasing demand into the hands of regional consortia has been common in the UK for local authorities, universities and regional health services for many years. As well as providing a forum for joint negotiations with very substantial buying power, the consortia act as centres for the exchange of knowledge, experience and professional expertise. Buying groups have been in existence in the private sector for some time, particularly in the retail trade, and there is some evidence of guarded moves developing elsewhere. There may be much for supply managers in private sector business to learn from their public counterparts.

The Consortium for Purchasing and Distribution is a local government supplies organization based in Trowbridge, Wiltshire. It services a wide range of customers in the public sector including schools, social service homes, council offices and libraries. Its distribution area extends from Cornwall in the South to Anglesey in the North, and across to London in the East, covering in total 17 000 square miles. The stores operation offers over 5000 stock lines held in a warehouse measuring 63 000 square feet. The consortium supplies a wide selection of consumer and consumable products such as office and educational stationery, cleaning products, sports and games equipment, and computers. Stores turnover exceeds £30m pounds and goods are distributed by the group's own transport fleet.

The Joint Consultative and Advisory Committee on Purchasing for the Universities of Scotland and Northern Ireland was set up in 1974 with a remit to promote co-operation within the higher education and research communities in order to obtain the maximum benefits available in the purchase of materials, equipment, furnishings and services. Commodity groups include computer; laboratory supplies; stationery and office supplies; textiles, cleaning materials and protective clothing; workshop and maintenance supplies. This consortium does not operate a central store but distributes its agreements for buying action at institution level. It operates a computerized purchasing information system.

Consortia like the Consortium of Purchasing and Distribution can act like a network sourcing arrangement and work quite well provided contact is not lost entirely with the tiers of manufacturers and suppliers lower down the pyramid. The Joint Advisory and Consultative Committee on the other hand, while providing the consortium benefits of aggregation of spending power, also concentrates on the development of the supply management organizations within the individual institutions which are its constituent members.

Implications of international free trade agreements for purchasing in the public sector

The World Trade Organization which replaced the General Agreement on Tariffs and Trade (GATT) in 1995 is the widest of a series of institutions set up to liberalize world trade. Left to their own devices, most governments are subject to too many political pressures to protect local producers to ever act entirely in the selfless interests of purely global issues. The public procurement directives of the European Community or the complex strictures of the North American Free-Trade Agreement can either be looked upon as an unwelcome intrusion of bureaucracy, or as powerful tools. With patient explanation they can be harnessed to help encourage the most recalcitrant senior executives and academics to sit down and devote time to defining their requirements in close detail, and agreeing in advance the criteria against which the final contract award is going to be made.

European Union policy on public procurement

The Treaty of Rome, which set up the original European Economic Community, contains in Article 30 a provision prohibiting the restriction and impeding of imports from other member states. To speed up the achievement of a true open market, several major directives have been created and implemented by most member states.

The first of these was the Supplies Directive issued towards the end of 1991 to cover public supply contracts of 200 000 ECU and above (the ECU equivalent of 130 000 special drawing rights and above for a GATT contracting authority). GATT contracting authorities in the UK are mainly bodies controlled directly by central government. In the same year the Works Directive was issued applying to proposed public works contracts where the estimated value of the contract is 5 000 000 ECU or above. The Services Directive followed in 1993, with the same 200 000 ECU threshold as the Supplies Directive. In 1994 these three directives were brought together in the Consolidated Supplies Directive. Every two years the national currency equivalents of the thresholds are revised. The basis for conversion into national currencies is the average daily exchange rate over a two-year period to the end of the previous August.

The Consolidated Supplies Directive introduced for all contracting authorities the requirement for prior information notices, indicating purchasing requirements subject to the directive for the forthcoming financial year. As well as its intended purpose of alerting suppliers to potential demand, this is a useful stimulus to forward planning, particularly in large decentralized organizations.

The contracting authority is required to publicize its requirements in the official journal of the European Communities. Adequate time must be allowed for expression of interest and submission of tenders. The minimum periods are laid down in the regulations. There are three possible procedures: an open procedure where anyone who is interested may tender; a restricted procedure where only those selected by the contracting authority are allowed to submit bids; and the negotiated procedure which only applies in certain particular circumstances. The contracting authority is required to award the contract on the basis either of the offer of the lowest price or the one which is the most economically advantageous. Where the intention is to make the award on the basis of the offer which is the most economically advantageous, the criteria on which the decision will be based must be contained in the contract documentation where possible in descending order of importance. Allowable criteria for judgement include price, delivery date, running costs, cost effectiveness, quality, aesthetic and functional characteristics, technical merit, after-sales service and technical assistance. Where there is a requirement for compliance with technical specifications, these must be defined by reference to European specifications except under certain circumstances.

How effective is this sort of strategy? A research team from the University of Birmingham (Furlong, Lamont and Cox 1993) looked at the particular effect the European Single Internal Market was having on small to medium sized enterprises in the Humberside area in the UK. This size of company has been targeted as amongst the major beneficiaries, since they were assumed to be the group most likely to have suffered from barriers created by protectionist national procurement strategies. The Birmingham research did not find that all the objectives were being achieved:

> The compulsory competitive tendering/public procurement reforms create opportunities and problems for private and public sector. Clearly they ought to mean more opportunity for potential suppliers to participate in public tenders, but unless they are aware of the increasing propensity of the larger purchasers to prioritize technical qualities, reliability, and security of delivery, the local economy is unlikely to benefit. On the contrary, the reform of purchasing procedures may

disturb established supply chains with the public sector to the detriment of local small and medium sized enterprises. The lack of awareness of the specific impact of the single internal market reforms among local small and medium sized enterprises increases this danger. At the same time, the public sector and the utilities face increasing costs in meeting the legal requirements of the public procurement reforms, which they do not see as an optimal purchasing strategy in any case. The large private sector companies interviewed all claimed to have strategies in place to respond to the single internal market; they were uniformly sceptical of the impact of the reforms, which they, like the public sector organizations, regarded as more concerned with a 'level playing field' for existing large suppliers than a practical attempt to restructure markets in favour of small and medium sized enterprises.

Non-traditional areas and 'protected' services

Even when the supply management function is fully recognized for its contribution, and given early involvement in all the typical areas of 'bought-out' expenditure, there are likely to be 'protected' services considered by some to be too specialized to come under normal procurement rules. These vary according to the territorial jealousy in particular management sectors, but will include some or all of the following:

- accounting, auditing and book-keeping services;
- advertising;
- architectural services, planning, landscaping;
- building cleaning and property management services;
- design contests;
- education and training;
- financial services including banking and investment, and insurance;
- health and social services;
- hotel and restaurant services;
- legal services;
- management consultancy;
- market research and public opinion surveys;
- recreational, cultural and sporting services;
- postage, mailing and courier services;
- publishing and printing;
- research and development consultancy;
- security;
- sewerage and waste disposal;
- telecommunications services;
- travel and transport.

The Centre for Advanced Purchasing Studies at Arizona State University goes so far as to include pensions and taxes as legitimate areas for supply management involvement. The suggestion is not that supplies take all the above and other things on board as their prime responsibility, but rather that the normal procurement questions should be asked. What are the cardinal points in the deliverables? Are they specified in such a way that several suppliers can bid? Effective and formal control should be exerted and demonstrated to ensure that:

- The correct nature and level of requirements are being specified.
- The acquisition is properly authorized with all due regard to budget.
- Value for money is being obtained.
- Sufficient controls are in place to ensure that the service received is suitable for the function intended and is within the prescribed timescale.
- The organization's ethical code is fully complied with.

Part Three

Strategic Supply Sourcing

4 To make or not to make – the strategic choice

All organizations need to consider very carefully what their chosen role really is. Where are their areas of specific expertise? What is it that differentiates them from the rest? What are the core activities that management resources should be dedicated to, to preserve that leading edge? What are the non-core activities that might be better done by a supplier who leads and concentrates in that particular field? Today manufacturing industry focuses on learning how not to make things. How not to make the parts that divert a company's resources away from cultivating its real skills and future potential.

It certainly wasn't always the case. Vertical integration is the philosophy of buying-in as little as possible other than basic raw materials, and carrying out all the manufacturing processes under direct internal control. Henry Ford started out as a specialist assembler of cars, buying engines and chassis from the Dodge brothers, and other sub-assemblies from elsewhere. However by the time he opened the legendary River Rouge complex in Detroit in 1931, he had changed his tack and resolved to be independent of all suppliers. In *The Machine that Changed the World* (1990) Womack, Jones and Roos record:

> Ford pursued vertical integration partly because he had perfected mass-production techniques before his suppliers had and could achieve substantial cost savings by doing everything himself. But he also had some other reasons: for one, his peculiar character caused him to profoundly distrust everyone but himself.
>
> However, his most important reason for bringing everything in-house was the fact that he needed parts with closer tolerances and on tighter delivery schedules than anyone had previously imagined. Relying on arm's-length purchases in the open marketplace, he figured, would be fraught with difficulties.

Burt and Doyle (1993) add some cautionary observations:

> Frequently there is no easy or clear cut answer to the challenging question, 'Should we make this product or service or outsource (buy) it?' Several years ago, a president of the Ford Motor Company commented, 'At Ford we wasted millions making items we should have bought and buying items we should have made. But we could never figure it out before the fact.'

In the early 1980s, General Motors, Ford, and Chrysler were all confronted with make-or-buy decisions for their semiconductors. Interestingly enough, one chose a pure buy, one chose to invest heavily in manufacturing capacity, and one chose a hybrid approach without a manufacturing investment. In retrospect, it would appear that each decision was correct based on the unique circumstances at each company. Interestingly, with ten years of hindsight, it appears that all three strategies have been successful.

Osborne and Gaebler (1992) stress the difference between management and operations, and the quite separate issues of steering and rowing in an organization:

> Steering requires people who can see the entire universe of issues and possibilities and can balance competing demands for resources. Rowing requires people who focus intently on one mission and perform it well. Steering organizations need to find the best method to achieve their goals. Rowing organizations tend to defend 'their' method at all costs.

Argenti (1974) examines the problem from a consideration of centrifugal forces within the organization:

> It is a phenomenon found mainly in the larger organization; namely the difficulty of holding the organization together as a coherent whole. It is not only a matter of maintaining control – manifestly this must be more difficult for the chief executive of a large organization than a small one – there is also the problem of deciding which new activities will best complement the existing ones, how the existing ones should be altered to maintain the organization's balance in a changing environment...'

The simple make-or-buy decision is in fact an extremely complex one involving the need to maintain or improve cohesion in the organization in the eyes of customers, employees and shareholders, as well as the vital requirement of identifying and concentrating on core activities.

Straightforward subcontracting or facilities management

Contracting out some or all of the manufacturing processes or service provision on a long-term basis is a quite distinct strategy from simply off-loading work during times when demand exceeds internal capacity. To be cost effective it requires a dismantling of the part of the asset base dedicated to these peripheral activities, and an abandonment or at least a serious dilution of the associated skills and capability. In return an organization must ensure that the subcontractor chosen brings access to much improved abilities, greater investment in equipment and technology, and increased flexibility. As a specialist in say, contract manufacturing, the new partner should be able to provide:

- An established quality assurance system with regular internal audits, and management review, backed by approval status in the BS 5750 or ISO 9000 series.
- Access to a wide range of up-to-date, well maintained, and calibrated machinery, process plant, and test equipment.
- The full range of specialist manufacturing skills with ongoing skill development programmes.
- A sophisticated communication system with comprehensive progress reporting.
- An integrated materials management system.
- The flexibility to absorb increases and decreases in demand levels as requirements change.
- Quick reaction to new demands to get your products to market without having to wait for investment decisions and extended lead-times for the purchase of new plant and equipment.
- Advice and guidance on new developments in subcontract manufacturing.

Facilities management seemed to start life as a description for the day-to-day running of an organization's computer network. This usually included hardware and software maintenance, and sometimes provision of new equipment and packages. It now covers many more of the activities that its name actually suggests, in some cases extending to everything from gardening and security to the provision of car pools and even secretarial services. Specialist suppliers in this field include P&O Total Facilities Management (P&OTFM). A successful relationship between P&OTFM and computer giant Digital was reported in Purchasing and Supply Management (Tulip 1991).

> *Case study* – Total facilities management:
>
> An important consideration when P&OTFM won the contract with Digital, was that the customer did not want a 'big bang' style change and especially the changeover had to be transparent to Digital's customers despite the fact that their first contact through reception or switchboard would now be with P&OTFM employees. Many of the staff in fact moved over to P&OTFM from Digital, but P&OTFM also brought in some of its own managers, and

in addition, can use its position as part of the larger P&O Group to utilize seconded specialists for the management of specific projects – a specialist from sister company Bovis, for instance, to supervise the fitting out of a new building.

Although the P&O Group includes leading companies in most of the areas covered by a facilities management contract, from building work (Bovis) and catering (Sutcliffe) to vending services, security services, laundry and washroom services and even tropical plants for offices, P&OTFM's strength is in selecting the most cost effective and appropriate companies from the whole marketplace to tailor the appropriate package for the individual client.

Performance monitoring comes in two forms. Firstly and obviously there are the usual financial measures of performance to budget and cost savings achieved. The second measure is a self-score test, a sort of exam paper, that P&OTFM's managers can use to assess performance on a continual basis – whether the washrooms are clean, how long it takes for the switchboard to answer the phone, response time to equipment failures, etc. At intervals the client will come in and administer the same test.

The score test covers essentially anything that you can assess by walking around and looking. Equally important to a customer-oriented client like Digital, is the question of staff attitudes, and this is the subject of continuous review with the client, and is addressed by considerable training effort.

Understanding the strategic implications of make or buy

The advance of technology, and the development of business skills across the whole spectrum of activities, have simply made it impossible for any organization to do everything for itself. The trend is progressively to a modular status with non-core activities subcontracted to specialists. The pressure of a rapidly changing world demands agility and flexibility. The best results will come to organizations who put their best efforts into the areas in which they excel and have a leading edge. Peripheral activities to which they can add no value are best subcontracted to people whose speciality they are. Creating real competition in the provision of products or services to which no value is added, can provide access to innovation in the marketplace as well as accountability and lower costs.

Management effort that has been bogged down with the day-to-day tasks of running the system can be freed up to think about how it should be run. Managers can be released from having to confuse activity with action. Instead of going home exhausted after a day spent fire-fighting problems at the detail level, they can relax after reviewing progress with the specialist contractor who is now running that part of the business with minimum hassle. It might be the director of human resources who is no longer having to cover for key staff bogged down organizing staff relocation, or having to devote valuable time to temporary staff recruitment. It might be the management information systems manager who has been freed up from having constantly to react to problems with the management of the complex computer network. It might be the production director concerned about whether limited investment resources should go on replacing the ailing laminating press in the printed circuit board manufacturing unit, or make a real difference if only he could earmark it for the latest upgrade of software for his production planning team.

As Chapter 10 on global sourcing shows, we are all working in a global market whether we like it or not. If there is no option but to strive for world-class standards, and since it is more than likely that these will only be achieved in the areas where the best talent is deployed, then it doesn't really make sense to have too much vital resource tied down in the struggle for mediocre success in peripheral activities. Where such activities are readily available and can be harnessed effectively, they should be sourced from an external supplier. However the process needs to be managed very carefully. There are significant implications for personnel relations and motivation. Some individuals will be directly affected and will at best have to face some uncertainty, retraining, and transfer to another part of the organization. The process is likely to have some impact on all staff and can slow down or even derail initiatives like total quality management.

Of equal importance, there are major implications for the supply management function itself. The clerical scenario outlined in Chapter 2 is just not capable of handling the demands of external resource management generated by a progressive make-or-buy strategy. The carefully calculated transfer of more resource provision to the hands of external suppliers, requires a matching increase in the capability of the supply management function which will have to be charged with making sure that they perform.

What to make, and what to buy?

In the ideal world, organizations would concentrate fully on their core, or prime business activities. Other services and support facilities would be handed over to the very best providers in the relevant fields. These suppliers would be chosen by cross-functional source selection teams after a careful and comprehensive specification of the requirements. Non-core or peripheral activities could include:

- Professional support services, including financial and administrative services, travel, human resource support, staff development and training.
- Facilities management including responsibility for computer and communications networks, hardware and software provision and maintenance, data processing skills.
- Building and plant maintenance, catering, cleaning and security.
- Non-strategic manufacturing.
- Logistics and distribution.

Several major difficulties are likely to occur. For many of these activities, there will be some internal provision already in existence. In some cases it will simply be a distracting and time consuming adjunct to an essential core element. In others it will have developed into a sizeable semi-autonomous structure consuming a considerable amount of management time, talent and investment. The status of the internal facility will be somewhere in the following range:

- Highly rated by its internal customers and providing 100 per cent of the requirements.
- Mandatory instruction to use, mediocre but reasonably effective.
- Used by some internal customers, while others already use external providers.
- Only used by traditional customers, slow and inefficient, most business already goes outside.

One major difference between external and internal providers of service is that external providers have a trained sales staff. They are also likely to be much more demanding of a full specification of all aspects of the work to be carried out. This may be something that the internal facility has never had to opportunity to work to. One of the major benefits of any form of market testing is the discipline which has to be adopted of producing a clear definition of needs and an exhaustive functional specification. In many areas of the UK public sector, the process of market testing established internal services has stimulated a fresh examination of service requirements and a significant transformation in performance levels. This might be seen as a useful by-product of a make-or-buy strategy. However this would be missing the original objective. The fact that the management and workforce of an internal non-core activity can demonstrate under severe pressure that they can compete with the outside world can be taken to mean two things. Either that there is no really good external alternative, or that the talent displayed should be transferred to generate far greater returns in the main value-adding activities of the organization. This latter was the main reason for looking at a make-or-buy strategy in the first instance.

Ironically the internal facility which is performing well and is highly rated by all of its internal customers, is probably the one which can be sourced outside most effectively. Just as when processes are being computerized, the ones which are fully understood, safely under control, and working well manually, are much preferred by programmers to the complex tangled operations which prove difficult, and fail to work because no-one has ever taken the time to sort them out. However it is inevitably the activities at the bottom of the range which are selected as the first candidates for make-or-buy analysis. Because they are only used for a proportion of the organization's requirements, it is usually easy to prove that the effective price of their efforts, as calculated by dividing their operating costs including overheads by the low number of jobs that they actually get, is very high.

The problem with this approach is that of inactivated capacity. From this sort of cost analysis angle there may actually be savings to be made from bringing inside more of the work which is currently going out to external suppliers. This would work on the basis that because the internal facility is loaded below capacity the proportionate spread of overhead cost is reduced by being spread over a larger number of jobs. Fixed overhead costs have to be met whether or not the facility is up to capacity. Cost comparison alone should not be the final deciding factor. There are many different aspects to be taken into account. The internal facility may in fact be handling all the most difficult work and providing a patient and vital service to engineering design, or some other major core activity. There may be aspects of commercial secrecy to be protected, or a particular skill involved which it is desirable to retain within the organization. Management roles in the non-core activity may be a valuable training ground for junior executives who can have a little freedom to make mistakes and try out ideas without endangering the main business. The analysis needs to be fair and unblinkered.

The issue of what to make and what to buy is very much a strategic one requiring full executive backing and clear communication. In the context of partnership relations, Chapter 5, and strategic negotiation, Chapter 6, it should be taken from a position of a well developed supplier relationship with clear cost and capability awareness, far removed from the blind ignorance in the traditional adversarial confrontation with suppliers. The whole object of a partnership with a supplier is that by working together, costs and risk can be reduced and the customer's requirements can be met more readily. In *Beyond Partnership*, Richard Lamming (1993) advocates a move from the traditional practice of gradually cherry picking the operations of suppliers, to increase control of added-value at their expense:

> The basic problem with the make-or-buy decision was traditionally that the customer rarely knew, as a result of the choice, how much value was being added and at what cost. Cost accountancy within the organization was generally not good enough to show these factors accurately, so the make option would be more influenced by political factors (e.g. using existing capacity – including labour – because it was there) than by genuine cost/value calculations. The extreme of this is, of course, the stagnation of vertical integration in mass production, in which the supreme factor was ownership of the process: a mixture of myopic greed and insecurity.
>
> The buy option would also not provide the necessary value/cost data, since all the buyer was provided with was the price – a complex factor hiding many different costs.
>
> A developed relationship, however, should be able to provide better cost/value data through the process of the two parties working closely together, sharing information, etc.

The question of cohesion is even more difficult. The concept of the virtual organization of the future with no boundaries at all between functions and employers can conjure insecurity and lack of commitment for all but the most self-assured. The traditional experience of most people has been to work in a reasonably self-contained structure which gave the feeling of security partly by its size and breadth of activity. In the earliest organizations the patronage of the employer might provide the only access to decent housing, schools and social benefits. No one would advocate a return to this, but as non-core activities are increasingly stripped away to be handled by outside agencies a little consideration is necessary to ensure that some of the glue remains.

The need for strategic supply management

When organizations do and make for themselves practically everything they need, the requirements placed on the purchasing department are very minor. There may not even be a proper purchasing department at all. The transformation from a mainly make and do to a largely bought in status demands a considerable upgrading of the supply management resources. Deciding to transfer non-core activities to suppliers who specialize in that particular field brings the responsibilities of harnessing and managing external resources with skills and abilities quite different from those of controlling a captive internal activity. The immediate reaction of reassigning staff without retraining, from internal management positions to responsibility for procuring the resource from outside can misfire badly. Part of any make-or-buy decision must be to recognize the need to boost the resources of the supply management function.

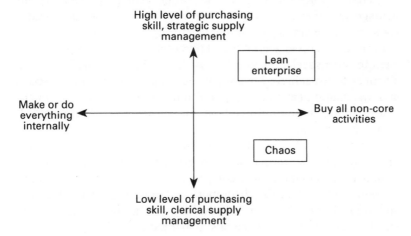

Figure 4.1   *The implications of make-or-buy for supply management expertise*

Figure 4.1 illustrates the make-or-buy choice along the horizontal axis, and the status of the supply management function displayed vertically. Low levels of purchasing skill and resource may be a possible option when a very large percentage of activity is carried out purely within the organization. However as the proportion of bought-in activity rises, the strength and expertise in the supply management function must be increased significantly if something approaching chaos is to be avoided. Too rapid a transition without the accompanying upgrading of the purchasing effort, will first bring doubts and fears to the supplier relationship, quickly followed by delays and cost escalation.

5 Strategic partnership

Introduction

Organizations cannot sustain competitiveness and success in a global market without the support of their suppliers. When given the opportunity, suppliers can have a significant influence on, and make an important contribution towards total cost management. In a strategic partnership role, suppliers will enhance the essential elements of on-time delivery, lead-time reduction, total quality management, flexibility, and new product introduction supported by leading edge technology and manufacturing excellence.

In order to access a source of differential advantage, organizations need to form special relationships with suppliers. Formation of such alliances is not achieved overnight, but requires a carefully prepared and systematic plan to develop and nurture the partnership. Such a course adopts a long term collaborative strategy as a key part of the overall supply plan.

This chapter offers an overview of the existing literature on collaborative relationship formation, identifying its evolution and its contribution to an organization's competitiveness and sustained success. Sections will explore the theoretical underpinnings in greater detail and argue that the linchpin for advantage in the end market is strategically linked with the choice of supplier partnerships.

Evolution of the collaborative relationship

In traditional organizations, buyers have favoured simple transaction exchange relationships with their suppliers. These involve multiple sourcing strategies that split the purchase of each item among two or more separate sources. It was considered to be the prerogative of the buyer to define the exact needs of their organization and the specifications of the products to be purchased. The only job expected of the supplier was to meet these requirements at a competitive price. Relationships with suppliers were essentially short term, valid only for a specific transaction. The relationship was adversarial and designed to play competing suppliers off against each other for price concessions. Suppliers were to be kept keen and hungry. There was frequent switching of suppliers. Sources tended to be domestic, with the focus only on price, quality to match the specification, and delivery. The orientation was clearly towards gaining short-term advantage for a specific transaction. There was a lack of long-term commitment on either side, with little concern for the interest of the other party, and hence a high degree of uncertainty and volatility in the relationship.

In this era of transactional exchange relationships, the power was perceived to be primarily with the buyer. As such many researchers focused their attention on studying supplier attributes, bid character- istics and choice strategies used by buying organizations to select suppliers on a transaction by transaction basis (Cardozo and Cagley 1971; Copley and Callom 1971; Crow, Olshavsky and Summers 1980; Dickson 1966; Gronhaug 1977; Hakan and Wootz 1975; Scott and Wright 1976; Westing, Fine and Zenz 1969; Webster and Wind 1972).

However the 1980s saw the emergence of a new world character- ized by rapid advances in technology and a breakdown of many traditional barriers to communication, trade and travel. The ideal of global competition became much closer to reality. Incessant striving for better quality was no longer just a virtue but a necessity for the very survival of organizations. Integrated management of all functions became a success requirement in which all departments had to work together towards the common goal of satisfying the needs of external customers in the best possible manner. This dynamic environment forced changes not only in the internal workings of organizations but also in their attitudes and behaviour towards suppliers.

They realized the futility of the traditional concept of maximizing short-term gains in each individual transaction, and keeping suppliers guessing. Further they came to realize that there were vast potential benefits in developing stable and strategic partnerships with selected suppliers through mutual and long-term commitment of resources, common interest and loyalty. Such arrangements could save the energy expended on managing numerous small transactions individ- ually to concentrate on handling much larger slices of the external resource pie. By working together organizations can make a much better job of satisfying the requirements of their end market, and thus increase their market share. Organizations realized that they were losing much more than they were gaining by treating products and specifications as their prerogative alone. Instead, by opening up their design departments and supply problems to their selected suppliers, a synergy resulted generating new ideas, solutions, and new innova- tive products. Thus began the era of relationship management.

Managing external relationships through supplier partnership or strategic partnership sourcing can be defined as the strategic establishment, systematic maintenance, and proactive enhancement of close, mutually beneficial, long-term business exchange relation- ships with a limited number of carefully selected partner firms. Such relationships are truly two-way in nature, and are equally meaningful from the buyer's and seller's point of view. External relationship management is characterized by the use of few or just one source of supply for each purchased item, very rare switching of supplier, and strong, mutual long-term commitment of both trading partners to the exchange relationship (Crosby and Stephens 1987; Dwyer, Schurr and Oh 1987; Jackson 1985; Shapiro 1985; Speckman and Johnston 1986). Figure 5.1 shows the evolution of the collaborative relationship.

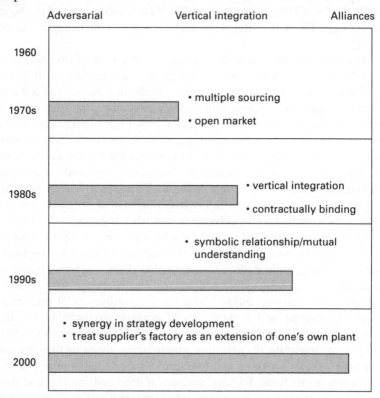

Figure 5.1 *Evolution of collaborative relationship*

One of the major benefits of supplier partnership is the synergy created between two organizations working together on common problems to achieve common goals. Such synergy can be expected to result in a constant improvement in product quality through careful monitoring and co-operative analysis. Continuous innovative effort can be anticipated to upgrade products, develop new applications, and maintain both organizations' competitiveness in the marketplace. These factors have a direct impact on cost reduction, profitability increase, and market expansion for the products of both buyer and seller.

Types of partnership grouping

While it is common to think of a simple partnership between one buyer and one seller, in practice the market is much more complex. Most buying organizations will have many suppliers, some for similar if not identical products. Similarly suppliers will usually have a number of different customers for the same or similar products. There are generally two main types of partnership grouping as illustrated in Figure 5.2.

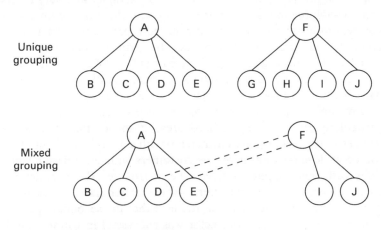

——— primary partnership relationship

– – – secondary partnership relationship

Figure 5.2 *Types of partnership groupings*

In the first example in Figure 5.2, Organization A is a market leader with unique primary partnership arrangements with Suppliers B, C, D and E. Organization F is a market follower but has developed its own group of suppliers, none of whom trade with organization A which is F's competitor in the market. In the second mixed grouping which is much more common, A has primary partnerships with Suppliers B, C, D and E, but F buys from Suppliers D and E. However because of their primary link to A, F can only establish secondary partnership relationships with D and E.

These mixed groupings tend to be the norm with suppliers often forming relationships with customers who may be in competition with each other. Where the customer is not powerful enough to form truly unique relationships where mutual benefits can be fully exploited, the gains from partnering will have to be shared. However the main attraction may be the access to innovation and efficiency spun-off as a result of the supplier's collaboration with the dominant primary partner.

In general, only market or technology leaders can form and sustain primary partnerships with the best suppliers. Market followers, and niche differentiators must choose either to set up their own independent primary partnerships with different suppliers if they have enough business to sustain their interest, or form secondary partnerships with suppliers to the market leader. If the latter course of action is the only one possible, it can still bring major gains. However, secondary partners are usually unable to sustain the momentum of the relationship if the primary partner pulls out. For example, in a very diverse and low-volume industry sector like defence, there is seldom enough business to justify the investment from both parties to form a unique grouping. Defence contractors can be primary partners usually because of technological edge in a particular niche, but in general there is insufficient business to be other than an influential secondary partner for most product and material requirements.

However being a secondary partner can be fraught with danger particularly in a very specialized area. If the dominant customer decides to break a primary partnership with a supplier and cut off the source of development drive, the customers with secondary relationships with that supplier may well be in trouble. The supplier may collapse completely or will certainly no longer have access to the necessary resources to maintain the lead that the secondary partners require. A UK defence contractor was successful in winning all the UK Ministry of Defence requirements for night vision goggles for airborne applications. The supplier selected by the contractor for the critical image intensifier tube components was a US manufacturer. This supplier led the field largely because of its success in winning a very significant US Department of Defense military programme. Two years later the US supplier lost out in the competition for the next major phase of US procurement. The British defence contractor with several years of its contract still to run found its secondary partnership status rather exposed (Chadwick 1994).

On the other side of the coin, the same UK defence contractor was a leader in avionics display technology. The severe environment and very limited space in the cockpit of a military aircraft demand some very specialized technology including very compact, very high voltage power supplies to drive the colour cathode ray tube displays commonly used. The defence contractor has a primary partnership with a small Scottish supplier which at one time was an internal division of the customer. The defence contractor does not have enough power supply business to make the relationship a unique one. The small manufacturer has found and created three secondary partnerships with two other UK defence customers and an Italian one. However it is unlikely that the business for the other three could be sustained if the primary partner pulled out. This series of relationships is shown in Figure 5.3.

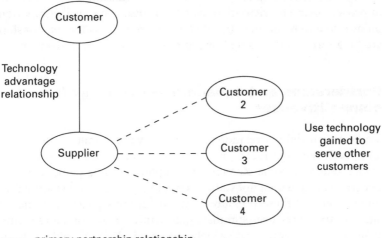

——— primary partnership relationship

– – – secondary partnership relationship

Figure 5.3 *Primary and secondary relationships*

Sometimes this apparently dominant role can be taken by the supplier, regardless of its size, if it has a sufficient edge in technology. An example here is a small Swiss company which produces very advanced printed circuit boards for many much larger defence contractors. This supplier is strongly proactive in formalizing partnership relations, but the loss of some of its customers would not have a very significant effect on its status with the others.

Burt and Doyle (1993) comment:

> Any one manufacturer typically not representing more than 15 to 20 per cent of its suppliers' business encourages suppliers to have important relationships with other customers.

Peter Hines in *Creating World Class Suppliers* (1994), comments on the apparent risk of the benefits of supplier development work done by one customer leaking out to help competitors, but observes that:

> if each of the firms within an industrial sector, or indeed between interlocking sectors, spend a considerable amount of effort on supplier development then the beneficial spread effects from one customer's assistance will be matched from that given by another. As a result the subcontractor will become better and both customers will gain. It is therefore no coincidence that the sectors in which Japan has shown the greatest degree of manufacturing success, such as automotive, consumer electronics and machine tools, all hold a significant number of strong customers all committed to supplier development.

The multiple relationships between buyers and suppliers are in fact stimulating the vendor base to be creative, innovative and responsive. All parties should gain from the cross-fertilization of ideas and improved market orientation which ensues. The really important point is that none of these benefits will accrue unless the relationships are long-term and sustained by joint efforts to seek improvements.

Partnerships and collaborative strategy for competitiveness

To be worthwhile, a relationship must develop a culture that drives and measures continuous joint cost reduction efforts. This normally means retaining some element of competition. The global competitive model is dynamic not static. Economic pressures constantly drive innovation and these pressures must be acknowledged and encouraged. Market pressures stimulate competitive innovation and continuous improvement. It is widely accepted that the old vertically integrated organizations mostly failed because the internal divisions with their captive customer base eventually succumb to sloth and inefficiency as a direct result of not having to compete in the real market. Weakness in cost accounting and allocation systems cut them off from a clear view of just how badly they were doing. The absence of contact with external customers and suppliers eliminates the vital stimuli necessary to force technological growth. General Motors, IBM and Philips have all had to carefully re-examine their supply management strategies.

So how can the benefits of partnership relations be realized while maintaining the necessary input of competition? Firstly, make sure that all the costs of dealing with a supplier are measured and fully taken into account. Secondly, ensure that the partner/supplier is able to make enough profit to contribute to advances in technology on an ongoing basis. Finally, a culture must be established which drives and measures continuous joint cost reduction efforts.

When this is achieved, the partnership will already be producing the best possible price and should be able to stand the test of competition. If not, and if the trend is not moving ever closer to this goal, then it may not be the best partnership and ought to be put under serious review to see if a change should be made. The important factor is the first one above, that all the costs and benefits are properly taken into account. There will probably always be occasional occurrences of spot prices in the market which look better at first sight. There is also the constant danger of the larger partner pulling rank. For example a major aerospace contractor includes the following scarcely veiled threat in its formal supplier collaboration document:

> It should not be assumed that simply because costs are logically and fairly built up that it will in all eventualities be logical and fair to pay a price based on these costs. The goal is to continually drive costs down.

The concept of partnership and better supplier-customer relationships comes in many forms and under a variety of names including: supplier collaboration, preferred suppliers, comakership, and partners for profit among many others. Some imply a more permanent arrangement and some a relationship with greater depth. The overriding principle is that teamwork is better than combat. If the end customer is to be best served, then the partners must come to an agreement to work together, and both must win. A strategy of collaboration only works because both parties have an interest in each other's success. Like all the very best ideas, it is a simple one. The rewards are immense, but it demands considerable commitment, work and patience. Strategic partnership can help to:

- achieve world class quality standards;
- cut lead times and increase flexibility in response to market fluctuations;
- slash stock and administration costs and bolster cash flow;
- plan better through long-term information rich relationships;
- reduce production downtime and boost capacity;
- improve time to market;
- innovate through improved access to information and technology;
- reduce most forms of procurement risk.

Collaborative strategy can improve the competitive position by bringing down cost, eliminating waste, boosting quality and making both partners more responsive to customers' needs. It means rejecting the master–servant syndrome where the supplier is merely told what to produce and the customer is only told the price. Instead, the partners agree on common goals and work to build up the commitment, trust and mutual support necessary to achieve them. Further the partners must regard themselves as part of the same team with the same aim: to ensure that their link in the supply chain is strengthened so that the end customer is not only satisfied but delighted. And though the size of the partners may differ, perhaps significantly, both have the rights and responsibilities of making the partnership work. The concept may be customer-driven or supplier-driven. Some organizations embark on a partnership arrangement at a customer's behest and then go on to initiate similar relationships with their own suppliers or with other customers. Supplier partnership might not even be an explicit aim but comes about as a by-product of another strategy such as just-in-time supply.

In the manufacturing sector partnership, sourcing builds the trust needed for a supplier to be invited to deliver directly to a production line without buffer stocks or goods inwards inspection. In the service sector, it may allow a supplier to get inside the customer's business to assess their needs directly from the user and to deliver the service without detailed supervision. Key distinguishing features in strategic partnership include:

● cost versus price;
● long-term versus short-term;
● quality checks versus quality control;
● single sourcing versus multiple sourcing.

Thus forming strategic partnerships with suppliers is not an end in itself but rather a means to the end of achieving increased competitiveness and enhancement of quality. It is not a panacea for the fundamental problems of marketing and production. It is certainly not a soft option. Nor does it replace good management or good purchasing practice, rather it complements them. Though purchasing should not be adversarial, it must remain aware. Strategic partnerships will only work if neither party feels that they are being exploited. Both parties must feel secure that the relationship is on a sound footing and that it will continue for the foreseeable future. There must be an atmosphere where problems can be discussed frankly and constructively. In a strategic partnership a disagreement must signify the realization of an opportunity for improvement rather than the end of a relationship.

Study of eight multinational organizations

To investigate the practical benefits of close supplier relationships being experienced by a range of companies across the manufacturing spectrum, a short study was carried out. This exercise involved in-depth interviews with eight multinational firms, and where directed, with one of their partnership suppliers. Information gathering was based on a loosely structured questionnaire designed to tease out facts about the partnerships and to allow the researchers to explore more deeply and to understand more fully the attitudes and motives behind the firms entering into such a relationship. Researchers asked the buyer from the partnership to identify an associated supplier for interview. This supplier contact was interviewed using a similar questionnaire to provide a picture of both sides of the relationship. Table 5.1 lists the companies involved in the study.

Table 5.1 Companies involved in the study

Buyer	Supplier
Polaroid	Silleck Mouldings Ltd
Philips BCS	Sanko Goesi Ltd
IBM	Foam Plus Ltd
OKI	Plastic Engineers Scotland Ltd
Compaq	Keytronics Ltd
Philips Lighting	Cullen Packaging Ltd
Motorola	No single supplier given
National Semiconductor	No single supplier given

Polaroid (UK) Limited

Polaroid's principal business is in the manufacture of instant imaging products, such as photographic films and cameras, lenses for use in optical equipment, and sunglasses. The specific area of business to which the researcher was directed was the camera division where the company manufactures instant image cameras for the European market.

The partnership concept is one in which Polaroid believes world-wide. It is a crucial part of the company's materials management strategy, and is endorsed at the highest level.

Polaroid (UK) Ltd have various partnerships including one with Silleck Mouldings Scotland Ltd, a manufacturer of plastic injection mouldings. The company produces plastic parts which make up the main chassis of the camera and are hence critical to the overall image and durability of the final product. Polaroid has fifty UK-based suppliers of which fifteen are considered to be partners. Polaroid has a very positive view of its partnership with Silleck. The relationship is seen as having contributed to total cost reduction, enhanced service performance, improved quality, reduced risk, reduced time to market, and reduced inventory costs. The relationship was considered to be strong by both parties and has been built on mutual trust developed over time. Both partners felt that they had genuinely increased their competitiveness as a direct result of working together as partners.

Philips BCS

Philips BCS is a part of Philips Electronics and Associated Industries Ltd. The parent company, NV Philips Gloeilampen Fabrieken has its headquarters in The Netherlands, with production sites throughout Europe. Philips BCS is specifically concerned with the production and marketing of telecommunications equipment.

The partnership concept has become a crucial part of the drive towards excellence at Philips BCS, and follows an increasing awareness of the importance of the contribution of the purchasing function to the success of the firm. Implementation of the partnership philosophy involves the entire management team, but is very much driven by purchasing.

Philips BCS have a number of partnerships, one of which is again with a plastic moulder, Sanko Goesi Ltd. The plastic components make up the body of one of the telephone products and as such are important to the success and durability of the product in the marketplace. The company has eighty-three suppliers in total and considers nine of these to be partners.

The Philips representative spoke positively of the partnership with Sanko Goesi, which is considered to have met the objective of the relationship. This was to reduce time to market and enhance competitiveness. Additional benefits have been total cost reduction, improved quality, and reduced stock holdings made possible by daily deliveries.

IBM UK

IBM's Greenock plant produces display terminals, keyboards, logic cards and a wide range of computer systems.

The partnership concept is endorsed from the highest executive level and is seen as a key factor in IBM's materials management strategy. IBM has 120 strategic suppliers in the UK, of whom the majority are considered to be partners. Packaging manufacturer Foam Plus Ltd has been a supplier since 1985 and a formal partner since 1992. This relationship is expected to continue indefinitely.

The supplier is the single source for all IBM UK Ltd's foam packaging needs, which account for around 1 per cent of product costs. The partnership has resulted in total cost reduction, enhanced service performance, and reduced inventory. The supplier has also contributed up-to-date technical knowledge of packaging legislation, and drop test requirements.

OKI (UK) Ltd

OKI's principal business in Scotland is the manufacture of computer peripheral equipment including dot matrix printers for the European market.

OKI (UK) believes in the benefits of getting close to their suppliers, but is reluctant to describe any of their relationships with suppliers as partnerships. The company has a preferred vendor programme which has three levels: proactive, approved, preferred.

There are seventy-one suppliers of which between 65 and 70 per cent have reached preferred status.

One of OKI's preferred vendors is a plastic injection moulder, Plastic Engineers Scotland Ltd. This relationship seemed to be a little one-sided in the buyer's favour rather than a shared fifty-fifty partnership. However it is perceived by OKI as being mutually beneficial. The respondent did not try to make the relationship look more like a partnership than it was, and the researcher gained the feeling that although co-operation and the partnership philosophy make good business sense, they are in fact very difficult to achieve in practice. There seemed to be some scepticism that a true state of partnership could actually exist. The researcher felt that perhaps too much emphasis was being placed on cost accountability via cost modelling, for the relationship to be a fully trusting one. No matter what cost analysis the supplier came up with, OKI's cost model could find scope for greater cost reduction. This may have been a consequence of benchmarking against OKI's suppliers in Japan.

The relationship is however acknowledged as benefiting OKI in the three areas which OKI have identified as being critical to its continued competitiveness, those of cost reduction, service performance enhancement, and quality improvement.

Compaq Computer Manufacturing Ltd

Compaq is principally engaged in the manufacture of portable and desktop computer systems for the European market.

The partnership concept is fundamental to Compaq's purchasing policy, and strongly underpins the company's initiative to become more competitive in all its markets. This philosophy is endorsed throughout the organization and is operated actively in the USA, Europe and the Far East.

Compaq has partnerships with all its suppliers, one of which is Keytronics Ltd, a manufacturer of computer keyboards. This supplier is said to have benefited Compaq in every way including time to market, service and quality performance, reduction in total cost, and the advancement of the technological status of Compaq products. This is a relationship that both parties are proud of, not just because it fitted the profile of a strong supplier partnership, but because both parties have had to work hard with each other to get there, and both parties are now reaping the rewards of their efforts.

The Compaq document of understanding used to define the relationship it has with its partner suppliers is included as a Case Study at the end of the chapter.

Philips (Lighting) Hamilton Ltd

Philips (Lighting) is involved in the manufacture of lamps and associated hardware. Philips chose to describe the relationship which they have with packaging supplier Cullen Packaging Ltd as a co-makership partnership agreement. This is a relationship which is not particularly close other than for the basic needs of the business.

Philips has fifty suppliers of which ten are considered to be partners. Cullen has been a supplier since 1992 with a co-makership agreement since 1994. The relationship is expected to continue as long as the supplier provides the best quotation when the contract goes out to tender each year.

The researcher felt that this relationship, though described as having co-makership status, was in fact a typical example of traditional purchasing practice based on lowest price wins. The fact that the contract was tendered annually seemed to support this. Furthermore, the lack of interest in developing the relationship, appeared to provide evidence that neither party could see the potential mutual benefits. Though firm belief in the partnership philosophy was claimed, it seemed to be contradicted by practice.

The buyer in this case perceived to have gained benefits from delivery performance improvement, and the achievement of a stable price despite upward movement in the market.

Motorola Ltd, MOS memory and microprocessor division

This division of Motorola is primarily concerned with the manufacture of metal oxide semiconductor devices for the computer industry. The company has an 'overriding fundamental objective' which is to provide total customer satisfaction. This goal permeates everything Motorola does and is seen as especially important in the supply management process.

Motorola believes in the benefits of achieving closer relationships with suppliers, although the company does not like to use the word partnership. The company has a preferred vendor programme which has three levels: preferred suppliers (green); restricted suppliers (yellow) and suspended suppliers (red).

The researcher was not directed to a relationship with one specific supplier, so the format previously used was tailored slightly. The collaborative relationships which Motorola conducts with its suppliers are seen to be positive. Working closely together has become an essential factor for firms in Motorola's sector of industry, and the company has been active in this direction for a long time. Thorough preparation was seen as a very important ingredient for success, and the investment in resources necessary had to be weighed against the potential benefits. Although the corporate policy is very much towards closer relationships, the 'partnership' had to be achievable at the right price.

National Semiconductor (UK) Ltd

National Semiconductor is a leading designer and manufacturer of integrated circuits for a wide range of computer and microelectronics applications.

The company has strongly pursued the supplier partnership philosophy since the late 1980s, and is proud of the leading role which it has played in developing this concept in an industry traditionally shrouded in secrecy. National Semiconductor is for its own part closely involved with many of its customers in a key partnership role.

The research showed clearly that the traditional adversarial approach was steadily giving way to a more advanced approach, though full wholehearted adoption still had some way to go. Benefits have been realized in many areas including total cost reduction, reduction in inventory, increased service responsiveness and higher quality, in the fields of capital equipment as well as materials purchasing.

Analysis of findings

The findings from the survey are shown in Tables 5.2 to 5.8. Seven propositions are used to summarize potential benefits of the relationship:

1 That supplier partnerships contribute to improvements in the quality of inputs and to the final product.
2 That supplier partnerships contribute to reducing the total cost of ownership.
3 That supplier partnerships contribute to enhancing customer service.
4 That supplier partnerships significantly reduce the risks involved in procurement.
5 That supplier partnerships contribute to the technological superiority of the product.
6 That supplier partnerships contribute to reduction of the time to market for the buyer's products.

7 That supplier partnerships contribute positively to competitive position.

For each proposition the assessment of contribution judged by the companies surveyed is marked as:

> Significant improvement.
> Considerable improvement.
> Modest improvement.
> No improvement.
> Detrimental effect.

Proposition 1: That supplier partnerships contribute to improvements in the quality of inputs and of the final product.

Both the literature and the findings have highlighted quality as a key factor which makes an impact on an organization's competitiveness. Table 5.2 illustrates that quality was judged by all the correspondents who measure it, to have improved in some degree as a result of their supplier partnership.

Table 5.2 Analysis of quality improvement due to supplier partnership

Buyer and supplier	Quality improvement
Polaroid and Silleck	Significant improvement
Philips BCS and Sanko Goesi	Significant improvement
IBM and Foam Plus	Not measured
OKI and Plastic Engineers	Significant improvement
Compaq and Keytronics	Considerable improvement
Philips Lighting and Cullen Packaging	Not measured
Motorola and Suppliers	Considerable improvement
National Semiconductor and Suppliers	Considerable improvement

Proposition 2: That supplier partnerships contribute to reducing the total cost of the relationship to the buyer

The main factors cited as giving rise to total cost reduction as identified in the literature and findings are depicted in Figure 5.4. Table 5.3 shows which companies have reduced the total cost of the relationship and attributed this to the closeness of their partnership

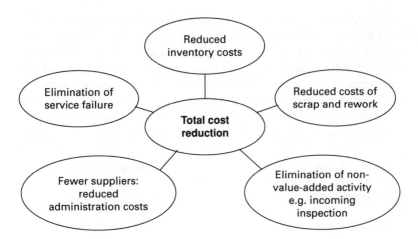

Figure 5.4 *Contributions to reductions in total cost*

Table 5.3 Analysis of total cost reduction due to supplier partnership

Buyer and supplier	Total cost reduction
Polaroid and Silleck	Significant improvement
Philips BCS and Sanko Goesi	Modest improvement
IBM and Foam Plus	Significant improvement
OKI and Plastic Engineers	Considerable improvement
Compaq and Keytronics	Significant improvement
Philips Lighting and Cullen Packaging	Modest improvement
Motorola and Suppliers	Considerable improvement
National Semiconductor and Suppliers	Considerable improvement

with the supplier involved. Without exception the respondents have seen a reduction in total cost since forming a stronger relationship with their suppliers.

Proposition 3: That supplier partnerships contribute to the enhancement of customer service.

The most common service performance indicator used by the buying firms was the percentage of shipments received on time. On time delivery was judged to have been achieved if consignments were delivered within a certain time frame, with early and late delivery both counted as failures. Other factors used to measure service performance include the number of administration errors, and consignments received incomplete. All the companies who responded with measured results showed that developing a better understanding of each other through working together as partners has improved customer service levels. This is summarized in Table 5.4.

Table 5.4 Analysis of improvement in customer service due to supplier partnership

Buyer and supplier	Improved customer service
Polaroid and Silleck	Modest improvement
Philips BCS and Sanko Goesi	Significant improvement
IBM and Foam Plus	Significant improvement
OKI and Plastic Engineers	Considerable improvement
Compaq and Keytronics	Considerable improvement
Philips Lighting and Cullen Packaging	Considerable improvement
Motorola and Suppliers	Not measured
National Semiconductor and Suppliers	Not measured

Proposition 4: That supplier partnerships significantly reduce the risks involved in procurement.

The level of perceived risk can go both ways, as seen from Table 5.5. Two respondents considered that they had increased risk by putting all their eggs in the one basket of a single source supplier. The others take the opposite view considering that the closer relationship provides much better understanding and communication, and should lead to early awareness of any potential problems.

Proposition 5: That supplier partnerships contribute to the technological superiority of the product.

The fact that only half the buyers felt that the partnership contributed to technological improvement (Table 5.6) suggests that although the suppliers were judged to be contributing very positively in other areas, they were perhaps not being given the chance to contribute to improvements in the technology of the product itself. In the case of Polaroid, Philips BCS, OKI and Philips Lighting, suppliers were not

Table 5.5 Analysis of risk reduction due to supplier partnership

Buyer and supplier	Risk reduction
Polaroid and Silleck	Considerable improvement
Philips BCS and Sanko Goesi	Significant improvement
IBM and Foam Plus	Detrimental effect
OKI and Plastic Engineers	Detrimental effect
Compaq and Keytronics	Significant improvement
Philips Lighting and Cullen Packaging	Considerable improvement
Motorola and Suppliers	Modest improvement
National Semiconductor and Suppliers	Considerable improvement

Table 5.6 Analysis of technological improvements due to supplier partnership

Buyer and supplier	Technological improvement
Polaroid and Silleck	No improvement
Philips BCS and Sanko Goesi	No improvement
IBM and Foam Plus	Considerable improvement
OKI and Plastic Engineers	No improvement
Compaq and Keytronics	Significant improvement
Philips Lighting and Cullen Packaging	No improvement
Motorola and Suppliers	Significant improvement
National Semiconductor and Suppliers	Significant improvement

involved at any stage of the component design, and as such had no opportunity to contribute to advances in technology.

Proposition 6: That supplier partnerships contribute to reduction in time to market for the buyer's products

The responses shown in Table 5.7 show that supplier partnerships can significantly reduce the time to market for an end product. Good examples are evident in both the Compaq and Philips BCS cases. In other areas particularly where packaging is involved there is less potential.

Table 5.7 Analysis of reduction in time to market due to supplier partnership

Buyer and supplier	Reduction in time to market
Polaroid and Silleck	Modest improvement
Philips BCS and Sanko Goesi	Significant improvement
IBM and Foam Plus	Modest improvement
OKI and Plastic Engineers	Modest improvement
Compaq and Keytronics	Significant improvement
Philips Lighting and Cullen Packaging	Modest improvement
Motorola and Suppliers	Significant improvement
National Semiconductor and Suppliers	Significant improvement

Proposition 7: That supplier partnerships contribute to competitive position.

Table 5.8 shows that all the respondents felt that their competitive position had been enhanced, and five saw this as a significant improvement.

Table 5.8 Analysis of the contribution of supplier partnership to competitiveness

Buyer and supplier	Competitiveness
Polaroid and Silleck	Significant improvement
Philips BCS and Sanko Goesi	Significant improvement
IBM and Foam Plus	Considerable improvement
OKI and Plastic Engineers	Considerable improvement
Compaq and Keytronics	Significant improvement
Philips Lighting and Cullen Packaging	Modest improvement
Motorola and Suppliers	Significant improvement
National Semiconductor and Suppliers	Significant improvement

Summary of companies in the survey

Table 5.9 provides a summary view of the results from the eight companies assessed against each performance factor.

Table 5.9 Summary results of all companies assessed against performance factors

Company	Performance factors						
	Quality	Cost	Service	Risk	Technology	Time	Competitiveness
Polaroid	Significant	Significant	Modest	Considerable	No improvement	Modest	Significant
Philips BCS	Significant	Modest	Significant	Significant	No improvement	Significant	Significant
IBM	—	Significant	Significant	Detrimental	Considerable	Modest	Considerable
OKI	Significant	Considerable	Considerable	Detrimental	No improvement	Modest	Considerable
COMPAQ	Considerable	Significant	Considerable	Significant	Significant	Significant	Significant
Philips lighting	—	Modest	Considerable	Considerable	Modest	Modest	Modest
Motorola	Considerable	Considerable	—	Modest	Significant	Significant	Significant
National semiconductor	Considerable	Considerable	—	Considerable	Significant	Significant	Significant

KEY

⭐ = Significant improvement   ☹ = No improvement

😀 = Considerable improvement   — = Not measured

😐 = Modest improvement   💣 = Detrimental effect

Characteristics of relationship integration

The key factor for success in the partnership is the ability of the parties involved to integrate closely with each other. Organizations which strive towards achieving the goal of closer integration, or partnership with their suppliers, find significant improvements in a wider range of performance factors, thus making significant steps in their ability to become more competitive. Table 5.10 outlines the characteristics of high and low levels of supplier integration. Using the factors outlined for the eight companies surveyed, a plot of their position can be made in the supplier integration spectrum illustrated by Figure 5.5.

The partnership spectrum was gauged by considering the degree of integration of the buyer and supplier. The level of integration was based on the position which the company's relationship with its supplier took between the polar alternatives of low and high as defined in Table 5.10. Out of the eight original equipment manufacturers studied, a range of partnerships with suppliers emerged. Based

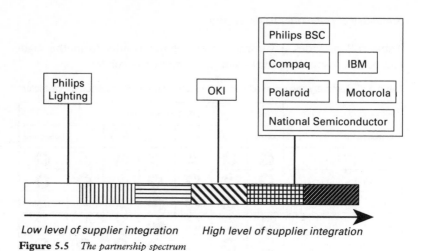

Low level of supplier integration   High level of supplier integration

Figure 5.5 *The partnership spectrum*

Table 5.10 Characteristics of supplier integration

Low level	High level
Infrequent communication	Frequent communication
Lack of fully co-operative attitude	Top level support of integration
Inflexible attitude towards supplier	Multifunctional acceptance of co-operation
Lowest price orientation for supplier selection	Philosophy of total continuous improvement
Supplier has no involvement in design decisions	Total cost orientation
Inability to see supplier's needs	Formal supplier evaluation programmes
	Early supplier involvement in design of products
	Empathy with supplier

on the literature and the survey findings, the authors propose a framework to identify and summarize the working criteria for a successful partnership. This is depicted in Figure 5.6. The diagram illustrates the main factors which can contribute to successful partnerships and through them to enhanced competitiveness.

Factors for a successful partnership

In developing their choice of supplier strategy, organizations need to assess the potential competitive advantages to be gained from the relationship. Figure 5.7 is a matrix of mutual trust versus profit orientation from opportunistic short-term to long-term and

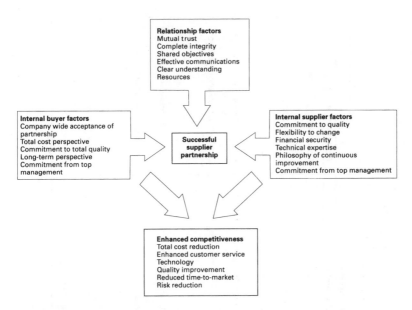

Figure 5.6 *Summary of factors for a successful partnership*

sustained. Finally Table 5.11 provides an overview of the supplier strategy characteristics which are considered to be important in assessing the type of stance an organization makes with its vendor base. Developing a supplier partnership is not a quick fix, and if it is to work to best effect, it requires a considerable amount of change inside the organization as well as in its external relationships.

		Degree of trust	
	Poor	Average	High
Short	Opportunistic strategy		
Medium		Contractual strategy	
Long			Collaborative strategy

Degree of profit orientation

Figure 5.7 *Matrix on choice of strategy with suppliers*

A partnership strategy needs to be driven from very high up in both organizations but will still not show the best results unless it receives

Table 5.11 Summary of strategy characteristics with suppliers

Characteristics	Strategy with suppliers		
	Opportunistic strategy	Contractual strategy	Collaborative strategy
Tools	No document	Document of contract	Document of understanding
Contractual relations	Free-for-all and formal/rigid	Very formal/rigid	Informal/flexible
Risks	Taken alone	Taken separately	Shared
Length of contract (time)	Spot/very short-term orientation	1–3 years mid-term/long-term orientation	Over 3 years/long-term orientation
Supplier selection	Multisourcing/competitive bidding/tendering	Dual sourcing/triad sourcing/tendering	Single or dual source/negotiation
Suppliers per item	5 or more	2 to 3	1
Communication	Guarded or sporadic	Some degree of cautiousness	Open and continuous
Control	Via initial terms	Legally binding	Ongoing mutual adjustments
Negotiation	Win–lose	Win–win	Win–win
Joint activities with suppliers	Little or none	Extensive	Very extensive
Trust	None	Legal obligation (average)	High

the full support of staff across all functions. Supplier partnerships can significantly enhance competitiveness when trust and long-term orientation are in place to nurture and sustain them. An organization which achieves this is in a strong position ultimately to achieve a source of differential advantage in the marketplace.

Case study – Partnership at Compaq – The document of understanding

Evolution
With experience gained in work at Rolls-Royce, Honeywell, Polaroid and Digital Equipment Corporation, the purchasing team at Compaq knew that a change could be made away from the adversarial business environment which promotes and sustains extra costs and generates waste and duplication. Ken Linn, who led the team, devised and implemented the document of understanding as the means of making that change happen.

Concept
What was needed was a shift in philosophy away from the traditional confrontational approach to a signed and documented commitment from the top levels of an organization to participate on a journey of continuous improvement, and to embrace a partnership approach, philosophy and style to conducting business. The means of achieving this was to produce a simple declaration of mutual co-operation, the document of understanding.

Significantly the document of understanding has no end date. It is not a contractual or legally binding document. All it does is to commit companies to an endless unrelenting journey to world class continuous improvement programmes.

Examples
A supplier investment programme to commission a robot-equipped paint line in a clean room environment to meet Compaq's cosmetic specification which was the highest in the industry. The supplier invested several hundred thousand pounds. Compaq sell more computers and the supplier sells more parts.

A containerization programme for top covers for personal computers, developed because of the close working and extended time frame that only partnership

---

relationships can provide, made a return on investment of many hundred thousand dollars per year.

The 'drip' process is a direct feed of hardware from suppliers straight onto Compaq's manufacturing work stations. By establishing mutual trust between two suppliers, Compaq brought together an established US supplier with a competing local UK hardware manufacturer to form a joint collaboration with each other as well as with Compaq. There are benefits to all three.

To Compaq the gains are:
- one corporate supplier;
- one corporate design;
- standard corporate pricing;
- local supplier totally manages UK hardware requirements;
- reduced purchase order, invoicing, and inventory holding activity

To the US supplier the benefits are:
- continues as the Compaq corporate supplier;
- opens up the European market for sales via the local supplier and its distribution network.

The benefits to the local supplier:
- Access to US technology and supplier patents;
- becomes a value added partner to Compaq;
- opens up the US market.

Direct ship

Compaq arrange for display monitors to be shipped directly from the European supplier direct to dealer outlets. Savings in freight, duty, double handling and inventory carrying are enormous.

Elimination of incoming inspection

Over a four-year period Compaq eliminated the need for 95 per cent of incoming inspection. The floor space released now earns money by being used for manufacturing. The human resources freed up now work even more closely with suppliers at the suppliers' premises.

Vendor base reduction
A very small vendor base of key suppliers has been developed. This has been accepted across the whole corporation and documented in the world class supplier process programme.

Obstacles
Change in any form is one of the most difficult things for people to accept. Change can quickly generate fear and stress. Partnership can be hard work, physically, mentally and emotionally, and inside as well as outside the organization. It is certainly more difficult than issuing and receiving dogmatic instructions. When things get tough there is always a tendency to revert back to traditional behaviour. Compaq has behaved in the same way that it has preached and over time its suppliers have learned to trust it.

Conclusion
Compaq believes firmly that continuance of traditional business practice and adversarial relationships often result in situations from which neither side gains. Through hard facts and hard earned experience Compaq can demonstrate that partnership relationships can result in long term gains to the benefit of both parties, even where competitive situations exist. Both customer and supplier must be prepared to break the mould.

6 Strategic negotiation

Introduction

The traditional concept of negotiation as a tactical process of persuasion by the five processes of logic; emotion; power coercion and threat; bargaining; and compromise has probably earned more money for consultants and management training schools than any other single misunderstanding. Michael Edwardes in his book *Back from the Brink* (1983), describing his time as chairman of British Leyland quotes one speech to the trade unions:

> If your objectives are the same as mine then how can it be that hundreds of vehicles can be lost in one week because managers and workforce find themselves unable to agree on overalls, while the business goes to ruin?'

The persuasion process with its role play and body language, is really just a short-term skirmishing tactic tarnished with deception and confrontation and inevitably negated in the long-run as every dog has its day. If it is now widely accepted that confrontation and mistrust between management and workforce is the wrong way to get the best out of human resources, it may just be that the same axiom applies between buyers and sellers. Especially buyers and sellers whose future survival is inextricably bound up in each other's success.

Strategic negotiation is a quite different process altogether. It starts with the simple premise that two organizations want to investigate the potential advantages in working together towards specific goals. So it has to start by sharing information on these goals. It is an open process which seeks and provides information. It is not naïvely trusting and it is very demanding of facts and the evidence to back them up. It requires a very clear understanding of the organization's own objectives, and exhaustive preparation.

We need to get away from the pre-conception that good supply management staff immediately create savings by engaging suppliers in some mystical head-to-head intellectual or physical confrontation to reduce prices. Every experienced old fashioned 'buyer' can bring in a sales representative, or better still a sales director, and by some means or other get a small percentage off the price. This is actually quite good fun, but it is not strategic negotiation. Strategic negotiation is about defining the principles governing relationships with suppliers. It is about selecting eligible suppliers, and most of all it concerns working with suppliers to help to bring about ongoing improvement in capability and performance. Done properly, the quick money-off deal, will be replaced by a major change in the way which the whole business or organization operates, with very significant reductions in both internal and external costs. Risk will be substantially reduced, and the prospects of survival and growth increased enormously.

Why are we in this business? Core aims and core business

In Chapter 4 the strategic choice 'To make or not to make' was examined. Being at peace with our choice of destiny means that we can learn to see our suppliers as opportunities and not threats. In manufacturing industry the 'Just-in-Time' philosophy forced everyone not just to reduce stocks but to wonder why stocks were there in the first place, to step back and to take a fresh look at the whole business and its objectives. Strategic negotiation can only take place once the core aims and core business of the organization are fully understood and available to be openly shared with the suppliers of external resources.

Gullible junior staff and slick sales representatives

An essential part of supplier appraisal should be an enquiry as to how the sales force assigned to deal with us is paid. Performance related bonuses and commission fees which are solely awarded on short-term product shifting or monthly invoice levels may not be the best spur to long-term mutual advantage. Piece-work bonus rates in manufacturing began to disappear before the First World War as Henry Ford spread his new mass production techniques across the Atlantic. Only in the strike-ridden motor car industry in the UK did pay rates connected directly to pushing work through as quickly as possible, survive into the 1980s. Rosabeth Moss Kanter in *When Giants Learn to Dance* (1989b) devotes a whole chapter to the changing basis for pay. She includes a wonderful story about Ross Perot told to her by an executive to justify his company's choice of entrepreneurial incentives rather than paying commission on sales results alone. Perot founded a company called Electronic Data Systems which he later sold to General Motors. 'This may be folklore,' the executive said, 'but when Ross Perot was a salesman for IBM, there was a cap on commissions. Perot had filled his quota by April or May one year, so he went to the boss to point this out and to seek additional commission. The boss turned him down. So Perot spent the rest of the year at IBM's expense, designing EDS.' Pay cheques for salesmen and others need to be balanced between individual performance and company performance. Kanter concludes that

> 'Ultimately, those pay systems that work will not be ones that encourage the competition-focused corporate cowboys to rise again, getting what they can for themselves without taking the broader goals of the company into account. Instead, the successful systems will be those that balance the drives for individual achievement with the co-operative effort of the whole corporate team.'

High-level organizations in manufacturing, service or the public sector should not in themselves be seen as targets for 'milking' but more as the focal points of a combined effort to provide the right levels of satisfaction to the ultimate consuming customer. Income must be generated to fund operations, re-investment, reserves and dividends, but much more will be gained over the long-term if short-term punitive raids are eschewed. The keiretsu system in Japan successfully achieves this by means of interlocking share holdings. (Burt and Doyle 1993) In the car industry in particular cross-ownership of equity share among assemblers, parts suppliers and even banks, eliminates any doubt that the long-term success of the final producer remains the prime interest of its most important suppliers.

Inexperienced buyers and junior staff whose purchasing or specifying activities may only be a small part of their duties are often guilty of short-term spot buying in breach of well prepared corporate agreements. Attempts at discipline from the centre are resented and become counter-productive. Divide and rule tactics bring fast talking salesmen a fast buck, but pluck another feather out of the goose which if understood better and cared for more wisely could go on to provide a steady supply of golden omelettes. Sniping at established price agreements won by competitors, can bring down any agreement no matter how fairly won and competently monitored, and serves to make all agreements more difficult to sustain. The end result is an overall loss of efficiency and ultimately the collapse of the whole castle. Potential suppliers who have lost out in a group or corporate deal would do better to help their competitor keep and consolidate the large slice of the expenditure cake, so that next time round there will be an even more solid portion to bid for and win. Dividing little crumbs off at the edges with 'loss leading' special offers may well crumble the whole thing away to no-one's advantage.

Delivering the commitment

Strategic negotiation is only possible when each party can 'put their money where their mouth is'. The classic situation where decentralized activity by holders of devolved budgets means that everyone has freedom to choose suppliers and negotiate away till their heart is content, is often given as a scenario where strategic negotiation fails to work. But if the agreements with suppliers are good, if they are presented in a well justified manner, and if they are communicated throughout the organization in a clear, readily accessible and easy-to-understand format, then the commitment will be able to be delivered. When supply management is recognized as a core function, and when staff in purchasing in devolved areas have the opportunity to spend some time in training at the function's centre and contributing to its development, agreements reached by strategic negotiation will gain staff commitment, because they will be recognized for their benefits and not seen as negative or restrictive.

The 'open kimono' approach

It seems very ironic that for years the West put Japanese industrial success down to cosy relationships between customers and suppliers, and even talked about the wisdom of 'getting into bed with your suppliers'. A culture so steeped in martial arts and personal honour seems hardly one that could find such a subservient approach to conducting business.

In the land of the shogun warrior, the loose ankle-length kimono with its sash and wide sleeves, was not just a practical, comfortable garment but also served as a means of containing and concealing a wide range of deadly armoury. The open kimono approach is not to show that you have come to the meeting with no weapons, but rather to show clearly the weapons that you have brought, prepared and ready for use. Strong leaders attract strong followers. Strong leaders are not afraid to shelter, rehabilitate, and develop weaker followers in whom they can see potential.

Being involved in a partnership relationship with a supplier exposes both parties to close examination and evaluation by the other side. Before entering into strategic negotiation, it is important for each party to ensure that their act is robust. Even if the kimono is not permitted to be open from the beginning, it will soon become transparent, if the negotiation is to be meaningful.

Charles Handy's 'Chinese contract'

In his book *The Empty Raincoat* published in 1994, Handy describes his first exposure to the fear and suspicion that formal, legal contracts bring. He was working in the oil industry, and had just agreed an agency deal in South Malaysia. 'Why do you want a legal document?', his counterpart protested. 'It makes me suspect that you have got more out of this agreement than I have, and are going to use the weight of the law to enforce your terms. In my culture,' he went on, 'a good agreement is self-enforcing because both parties go away smiling and are happy to see that each of us is smiling. If one smiles and the other scowls, the agreement will not stick, lawyers or no lawyers.'

But as Tom Peters observed in 1991, not everyone is ready for such trusting relationships:

> There is a rhetoric of partnership in the business world today – and then there is the reality... But we have many miles to go in translating slogans like 'strategic alliances' and 'borderless company' into competitive reality.

When I first moved from development engineering into purchasing, my new boss said that I should take care not to get sued, or to get into a position where I wanted to sue some supplier. I think there was a fairly strong inference about the effect this would have on my prospects of continuing employment. It seemed a rather strange statement at the time, but I guess it was my first lesson in strategic negotiation. Later in my career, when for the first time I became head of a supplies function, the Chief Executive of the company took me aside and said that while he received many complaints from our customers, he had never heard any protests from our suppliers. Perhaps because my predecessor had been a bit soft on our suppliers, the Chief Executive felt that they should feel a bit of the pain as well!

The myth of the persuasion process

The *Collins Dictionary* defines 'to persuade' as '1. to induce, urge or prevail upon successfully; 2. to cause to believe, convince.' The persuasion processes of logic; emotion; power, coercion and threat; bargaining; and compromise are all about role-play and trickery, being economical with the truth, or even deceit and fraud. Why should so many people who by choice of profession and place in the market have the same inextricably intertwined goals, waste so much time and energy turning their back on reality and trying to cheat each other? A recent briefing publication from an organisation too distinguished to be named here, cites one weakness of the first process logic: 'if logically the case can be proved then the logical outcome would be agreement – and that may not be what you want!'

The real problem is that bargaining between unequal partners can never be as effective as getting together to jointly solve problems. Bargainers hide things, keep things up their sleeves, exaggerate strengths, understate or cover up weaknesses and basically tell lies to trick and cheat each other. As early as the fifteenth century even the powerful Niccolo Machiavelli had discovered that persuasion just did not work. In *The Prince*, Machiavelli stresses the distinction between those

> 'who stand alone and those who depend on others, that is between those who to achieve their purposes can force the issue and those who must use persuasion. In the second case, they always come to grief, having achieved nothing'.

Machiavelli of course had other options up his sleeve, which fortunately are not open to buyers today. Why then are modern buyers so often encouraged to act as though they actually do have ultimate power?

There is a fascinating description of the multi-faceted buyer–seller relationship as a sort of Neanderthal village with many intersecting paths between large and small shelters inhabited by fierce giants with clubs, and cowering midgets who grow crops for themselves. The midgets needed to live near the giants for protection from wild beasts, but avoided contact whenever possible. The giants felt no qualms about taking the midgets' food, or even about killing any who accidentally got in the way. Some giants were very careless with their local midgets and had to wander further and further from their shelter to find new midgets to plunder. This usually brought them too close to the next giant who would emerge grunting fiercely and a fight to the death would ensue. Fewer giants meant less protection for midgets so their numbers began to decline as well.

A crack team of Neanderthal consultants managed to infiltrate the village, posing first as midgets and then as giants. While the midgets largely kept to themselves, meeting and mixing fairly infrequently, the giants never got together at all, and if they came within shouting distance it was to hurl insults and boasts. When the midgets did meet, talk was inevitably about survival, about how they hated the stupid giants and how they tricked them and outwitted them whenever they could. There was often talk about the weaknesses of particular giants and how easily they could be fooled and taken advantage of.

Talking to the giants was much more difficult and some consultants actually lost their lives, but data was eventually collected partly by interview and partly by observation. The giants basically cared only for themselves and to a lesser extent their sleeping partner if they had one. Everything else was a waste of space. The midgets were of no consequence. Why, if you killed a few, more soon came along. As the giants saw it, the midgets' food belonged to the giants by right because the giants were the lords and masters of the territory. Taking as much as they wanted was no more than a giant's entitlement. They were big and strong and could look after themselves. Why should they care about anything or anyone else?

Years later, a form of religion came to the valley, and life was seen to be sacred, so the deliberate killings stopped, but nothing much else changed. Over generations, communication improved and travellers appeared telling tales and showing evidence of the better ways of doing things which had developed in other valleys. Some isolated attempts were made to try the new ways, but they didn't really work very well, and anyway they were difficult and there wasn't really time to waste. In any case, the giants in this valley had always been superior to midgets, and the midgets, well they were becoming trickier every day. There was no way that you could ever trust them.

Achieving credibility: defeating dynamic conservatism

Just as leopards have very serious difficulty in changing their spots, moving from a conventional, confrontational form of negotiation to a truly strategic one, requires more than just a change of heart by the supply management department, and a few apparently willing suppliers. Supplier development for instance, has been around for a long time and is often employed as a means to introduce new competition, rather than to build a true partnership type of relationship. Chosen solutions must be aimed accurately at the root causes of the problem and not overly influenced by the more obvious symptoms on the surface. Joy Batchelor, Tom Donnelly and David Morris (1994) use the case of the imposition of a particular quality management technique by a powerful customer to illustrate this. Resistance is likely,

> when an organization feels threatened by, for example, the requirement for gaining a supply contract being the attainment of BS 5750. Therefore a supplier may comply, implement and achieve BS 5750, but the implementation of procedures without changing attitudes and behaviour (uncritical learning) will not foster a wider culture of total quality management within that organization. Therefore a state of dynamic conservatism exists where the minimum change has been implemented to appease a customer, losing the opportunity for a more long-term and fundamental change in behaviour.
>
> Dynamic conservatism is also a feature of many purchasing departments where instead of pursuing price, strategies may have changed towards putting pressure upon inventory, delivery times and increased quality. However a supplier who has experienced the old adversarial approach to purchasing will see that in effect, while the buyer may have changed the emphasis placed upon a particular criterion, the basic logic

to their approach in fact remains unchanged and no fundamental change has occurred within the relationship between the two parties. Therefore the need to change the perceptions of the customer is of equal importance to that of changing the perceptions of the supplier. If the supplier feels that the underlying motives of the customer have in fact remained unchanged, what motivation do they have to change their fundamental attitudes and behaviour over and above that which satisfies the customer in the short run?

Building a cathedral

Peter Drucker likes to recall a favourite story about the three stonecutters who were asked what it was that they were doing. The first replied: 'I am making a living.' The second kept on hammering while he said: 'I am doing the best job of stonecutting in the entire county.' The third one looked up with a visionary gleam in his eye and said: 'I am building a cathedral.'

How many of your suppliers are working towards the cathedral of your organization's mission and goals? How many are working hard to optimize their particular little bit of the supply chain or value stream without even glimpsing the greater whole? How many of your suppliers are simply trying like the first stonecutter, to make a living?

Stonecutters are not just operators whose contribution is limited to shaping and trimming unconnected blocks from the quarry. Masons depend on their skills and diligence. Architects and engineers have little of any use to contribute without stonecutters.

Over the last few hundred years, organizations have become reasonably skilled in dealing directly with employees and the science of human resource management has developed in many areas to understand the needs and desires of workforces. Going to the market to hire a few likely looking labourers on short term 'fees', has largely given way to the recognized mutual advantage to employer as well as employee of a rather longer-term arrangement with at least a little attention to sympathy with each other's needs. Countless books and articles have been devoted to management, motivation, leadership and coaching. Tom Peters cites one of the three secrets of long-term excellence as 'full use of the abilities of every company employee'.

What has all this got to do with external suppliers? In a word everything.

All suppliers are managed and staffed by people. Every aspect of responsible human resource management is relevant to working with suppliers. In a true partnership relationship, people should sometimes forget who their actual employing company is. The principle of strategic negotiation is based on this bedrock. Sallies into and out of the marketplace to plunder what we can at minimum expense to ourselves and scant regard to the other party is a Neanderthal village tactic. Even the fearless Vikings eventually tired of raping and pillaging and came up with the more acceptable strategy to both parties of extracting Dane-geld protection money.

Strategic negotiation is not just about ensuring that suppliers have access to all the information which is necessary to be full partners in the operation. It does not merely involve the clear articulation of performance objectives and expectations. Just like personnel management, it includes education and development of suppliers. Strategic negotiation works to increase the content and scope of the work carried out by the supplier. Satisfaction and motivation to perform well develop by growth in the content, scope and depth of work as well as recognition of good performance. Scope is the range of operations given to the supplier to complete. Work with a narrow scope contains few operations and is often highly repetitive. Broadening the scope increases the range of operations and hence makes the work more interesting without necessarily demanding more skills or increasing the responsibility.

Increasing the depth of work given to a supplier means that they have to plan and organize more activities, and does lead to an increase in responsibility and a heightened feeling of partnership as well as motivation.

Access to and full use of the abilities of the supplier does not come in return for payment for work done. Loyalty, satisfaction, motivation and innovation come in full measure only when suppliers expect, demand and crave to work with you for what they can learn and gain from working together to solve problems. All problems are joint problems: 'you dream the same dreams, you want the same things'.

The strategic negotiation process

The objectives of strategic negotiation are to put more work with fewer, better partner suppliers. To work with them to the common end of cost reduction, innovation generation, and market development.

The process needs a clear definition of the principles which are to govern relationships with suppliers; a means of selection of the most eligible suppliers; and an ongoing commitment and methodology to work with them for continuous improvement and development.

Requirements

- Investment of time, energy and resources.
- Extensive preparation and information gathering.
- Commitment from the top of the organization.

- Highly developed presentation and counselling skills.
- Open sharing of information and objectives.
- Pre-meeting communication to ensure no surprises.
- Listening to and stimulating supplier contributions.
- Clear cut, but realistic objectives.
- A systematic framework to be followed.
- Avoidance of any reliance on persuasive pressure.
- Production of an action plan with mileposts as well as final targets.
- Realization that flexibility is always required.

Considerations
- Objective review of supplier's present capability and performance.
- Assess further job opportunities at current capability level.
- Where will the supplier be in five/ten years time?
- Is there a sustainable level of business of mutual interest?
- Discuss and agree targets and objectives.
- Plan programme of coaching and development.
- Develop effective record of the supplier's development.

Potential drawbacks
- Empty paper exercise and waste of resources.
- Create fear and uncertainty.
- Can damage 'good' working relationships.
- Non-fulfilment of good intentions.

Case study - British Aerospace Defence, Dynamics Division (Lee-Mortimer 1993)

British Aerospace Defence, Dynamics Division has a mission to be the leading supplier in Europe of guided weapons and associated equipment. Essential to the drive for production improvement was a collaboration programme between purchasing and suppliers.

The lowest number of best-of-class suppliers was identified for all products and a long-term partnership developed. The collaboration programme has led to a major reduction in the number of suppliers from the original 4000 to 5000 base. Now over 80 per cent of the business is sourced with 50 collaborative suppliers, whilst the percentage of the product bought from outside has increased to 70 per cent on route to an eventual target of 90 per cent.

Roy Polson, managing director of printed circuit board supplier Manchester Circuits, cites three vital areas where significant benefits have been derived from the collaboration:

1 Technology. 'BAeDynamics was having great difficulty sourcing printed circuit boards for a missile system from within the United Kingdom. From a technology standpoint these boards were beyond Manchester Circuits' experience. But through the developing relationship we were able to get the chance to produce, at our own risk, some test cards. Although the first ones failed, we had shown enough to demonstrate our ability. Subsequently we went on to pre-production and production.

Importantly, throughout this process BAeDynamics provided encouragement to go forward with the project, and were very supportive with technical assistance. Moreover once we had proved our capability, they were quick to provide us with ongoing order commitment.'

Manchester Circuits was able to establish itself as a niche player in this particular technology, going on to win orders from several other customers.

2 Quality. At the start of the process of rationalizing the supply of printed circuit boards, BAeDynamics were suffering a defect rate of 30 to 40 per cent. Instead of the traditional solution of changing to another source, BAeDynamics worked jointly with Manchester Circuits to get to the root causes of the problems and eliminate them. In fact at least half the problems were found to be created by the missile manufacturer.

'The essential element in the relationship,' according to Roy Polson, 'is that the fear factor has been removed. With the collaboration programme there is a willingness to work together to improve the situation. The customer is prepared to invest time in the supplier, and this is not found at this level with other customers.'

3 Sales Growth. During a period of severe market recession Manchester Circuits' sales have nearly doubled when in other circumstances contraction, and perhaps even closure, could have been expected.

The next phases of the collaboration will include Manchester Circuits taking on more component design responsibility, a kanban supply link for all its products, and genuine continuous improvement where together the companies will work at achieving a 10 per cent per annum cost reduction throughout the whole supply chain.

Case study: Honda of America Manufacturing Inc.

Honda has striven to establish self-reliance in North America. Approximately 80 per cent of the cost make-up of products is purchased from outside suppliers. Around 800 personnel are dedicated full-time to supporting suppliers. Three hundred of these are in Purchasing and Logistics, 200 in Quality Control, and 300 in Engineering, all dedicated to the support of 246 suppliers. As well as extensive involvement at the design stage, monthly supplier performance reports are raised, detailing shipments with a record of any quality or delivery problems.

There are a series of Honda Improvement Programmes designed for suppliers with recurring quality problems, but the most strategic aspect of all is the Support and Development Group's 'BP' section. BP stands for Best Position, Best Product, Best Productivity, Best Partner and Best Price. BP is a systematic method to achieve all of these. A typical BP project is made up of a team of three Honda purchasing engineers and three engineers from the supplier.

An example of a BP success is the team set up to help a Parker Hannifin plant in Mississippi. A model line was selected where they made an air conditioner tube. Ten Parker employees made 1600 pieces per day on two shifts. The team brainstormed and gathered suggestions, many coming from the ten production workers. They implemented the good ideas at a total cost of $3700, most of which was for handling equipment. At the end of three months, a 100 per cent improvement was achieved. In other words 1600 pieces were made by five employees working only one shift. The ten production workers were so highly motivated because many of their ideas were used to make the improvements. The five who were displaced were given other jobs where they could help teach BP to their fellow employees. BP has now spread throughout all of the Parker Hannifin plants in the US. They call their programme 'Targets for Excellence' and have adapted it to fit their specific needs.

So far BP projects have been completed at more than fifty Honda suppliers. On average an overall improvement of almost 50 per cent in productivity, measured in pieces per person per hour has been achieved.

Once Honda of America Manufacturing select a supplier to make a part, they expect that supplier to make that part indefinitely. They typically do not send the part out for quotations or lower bids from other suppliers, and then beat the existing supplier down to that price. Rather they use the target pricing method. Together with the supplier, Honda develops cost tables from which the target cost is logically and systematically determined. For example with stampings, knowing how much steel is needed, working with the supplier, Honda determine the yield, the size of the press, number of hits and the type of finishing operations that are required. There are cost tables on every aspect of what makes up the price, and the supplier and Honda agree to what it is. Every specification change that affects the price upwards or downwards is then easy to agree to. When a part changes from one model to the next, a comparison is worked out between the old design and the new and the price is adjusted accordingly. Thus the supplier keeps the part model after model. The supplier's responsibility is to employ the latest in process and part technology, to utilize constantly continuous improvement technologies, and to consistently deliver 100 per cent quality, on time, and to meet development speed requirements.

In the Honda purchasing department is a raw materials group who have developed a raw materials supply system for suppliers. Raw material is purchased for suppliers and resold to them at a pre-determined price. By this method, Honda's purchasing power is leveraged to maximum effect and competitive, stable prices are maintained. Another positive feature is that the level of quality can be controlled.

Honda of America have many courses available to suppliers from their training centre, including problem solving, effective interviewing, coaching and counselling, blueprint reading, and many other technical courses. Should a supplier need assistance with electric power, gas or water supply, Honda's facilities department will help them as necessary. If they need assistance with environmental issues, safety regulations, finance or tax problems, administration or personnel issues, Honda have experts who go immediately to help.

As Dave Nelson, Vice President for purchasing at Honda of America Manufacturing says:

'Long-term relationships are two-way. We don't just make demands of our suppliers and never give anything in return. We look for opportunities to help and support our suppliers in any way we can. This is what develops the strong loyalty that we feel for each other. This is the essence of what long-term relationships are made of.

Since Honda suppliers' products make up about 80 per cent of the cost of a car, you can easily understand why our suppliers are an integral and vital part of Honda. In a real sense, they are Honda. Their success is Honda's success; their failure, Honda's failure.'

The marriage analogy: the seven-year itch

Just as suppliers need to gain broadening experience and development in a relationship, both parties must work hard to ensure that the spark of attractive magic that began the whole thing is periodically rekindled, or slow but steady decline in performance may ultimately lead to an expensive and potentially damaging separation. In many ways the analogy with a marriage is very close (Williams and Alderson 1992).

At the earliest stage of a buyer–supplier relationship the supplier is likely to be one of many, similar to 'dating'. Later the supplier will become one of a reducing supplier base, 'getting serious', developing to a preferred supplier, 'going steady', leading to a full partnership relationship analogous to 'engagement and marriage'. This ideal stage should be long-term but can be put under pressure if the degree of mutual commitment invested in the relationship declines. The danger is that complacency can set in and problems which are very minor at first are not addressed until too late. When one or other partner experiences dissatisfaction, a decline in commitment is likely.

Continuing the analogy, one or both partners may seek or become susceptible to the charms of other relationships. 'Secret liaisons and affairs' often lead to 'separation and divorce'.

For a marriage to remain stable and content, regular 'health checks' should occur where both partners address minor irritations. In a business partnering relationship regular performance reviews and maximum open communication must address these 'seven-year itch' issues and avoid the costly consequences of a messy break-up.

The culture of the common purpose

Strategic negotiation is the process of spreading the culture among suppliers so that the aims and objectives of their organization are the same as yours, and that together you are seeking to understand and to meet the requirements of the ultimate end-consumer.

It is always tempting to look towards Japan, and to carmaker Toyota in particular as the exemplar of shared objectives. Richard Lamming's book *Beyond Partnership* extends some of the work done earlier by Womack and Jones, and cites many examples of the success of well managed customer–supplier relationships focusing sharply on a common vision. However as Lamming points out in Chapter 7, of *Beyond Partnership,* there existed in Japan a rather special context and some particularly influential circumstances including:

> the determination born of the nationalism of a country rebuilding itself after a devastating war; the formation of the self-supporting groups to fend off foreign intervention, giving rise to a rare source of concern for mutual benefit; the early practice of reverse-engineering American and European products (learning and criticizing designs, etc.); the role of national initiatives – especially those of MITI; a protected domestic market; inspiration from American process innovators (Deming, Juran, etc.) frustrated by the lethargy of their own country; and some genuine brilliance of leaders such as Kiichiro Toyoda, Taiichi Ohno and Shoichiro Honda.'

But notwithstanding these positive pressures, the Japanese certainly took the job seriously and made sure that they were serious in the way that they went about tackling it. A fond memory of the early 1970s in the UK Defence Industry was the licence agreement signed by Ferranti for inertial platform systems based on gyroscopes to provide navigation information to the Self Defence Force aircraft. Although Ferranti had been building the equipment successfully for many years, it soon became apparent that our planning sheets and drawing sets were not as precise as we thought they were. The incoming telex machine would work overtime and the full length of an assembly work bench would be needed to lay out the list of detailed questions.

'Parts List *xxxx*, Item *yyy* calls for four three-quarter-inch long 4-40 unf pan head screws, – we can only find application for three, please explain...'

Attention to detail, questioning of assumptions and simply caring enough to get things right makes the difference between supplying customers, and delighting them enough to come back again and again. But it can only be done as a joint exercise. As Womack and Jones (1994) describe:

> The experience of Nissan's British subsidiary provides a striking example of what can happen when a purchasing department rethinks its mission. Nissan had serious problems during the 1989 production launch of the Primera, its first car designed for the European market, when several suppliers disrupted production by failing to deliver workable parts on time. The normal course of action in Britain would have been to replace the miscreants. Instead, Nissan's British purchasing department teamed up with the Nissan R&D centre to place supplier–development teams of Nissan engineers inside each supplier for extended periods to improve their key processes. Nissan's theory was that setting high standards and giving suppliers advice on how to meet them would produce superior results. Two years later, when Nissan began production of the Micra, a new small car, this approach had transformed these suppliers from the Nissan subsidiary's worst into its best.

So it is not just a phenomenon peculiar to the special circumstances of post Second World War Japan. To quote Dave Nelson, Vice President for Purchasing, Honda of America Manufacturing Inc., in a paper presented at the seventh Strategic Supply Management Forum in San Diego:

We have only two purchasing policies at Honda:
1 We purchase where we produce.
2 We buy from suppliers who help us to satisfy our customers' needs. We believe Honda suppliers are not simply selling their parts to Honda, they are selling their parts to our customers through Honda. We expect every supplier to develop the same care and dedication to customer satisfaction as we have.'

Conclusions

Strategic negotiation is used to create long-term partnership agreements in which both parties have identical objectives. It is partly investigative, partly checks and monitors, but most of all it is the tool that challenges and develops the buyer–supplier relationship. Strategic negotiation is a process of gathering information, sharing plans and expertise, and working steadily together to investigate and solve joint problems, to consistently deliver satisfaction and delight to the end-consumer of products or services.

7 Supply management's role in time-based competition

Introduction

Until the dreadful fixation with the 'five rights', which condemned purchasing for years to the wilderness of clerical techniques concentrated totally on acquisition, good buyers used to be sometimes regarded as 'the eyes and ears' of the organization. They would be alert to market changes in prices and availability. They could filter the approaches of sales representatives with the latest technical breakthrough and only permit the seemingly most relevant to disturb the desk of the senior designer. They learned to be aware of what was needed, and probably without realizing it, played an important role in the organization's design team.

Modern supply management must regain this strategic role and develop the best techniques possible to harness and harvest all the resources in the supplier base. As the rate of technological development accelerates, product life cycles are reducing steadily and the time available to bring new ideas to market is shrinking rapidly. Supplies have a vital role to play in every phase. But only if we are going to accept the challenge. It is not unusual to hear wails and protests about there never being enough hours available these days and cries of 'where is it going to end?'

Back in 1886, in the great days of railway rivalry for the lucrative London to Edinburgh passenger traffic, Neilson and Company in Glasgow received purchase order number E600 dated 23 January 1886, from the Caledonian Railway Company for one bogie express passenger locomotive to be delivered to Edinburgh by 1 April 1886, without fail. The delivery date was underlined twice. The quotation referred to was dated 22 January 1886, and the order acceptance was dated the same day as the order. EDI eat your heart out. We know that the delivery schedule was met because the locomotive, the famous Caledonian No. 123 was exhibited at the Edinburgh International Exhibition on 1 April 1886.

In *Railway Race to the North*, O. S. Nock (1958) records No. 123's subsequent performance in the 1888 race over a route which included climbs to both Beattock and Cobbinshaw summits:

But on the very first day No. 123 scored a resounding triumph; instead of the 112 minutes scheduled, she ran the 100.6 miles from

Carlisle to Edinburgh in 104 minutes, and stopped in Princes Station at 5.52 p.m. – 8 minutes early.

Nock goes on to describe how throughout the month of August, No. 123 did wonderfully consistent work, with an average time of 107.75 minutes, and average speed 56 m.p.h. This seems more than satisfactory for a locomotive built from scratch in under seventy days. There is no record of the precise role played by the supply management team at the Caledonian Railway Company, but the very simply worded order does contain some extra information added by another hand. Fairly vital information it is including the track gauge, and dimensions of driving wheels and cylinders. Was this a last minute decision on the specification perhaps, or an early example of engineering change control? In any event it is a rather old, but still relevant case of the importance of attention to detail and close working between customer and supplier.

Short time to any market then or now needs the earliest recognition of design innovation in component and service providers. David Burt and Mike Doyle in their book *The American Keiretsu* describe the wealth of innovation available from suppliers:

> The guard standing at the door of the technology gold mine is the firm's own technology paradigm. This paradigm blocks ideas from 'outside' and thereby prevents the early recognition and adoption of new concepts. Worse still, is the failure of many firms to recognize or to fully utilize the technology, engineering, and R&D available within their own supply base.

Management of development and pre-production phases is a hectic process of change, risk, and cost-optimization where close supplier involvement is a prerequisite. Closer attention to manufacturing constraints at the early stages of design reduces time to market by a much reduced level of engineering change orders and the concentration of the necessary changes at the very start before major material and tooling investments have been made. Short product life cycles demand the very best that logistics and supply chain management can achieve.

Harnessing innovation in the supplier base

There is a common complaint in purchasing offices about the high level of expensive single source components appearing on research and development parts lists. 'These engineers are so gullible, they have no conception of the cost of some of these items,' say the buyers, 'If only sales reps were banned from the labs!' On the other hand designers often see the buyers as a bureaucratic nuisance, and certainly not capable of any positive contribution. Many suppliers employ design-in specialists, usually well qualified technically to make the designer feel comfortable, and able to discuss problems and ideas among peers. Insecure buyers, often driven by pressure to make savings, rack their brains to come up with blocking strategies to thwart this upstream selling.

Another equally counter-productive process is neatly described in *The Machine that Changed the World* (Womack, Jones and Roos 1990), in the chapter based primarily on the research of Toshihiro Nishiguchi and Richard Lamming. The design process in the traditional mass-production company in the car industry succeeds to a fairly high degree in keeping the suppliers excluded for as long as possible:

> Then the product is planned in detail, down to the fraction of an inch (for example, the wheelbase and track) and the specific type of material to be used for each part (for example steel fenders, plastic steering wheel, aluminium engine). Next, detailed engineering drawings are made for each part, specifying the precise materials to be used (steel of a given gauge with double galvanized coating for the fenders, for example; thermoset plastic with carbon fibre reinforcement for the steering wheel; specific aluminium alloy for the engine block, and so forth). Only at this point are the organizations that will actually make the parts called in.

The consequences are fairly predictable:

> A key feature of market based bidding is that the suppliers share only a single piece of information with the assembler: the bid price per part. Otherwise suppliers jealously guard information about their operations, even when they are divisions of the assembler company. By holding back information on how they plan to make the part and on their internal efficiency, they believe they are maximizing their ability to hide profits from the assembler.
>
> Once the assembler designates the winning bidders, the suppliers set to work making prototype parts. The process is likely to uncover many problems, because the traditional mass-producer farms out the many parts in a complex component to many suppliers who may have no direct contact with each other. For example, until recently General Motors built practically all its own seats by ordering about twenty-five parts per seat from as many suppliers. When the parts were finally put together in the finished seat, it was not surprising that a piece wouldn't fit or that two abutting materials would prove incompatible.

The essence of harnessing innovation in the supplier base is to develop trust, not only between buying company and the best of the supplier base, but also and firstly between buyer and designer. So often the supplier is keen enough to initiate partnership moves with either the designer or the buyer, only to find the relationship soured and obstructed either by the insecure buyer thinking that the designer lacks appreciation of procurement and is threatening the buyer's job, or by the designer fearing that his traditional 'turf' is being invaded by an opportunistic supplier who seems to be favoured by the buyer, and who only understands a small part of the total picture.

These conflicts are from fault lines in the basic organizational structure. As described in Chapter 2, changes are needed to allow the supply management function to take the high level strategic role of defining the principles, forming links with suppliers and working to improve their performance at a level that transcends the day-to-day tactical issues. When source selection for important areas of supply is carried out by well managed cross-functional teams, there will be room for all parties to make their contribution, and clear up any doubts they may have. Only once complete confidence is established, can a positive, mutually-beneficial supplier relationship be built. Suppliers can then concentrate on managing the relationship to its maximum effect. Dedicated product development teams can be left to get on with the detail of the business.

Design for manufacture/design for cost/design for quality/design for time?

Inspirational world-beating products are not usually conceived when the pressures on time are paramount. However the winners in the time-based competition stakes are those who are organized enough to avoid as much waste as possible. Lack of information and hazy communications make ill-founded assumptions and avoidable mistakes commonplace. New ideas, developments in materials, the increasing potential of building block components, more and more extend the designer's view way beyond the limits of the organization's perimeter. As more of the innovation potential of the supply base is recognized and harnessed, good supply management of this area of the relationship becomes crucial. The fragile cease-fire painfully brokered in the well entrenched war between design and manufacturing in a vertically integrated environment, can seem like everlasting peace compared to the multi-sided conflict which can break out as more and more external resources become involved at the early stages.

The transition periods between design, development and early production are the critical areas to focus on to eliminate unnecessary time and cost. Even with the best computer-aided design tools running tests and simulations, there will always be a flurry of design changes and engineering amendments as the latest techniques are perfected and the customer requirements become fully clarified. The essential aim is to shake these out at as early a stage as possible.

Delays and costs rapidly accelerate if the changes are allowed to proliferate and impact on preparation for the start of the manufacturing cycle. Seemingly small amendments can reap expensive consequences if production tooling is affected or procurement cycles are put into abeyance.

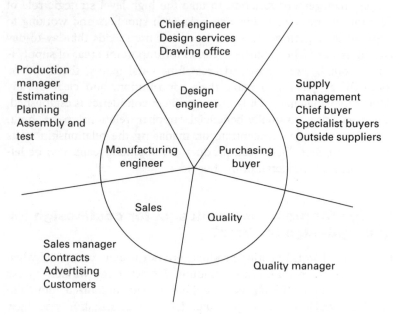

Figure 7.1 *A cross-functional design team*

Moving designers out of the vacuum to work with a cross-functional team is sometimes called concurrent engineering. It helps to ensure that a systematic approach is adopted giving consideration at the earliest stage to all aspects of the product's life cycle. It can have a significant effect on achieving the transition from design to production in a time efficient and cost effective manner. The team can be made up of representatives from design, supply management, quality, sales, and manufacturing, as shown in Figure 7.1. The resultant core design team, backed by the strengths of their respective functions, can operate to a set of defined procedures to:

● Establish a product timetable, and set cost targets.
● Hold a review at each stage of the design.
● Use checklists before moving on to the next stage.
● Complete and sign off a stage release certificate.

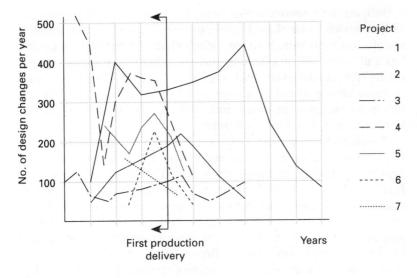

Figure 7.2 *Effects of the installation of a cross-functional design team*

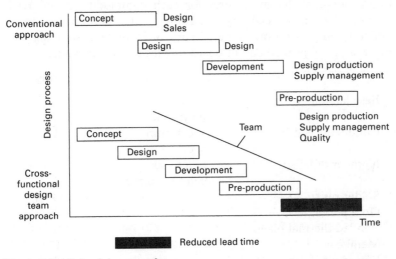

Figure 7.3 *Reduced time-to-market*

The strength of the process comes from all core team members representing the needs of their functions, and bringing in support where necessary. The supply management representative, for example, will involve key suppliers at the very earliest stage. Figure 7.2 shows how this process can bring progressively beneficial effects to a series of complex manufactured products in the defence industry. As experience develops, the date of the first production delivery can be steadily brought forward to shorten the time to market (Figure 7.3).

Bringing new products successfully to market often requires an earlier version to be phased-out in a smooth transition as customers transfer their preference to the latest offering. Supply management has a principal role in planning and executing the changing requirements for stock levels and purchase orders. Whether a hard changeover is planned or a more gentle transition by progressively incorporating new modules into existing products, the earliest involvement of suppliers is essential.

Designers have mostly been rescued from the isolation of their ivory towers, and the need to move away from the 'over the wall' approach is becoming grudgingly accepted if not widely recognized. Just as with internal departments like manufacturing, design engineers need to be brought slowly out of the vacuum to take full consideration of practicable constraints and abilities. New disciplines and checklists can be built in to the product design process. As part of their collaboration process British Aerospace Dynamics have introduced a 'Design Efficiency' scoring system. Working with their partner suppliers, BAe develop a set of design analysis criteria by listing potential design features for each commodity group. Each feature is given a weighting according to its additional technical difficulty, impact on raw material cost, or increase in sourcing risk. For example a printed circuit board might have features like:

		Weighting
Base laminate:	FR4	1
	polyimide	6
Conductor width:	> 0.15mm	1
	< 0.15mm	3
Number of layers:	two to six	1
	eight to sixteen	4
Solder resist		3
Gold plating		4
Bonded thermal plane		4
Metal core		8
Buried via holes		10

$$\text{The Design Efficiency} = \frac{\text{Number of design features}}{\text{Number of points scored}} \times 100\%$$

An eight-layer board in polyimide with normal conductor width, a bonded thermal plane and buried via holes, would score 8/25 x 100 or just 32 per cent. Designers would want to gain as high a score as possible, and rules can be set for the minimum below which approval or help becomes necessary.

Bidders' conferences: customers can be there too

Bringing suppliers together at the proposal stage of a major contract can reap major rewards in shortening product time-to-market as well as the cost and risk reduction focused on in Chapter 3. A simple example of this was a new avionics display for the export version of a military trainer aircraft. In the close confines of a cramped cockpit, space and heat dissipation are major problems. The precision investment casting forming the mainframe, and a high voltage power supply providing the extra high tension supply for the display cathode ray tube were significant components. A conference had been set up to look at cost reductions in these and other areas, but one of the main benefits came from the realization that it would be very much better to build the power supply directly into one of the mainframe cover plates. This provided a little more space for the power supply manufacturer, but more importantly eliminated completely two time-consuming sub-contracted processes in which the base plate of the power supply and the inside of the casting were finely ground to flat and parallel surfaces to ensure maximum transfer of heat away from the sensitive electronics (Chadwick 1993).

In another product, a conference brought together manufacturers of cathode ray tubes, high voltage power supply and the interconnecting cable and terminations, in a sub-group of the main activity. The atmosphere generated in a bidders' conference facilitates working together to focus on the end-customer's requirements and how the order can be won by best meeting them. In this case, discussion ranged around whether the two high voltage components could be permanently wired together, before coming up with a less drastic but rather neat solution. Several of the delicate electrical terminations were combined into one customized block, which still allowed disassembly for service and replacement. This required a little expenditure in tooling, but produced an improvement in reliability and a valuable reduction in assembly time.

Supply management's role as architect of the whole value stream, includes close attention to the detail of arranging meetings where problems can be investigated jointly and the very best solution found. In the period just prior to the launch of a major bid, there is the extra catalyst in the excitement of the competition to be won.

When teams of partner suppliers are gelling together successfully, the end-customer can be invited along as well. Just as bidders' conferences with suppliers flush out misunderstandings and invalid assumptions before real commitment is made, why not involve the actual customer as well? This is surely the means of focusing with ultimate precision. A good example happened when a defence contractor was striving to react to the shrinking military market brought about by the 'peace dividend' at the start of the 1990s by diversifying into new sectors of business.

Working with new suppliers and new customers at the same time meant that the learning cycle had to be done in parallel. What better way than to tackle it simultaneously? As a strategically important bid approached, the opportunity was seized to engage the help of key potential suppliers in some of the discussions with the potential customer. This three-tier cross fertilization of ideas stimulated shared problem solving on the difficulties of the proposed specification, and prompted valuable cost and time saving suggestions, which may otherwise never have appeared. It certainly seemed to work since, rather against the odds, the defence contractor won the business and a real opportunity to become established in an exciting and expanding market.

Supply management has an important facilitator role in not only improving understanding between customer and supplier, but also between and among suppliers and groups of suppliers. This is best and most easily done using the Japanese style of 'co-operative circle' or *kyoryoku kai* which have played such a significant role in the progress of the Japanese automobile industry. Peter Hines in his book *Creating World Class Suppliers* (1994) states:

> These *kyoryoku kai* can be viewed as communication, co-ordination and development tools that have successfully resulted in the deployment of successful Japanese management and manufacturing techniques throughout the complete network of supply over a period of several decades.

Like everything else, co-operative circles or supplier associations can produce marvellous results once they are established, but they cannot be created at the drop of a hat.

One useful approach is to cascade the bidders' conference idea down to the next tier of suppliers. By getting each prime supplier to identify the main cost and time drivers from their own supplier base, it is quite possible to arrange for them to set up a second tier bidders' conference. A lot of the ideas and resources generated for the top-level event can be repeated at the supplier's premises, harnessing more contributors into the common cause and introducing yourself and your company to this tier of secondary suppliers. Once it has been done for the first time, it is easier to repeat, especially if some good results have emerged.

Manufacturing myth and mystique: BOMs and JITs and things

To the interested non-specialist, procurement for manufacturing can seem to be impenetrably clouded by meaningless abbreviations like EOQ, MRP, MRPII, JIT, and OPT. All of them, in differing circumstances seek to avoid waste and reduce costs, and all of them play an important role in time based competition.

Economic order quantity (EOQ) calculations can still be used for items for in which demand is not dependent on other items. The cost of storing an item increases directly in line with the quantity of items held in stock. The cost of placing an order, receiving and clearing all the necessary paperwork is greater, the more individual orders that are placed. The simple formula is derived from a compromise where, at the lowest total cost, the cost of ordering is equal to the cost of storage:

$$EOQ = \frac{\sqrt{2 \times \text{Annual usage} \times \text{Cost of placing 1 order}}}{\text{Unit cost} \times \text{Cost of storage}}$$

In a manufacturing or assembly context, direct materials which are brought together to make up the final product or sub-assembly to be delivered to the customer, are said to have dependent demands. Requirements for these items depend directly on requirements for the end-product. For instance for each personal computer ordered from a PC manufacturer there is a related demand for a keyboard, and for the keyboard I am using, seven screws and seven washers to hold the assembly together. The number of screws to be ordered clearly depends on the number of PCs which the manufacturer has decided to make. Materials requirements planning (MRP) is the system used to calculate the demands for individual components which make up products and assemblies. MRP also provides a ready mechanism to reschedule orders for component parts to keep the inflow of material in line with changing needs for the end product.

Other than for the simplest of operations, MRP needs to be run on a computer, and there are many systems on the market. The basic MRP system makes use of a master production schedule (MPS) which specifies the individual end-products and the time periods in which they are to be produced. This is run against a bill of materials (BOM) for each end-product which specifies all sub-assemblies and the component parts and their quantities which are needed to make them. The BOM is sometimes thought of as a 'gozinto' chart. Seven screws and seven washers go into the keyboard, and one keyboard goes into the PC system etc., etc. It is important to know how long it takes to get each type of component and how long each stage of the assembly or manufacturing process takes. This 'lead time' information is included in the BOM so that the MRP analysis not only calculates how many items of each particular variety have to be ordered, but also when they have to be ordered to ensure that everything comes together to meet the demands for the final end-product. The final constituent of MRP is an inventory file which keeps a record of everything which is already in stock, or outstanding on order.

MRPII, which confusingly means manufacturing resource planning, is the development of materials requirements planning to include the various functions of production planning and control including capacity planning and shop floor control. It is said to be a total management control system integrated into the financial control system of the organization. Used on its own MRP assumes infinite capacity, so it has been improved to try to avoid the problems of overloads and underloads on machines, processes and people.

Incorporating some form of capacity resource planning requires the addition of elements including the routes through the plant for each product; the times required at each process or work station both for preparation and set up as well as carrying out the actual operation; delays required between each process; the capacity of each process or work centre; the work already loaded at each stage. There also have to be some rules for scheduling whether it be forward from the start date or backwards from the required delivery date. A comprehensive system also needs information on shift patterns, holidays and allowable and potential overtime availability with early warning where appropriate.

There are several additions that need to be made to the basic MRP system described on page 143. Right at the top comes the company business plan defining the medium and long term objectives of the organization. This links to the master production schedule. An element called rough cut capacity planning takes the immediate output from the master production schedule and compares the demands with the available resources at aggregate works or department level. If there is a complete mismatch on this crude measure, then changes are required in either the master production schedule or the extent of resources available. Rough cut capacity planning flags this up before the complex gears of the detailed analysis down below are engaged. It provides an excellent tool for 'What if?' analysis. Shop floor control looks after the issuing of works orders for manufacturing and assembly. Data entry during processing using operator keypads or similar means, keeps the whole system up-to-date as work proceeds and allows continuous comparison with planning objectives at both high- and low-levels.

The system is heavily dependent on good computer software and a manufacturing environment which is rich in planning, procedures and discipline. A well implemented system provides all the necessary information for total management control including finance, cash flow, human resource management and marketing. This integration allows constant feedback to ensure that plans are both practicable and up-to-date with the latest situation.

'Just-in-time' (JIT) is a philosophy for reducing inventory and waste, that came almost as the panacea to enable Western industry to shake off half a century's malaise and catch up and overtake the precocious Japanese. At its most simplistic level JIT is the scheduling of material and resources to arrive just when needed to support a requirement. It is the elimination of *muri* meaning excess; *muda* waste; and *mura* unevenness. However excess stocks, queuing delays, and imbalance have often been deliberately planned into our Western systems, as cautious and seemingly prudent safeguards against late shipments or uncertain quality from our suppliers. Processing in large batches is a chosen consequence of amortizing set-up costs over a larger quantity of items. These are classic examples of our penchant for optimizing the particular at the expense of the whole, or more succinctly, simply forgetting just what it is that we are trying to achieve.

Implementing JIT successfully demands a management and workforce that is ready and prepared for change. The overriding need is for a hunger for a philosophy of achieving excellence through continuous flow, elimination of waste and unrelenting quality improvement. Supplies' role is to ensure that the acceptance and benefits of change see no barriers or diversions at the inevitable boundaries between buying and supplying organizations. Commitment, new ideas and philosophies must flow both ways in a spirit free from hindrance or suspicion.

Optimized production technology (OPT) is a concept introduced by Dr Eli Goldratt in the late 1970s to attempt to define nine rules to gain effective control of a complex factory. OPT like JIT recognizes the need to balance flow, but introduces thoughts and guidelines about bottlenecks. Rule five: 'An hour saved at a non-bottleneck is just a mirage', is perhaps one of the most significant statements ever made in the history of production control. Goldratt also shows that lead times for individual jobs can only really be determined in relation to the schedules of all the other jobs being processed at the same time.

'Lean production', and thankfully lean is not an acronym, is a term coined by John Krafcik, a researcher on the International Motor Vehicle Program carried out at the Massachusetts Institute of

Technology from 1985 to 1990. The concept is of a system where waste and excess have been entirely eliminated. All resources, human, materials, space and complexity are put under the microscope and unnecessary cushion removed.

JIT and lean supply management

Taiichi Ohno is the production genius widely credited as having developed the very best lean production techniques at car maker Toyota. Working with Eiji Toyoda, Ohno studied every detail of car manufacturing in the West and set out to adapt and improve on what he saw. The case study is extracted from *The Machine that Changed the World* by Womack, Jones and Roos.

Case study: the Toyota press shop

More than sixty years have passed since the introduction of Henry Ford's Model A with its all-steel body. Yet, across the world, nearly all motor-vehicle bodies are still produced by welding together about 300 metal parts stamped from sheet steel.

Auto makers have produced these 'stampings' by employing one of two different methods. A few tiny craft producers, such as Aston Martin, cut sheets of metal – usually aluminium – to a gross shape, then beat these blanks by hand on a die to their final shape.

Any producer making more than a few hundred cars a year – a category that includes auto makers ranging from Porsche to General Motors – starts with a large roll of sheet steel. They run this sheet through an automated 'blanking' press to produce a stack of flat blanks slightly larger than the final part they want. They then insert the blanks in massive stamping presses containing matched upper and lower dies. When these dies are pushed together under thousands of pounds of pressure, the two-dimensional blank takes the three-dimensional shape of a car fender or a truck door as it moves through a series of presses.

The problem with this second method, from Ohno's perspective, was the minimum scale required for economical operation. The massive and expensive Western press lines were designed to operate at about twelve strokes per minute, three shifts a day, to make a million or more of a given part in a year. Yet in the early days, Toyota's entire

---

production was a few thousand vehicles a year.

The dies could be changed so that the same press line could make more parts, but doing so presented major difficulties. The dies weighed many tons each, and workers had to align them in the press with absolute precision. A slight misalignment produced wrinkled parts. A more serious misalignment could produce a nightmare in which the sheet metal melted in the die, necessitating extremely expensive and time-consuming repairs.

To avoid these problems, Detroit, Wolfsburg, Flins and Mirafiori assigned die changes to specialists. Die changes were undertaken methodically and typically required a full day to go from the last part with the old dies to the first acceptable part from the new dies. As volume in the Western industry soared after the Second World War, the industry found an even better solution to the die-change problem. Manufacturers found they often could 'dedicate' a set of presses to a specific part and stamp these parts for months, or even years without changing dies.

To Ohno, however, this solution was no solution at all. The dominant Western practice required hundreds of stamping presses to make all the parts in car and truck bodies, while Ohno's capital budget dictated that practically the entire car be stamped from a few press lines.

His idea was to develop simple die-changing techniques and to change dies frequently – every two to three hours versus two to three months – using rollers to move dies in and out of position and simple adjustment mechanisms. Because the new techniques were easy to master and production workers were idle during the die changes, Ohno hit upon the idea of letting the production workers perform the die changes as well.

By purchasing a few used American presses and endlessly experimenting from the late 1940s onward, Ohno eventually perfected his technique for quick changes. By the late 1950s, he had reduced the time required to change dies from a day to an astonishing three minutes and eliminated the need for die-change specialists. In the process, he made an unexpected discovery – it actually cost less per part to make small batches of stampings than to run off enormous lots.

There were two reasons for this phenomenon. Making small batches eliminated the carrying cost of the huge inventories of finished parts that mass-production systems

> required. Even more important, making only a few parts
> before assembling them into a car caused stamping
> mistakes to show up almost instantly.

The role of the distributor: time is money

The opportunity for close control and compression of the supply chain to make sure that users, consumers and customers communicate as directly as possible with creators and manufacturers is bolstered, and not obstructed by prudent use of well-organized stockists and distribution agencies.

As emphasized in Chapter 3, it is vitally important to get the low risk 'trivial many' ranks of requirements well-organized and fully under control. So many supply management teams can never find time for strategic issues because their resources haemorrhage away fighting the inextinguishable bush fires for mere day-to-day survival. Well planned and negotiated arrangements with a few good distributors, complete with regular performance reviews, can deliver the best range of common products, the best prices, the best levels of service, as well as that most valuable of all products: time.

Building a good relationship with a good distributor is a common way to reduce the supplier base, by developing the business so that the distributor acts almost as a buying agency, taking over much of the work of sourcing from third-party, seldom-used vendors, and absorbing the delivery and payment part of the supply chain. Zeneca Pharmaceuticals have formed such a relationship with a small number of laboratory supply companies including Fisons Scientific. They call this the Zeneca Pharmaceuticals streamline system. Once an effective system had been developed with blanket orders raised on an annual basis, and low-value requisitions sent by fax on a daily basis, discussions began as to how many of Zeneca's smaller suppliers were also on the Fisons Scientific database. In many cases Fisons were already obtaining better terms because of their greater purchasing power, in other cases the benefits for Zeneca were in the resulting smaller, easier to manage supplier base, and the ease and simplicity of bringing more of the purchasing transactions into the efficient 'streamline system'. Zeneca have not lost direct access to product information and innovative leads from the manufacturers of these products. It is simply established that purchase orders will now come via Fisons.

As early as the Autumn of 1937 when Adolf Hitler's Third Reich was planning to darken the world with a new European order, P. M. Sebestyen and J. H. Waring were establishing Radiospares Ltd in a lock-up garage in north-west London. Their first price list promised

'A Replacement for Every Job! and a 24 Hours' Service on top of it!' Their business was selling time and has been so successful that RS Components as it became known went on to become the largest distributor of electronic and electrical products in Europe.

Nowadays they have a three-volume catalogue which is available on CD-ROM with instant ordering via a fax modem. Orders received by 5 p.m. are despatched the same day, and for emergencies a courier service is available for delivery in three hours provided the customer is within thirty miles of one of the company's trade counters. Other offerings from suppliers in the same market include an automatic stock control and reordering system, the 'Fast system' from Farnell Electronics. This involves the use of barcode readers to monitor stock issues, and an automatic download each day to the distributor's computer to prompt the despatch of refill quantities if the agreed stock reorder level threshold has been reached. This approach seeks to address the perceived need, or feel-good factor in having some stock on hand locally to provide the instant responsiveness that many end-users, particularly in research and development see as a divine right. Having a local store may be anathema to many, but it can eliminate personal squirrel stores as even the most efficient quick response distributor finds it convenient to supply minimum pack sizes. It also gives ready information to ensure that price levels are commensurate with annual usage and not individual demand.

Like everything else, the logistical arrangements first offered may not suit particular requirements. It is very important to think through and define the most suitable arrangements to meet individual circumstances. Supply managers are supposed to clearly understand the need for a carefully defined specification with appropriate performance criteria to match real requirements. Choosing a logistics package to interface with distributor suppliers is a procurement exercise of some importance.

Key to successful acceptance and operation is the need to carefully consider the needs of the small as well as the large user in the organization. An overly centralized stance that a single source arrangement with one distributor saves money for the business as a whole but acts to the detriment of individual users, is not the best way forward. One important aspect of handling many small requirements is to ensure that there is a ready method of charging the cost to the correct account number. To achieve finely tuned control, it is often necessary to tie each transaction back to a specific job number or charge code. Raising individual orders with individually matched invoices is one means of achieving this, if hardly a cost-effective way when tackled manually.

Conclusions

Supply management has a very significant role in time-based competition. Where research and development is involved, there is a need to set up the very best links with suppliers using cross-functional source selection teams and making sure that the key design element is adequately covered. Prime suppliers are important, but there is an equal need to establish contact with lower tiers of suppliers to ensure that they understand fully what you are trying to do, and feel that they want to share in the task of reducing lead times and performing on time.

In manufacturing there is a wide variety of techniques available. Selecting the most appropriate for your organization's circumstances should bring closer supplier involvement to monitor and flag up potential problems before they occur, rather than leave you to expedite after the event.

It is part of the duty of every supply management team to eliminate unnecessary bureaucracy and provide a means of acquisition which is as efficient in time as possible. This is especially true with common everyday items. Time is valuable in every transaction. It does not have to be the drive to bring a new product to market. When needs are satisfied directly, staff can get on with their work and decisions can be taken and plans made without delay. The supply management role in time-based competition is to work increasingly closely with the best available suppliers to satisfy requirements in the best manner possible.

8 Managing risk in purchasing

Sources of risk in procurement

Risks can occur in all aspects of business and institutional management. With an increasing proportion of external resources contributing to ever more critical areas of our activities, exposure to risk in procurement must rise accordingly. Even more so than other problems, exposure to risk can lessen significantly when more information is brought out into open discussion. Perhaps the largest risk of all in supply management is to fail to carry out a proper risk assessment.

Supply management is essentially a process of bringing together diverse groups of organizations and people with different skills and experience to achieve tasks and requirements in an effective and economical way. Whenever information is passed from one mind to another there are problems of communication, and assumptions are made. It is so difficult for the expert in one topic to explain things in precise terms to someone who specializes in quite a different field. There is an exercise much loved by teachers and youth leaders of assembling a wide circle of youngsters just out of earshot from each other, and then causing a message to be passed from one to the other. When it eventually reaches the leader again it is often sufficiently garbled to have lost its original meaning altogether. The risks of an inadequate specification, and of inadequate control of its communication are the first areas which need attention.

The price arrangements made and final source selection bring the second series of risks. If a fixed price contract is agreed, then the supplier is assumed to be taking all the risk, and the buyer presumably paying for it. But what is the risk to the buyer of the supplier failing? Whenever prices are negotiated downwards, the seller will take some account of a perceived reallocation of risk, but is the buyer aware that it could really just be moving into his area of responsibility? Any sourcing selection brings exposure to the fragility of the supplier's financial position, and external market pressures which may act counter to the best laid plans of partnership. Single and multiple sourcing strategies each have a checklist of questions and balances to be analysed before the best decision can be made.

The purchasing transaction itself has its obvious legal and contractual implications. In many cases there will be currency exchange rate fluctuations to be considered. Any advance payments, or costs charged as progress milestones are reached, need to be safeguarded against adverse changes in the supplier's solvency status. There is the major risk that the work will not be carried through to completion, or may be delivered late, or may fail after delivery.

Nowadays there are the ever-increasing pressures on organizations to behave more responsibly towards the good health of the environment. The effects of legislation and powerful public pressure groups can bring rapid changes in the status of otherwise secure sources of supply. There are direct as well as indirect implications where products and processes carried out by suppliers in response to purchase order requirements may result in harmful emissions, toxic waste, or contaminated land.

Finally it is essential to cover the important if unsavoury topic of ethics in procurement, not only as a guard against the risk of corruption and fraud, but also to ensure that concern for the confidentiality of information is not allowed to hamper the effectiveness of relationships.

Carrying out a risk assessment

Before any major project is finally committed to contract, a formal risk assessment should be carried out. This will address all the major parts of the project from design and specification right through to review of performance after completion of the normal delivery and installation process. Checklists are a very useful aid in this but there is no real substitute for formal involvement of all participants from users, designers, manufacturers or providers, installers and maintainers in risk identification and reduction sessions. No general set of questions can ever be completely comprehensive.

Just as in strategic negotiation there is nothing worthwhile to be gained in tricking or bullying supply partners into swallowing unnecessary costs, the whole essence of risk assessment is to identify and reduce or eliminate risk. It only makes sense to transfer risk to someone else if the other party is in a position to control it better, or reduce its consequences.

The purpose of risk assessment is to understand and where possible measure the effect of potential risk. There are elements of qualitative as well as quantitative assessment. Qualitative issues should be listed as a series of written statements covering every stage of the project or task. The qualitative assessment is particularly valuable at the very earliest or conceptual stage of the project. Attention is focused on uncovering causes and likely effects of each potential risk. There is an immediate opportunity to abandon or redefine the work before any serious expenditure of resources has taken place. Where risks appear to be less than catastrophic, a simple impact and likelihood of occurrence table can be constructed. Risks which score high in both categories are dealt with first.

A simple example is a risk assessment for a source selection decision:

- How is the supply market in terms of number of potential sources?
- Does the available capacity now and in the future comfortably exceed our needs?
- How committed are we to the current supplier in specialist tooling or shared designs?
- How committed is the current supplier to our requirements and goals?
- What level of asset specificity exists?
- How closely does the current supplier meet our specification and quality needs?
- Is the current supplier financially stable?
- What environmental management issues are involved?
- Are there legal, social or ethical constraints?

It works quite well to score the eight factors twice. Firstly ranking the potential impact on a basis of low scores one; medium scores two; and high scores three. Then secondly on likelihood of occurrence, low scores one; medium scores two; and high scores three.

Where no specific checklists exist, a structured brainstorming session can be as good a way as any of identifying areas of potential exposure. Brainstorming should be broad ranging, but needs skilful management to make sure that all the key contributors are present, and that junior as well as senior staff feel comfortable and confident enough to throw in all their ideas. The normal procedure is for the leader to express the problem on a flipchart or black or white board. Before the process starts in earnest it is useful to restate the problem in as many ways possible to ensure that everyone understands it fully.

Basic rules of brainstorming are:

- As many ideas as possible should be generated.
- There are no suggestions which are too wild or too silly.
- Don't criticize other people's ideas.
- Make sure that everyone participates.
- Build on and add to earlier suggestions.
- All suggestions are recorded exactly as they are stated.

Sometimes it can be constructive to restart with one of the wildest ideas and brainstorm on that. At the end the group works through all the points distilling out the most relevant for further analysis.

Take care that exposure to risk is being considered at root cause rather than surface level. One of the greatest benefits of the 'just-in-time' approach to manufacturing is the much increased visibility of exposure to risk. The 'just in case' stocks, the safety buffer in the lead-time, the belt-and-braces of dual sourcing are definitely justified if the mistaken philosophy is simply to avoid risk rather than to investigate and deal with the root causes. It is only when all the buffers are removed from the system and material is being pulled forward just-in-time that the problems become clearly visible as the whole production line and entire work force grind to a halt.

Risks may be hidden like the jagged rocks well beneath the fragile hull of the ship. But how much longer will customers and shareholders be happy to sustain the burden of the expensive safety cushion of deep water that is currently being relied on? No matter how far your organization is removed from manufacturing, put on some 'just-in-time' spectacles and use their X-ray vision to penetrate the waste and precautionary excesses in your business. These are the just-in-case contingency provisions and extra time which have been allowed to creep in as an easier option than understanding and preventing the thing that just might go wrong. Even if you think you can afford the extra fuel and time to navigate around them today, unresolved problems tend to worsen and spread, and diversions become even more costly.

Quantitative assessment follows the qualitative ranking. Each risk is scored against increased cost; increased time; and reduced compliance or performance level. From this information a plot of likely expenditure against time can be made with both planned and worst case scenarios.

Risks associated with the specification

A specification can be defined as a statement of needs to be satisfied by the procurement of external resources. It should be sufficiently tight so that the product or service meets the user's requirements but not so exclusive that it closes the door to innovative proposals, or removes all scope for negotiation.

Where an organization is heavily involved in research and development, the prime responsibility for drawing up specifications will lie with the design department. There should be a carefully controlled design procedures manual which contains a range of checklists covering as many aspects of specification content as possible, but certainly including:

- adequacy of proposed design;
- producibility;

- safety;
- reliability;
- maintainability.

The use of these sort of checklists can help a designer to avoid a bad design but cannot in themselves ensure that he produces a good one.

In many cases the author of the specification will be the user. Even more care is needed here to avoid unnecessary risk. The most common problem comes from assumptions. Inexperienced purchasers are not really used to setting out a clear statement of their needs. It is rather hard work, and so much easier to just shop around for something that we assume will do the job. Sales representatives also make assumptions that they understand the user's needs. It is worth quoting the old adage 'to assume is to make an ass out of u and me'. The supply management team has the prime role in determining the answers to questions like the following:

- Is there a specification of requirements?
- Have these requirements been challenged, and changed if appropriate?
- Are the needs stated limited to the necessary and sufficient ones to achieve the purpose?
- Are they stated clearly and unambiguously?
- Are there sufficiently well-defined criteria for evaluation and acceptance or rejection?
- Does the specification provide an equal opportunity for all potential suppliers?
- Is current legislation complied with?

Risk in contracts

Contracts are formal agreements set up to ensure that defined things get done. But they can be made do more than that. The best contracts should create some incentive to do the work well, and to deal with the inevitable risk involved. At one end of the scale the fixed price contract can be seen to place all the risk with the supplier. At the other end a cost plus contract transfers risk to the purchaser. An incentive contract seeks to share the risks and if carefully set up, can be successful in stimulating innovative input to produce the very best value for money and a delighted customer who is very likely to return for more business next time there is a requirement.

Figure 8.1 shows an incentive contract where the agreed target cost is £100 000 and the agreed fee is £10 000. If the project goes entirely to plan the buyer will be happy to accept a final invoice of £110 000. The incentive to the supplier to improve on this is illustrated by the 50/50 share line. If costs can be reduced below £100 000, say by £10 000, then both customer and supplier benefit by £5 000. This takes the form of a final invoice reduced to £105 000 for the customer, and an increased fee of £15 000 for the supplier.

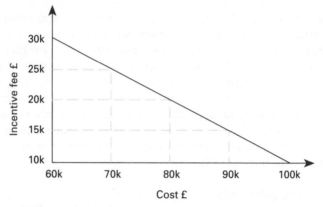

Figure 8.1 *Incentive contract*

One practical example of this sort of contract has been used for highway repairs. As part of their bids for motorway maintenance, contractors can be asked to include a rental of so many pounds per hundred metres of lane occupied per day. The incentive in completing the work ahead of schedule is to save rental payments for the periods when the lane no longer requires their occupation. The subsequent early removal of maintenance cones has the added bonus to both the travelling public and their perception of the highway authority.

Contract price adjustment formulae

The risk of changing costs over the life of a contract can be reduced by means of a price adjustment formula. This can be particularly useful when the work is complex and there is an extended time interval between placing the order and anticipated completion. It is very important not to think of these as escalation formulae. Costs can go down as well as up, especially if there is a high content of special materials which may be subject to commodity market fluctuations. Quotations are invited to be priced at the cost levels currently existing and available for examination and audit. This should remove the temptation for bidders to cover their risk by adding an extra percentage to cover unforeseen circumstances. All the normal price dissection, value analysis, and negotiation are necessary to ensure that the base price finally agreed really is the base price.

By this stage it should be clear how costs break down proportionately between labour and material. Indices need to be identified which relate as closely as possible to the nature of work involved. Many governments produce monthly statistics for a wide range of industries. Professional bodies and trade associations collect data and publish regular sets of figures for specialist areas of industry. Great care is needed in selecting the most appropriate indices. Historical data should be examined and graphed over a sufficiently long period to allow meaningful extrapolations to be made to assess likely future trends. The formula chosen will break the price down into labour and material content and can include a fixed element which is not subject to adjustment:

$$P(n) = P(o)/100[5 + 63S(1)/S(o) + 32M(1)/M(o)]$$

$P(n)$	Final price.
$P(o)$	Price at time of placing the order.
$S(1)$	The average labour index over the last two thirds of the project.
$S(o)$	The labour index at the time of placing the order.
$M(1)$	The average material index over the period from two fifths to four fifths of the duration of the project.
$M(o)$	The material index at the time of placing the order.

In this example a fixed element of 5% has been agreed and cost breakdown is calculated at 63% from wages and salaries and 32% material resources.

Working out averages for the indices $S(1)$ and $M(1)$ make the calculations slightly more complex, but provide a much more realistic assessment of actual costs than simply using labour and material figures adjusted right up to the end of the project. The logic behind this is that most of the material purchases will be completed between two-fifths and four-fifths of the way through the duration. Labour will be paid for as it is used so this proportion of costs should only be adjusted to the average level prevailing over the last two-thirds of the time. These details can make a significant difference where projects are scheduled to take many months or even years. As with many of the tools suggested in this book, the process of discussion and agreement between buyer and supplier to establish the most suitable formula, provides the very basis for working more closely together and understanding all the costs and risks involved.

There is usually a gap between the period covered by the calculated index and the date of publication. This delay is needed to collect and validate the data, and can be as much as three months. This means either a considerable delay in raising and agreeing the main invoice, or the submission of supplementary documentation three months or so after the completion of the project. To avoid this it is helpful to agree to work to the indices published at the dates in question, rather than those specifically for the dates. In other words if a contract began in February, the start point would be the latest figure available in February, probably December's, and the other analysis points would use data offset backwards by the same time periods. It is then possible to raise the final invoice at the date of delivery and include the final calculation of adjusted costs.

Purchasing in other currencies

When all the normal criteria have been satisfied for source selection and the ordering decision is taken to buy from a supplier in a foreign country, there are several new risks to be faced. The first of these concerns providing funds for the eventual payment. There is least risk by buying the foreign currency forward immediately, thus securing the same exchange rate which made the purchase acceptable in the first place. For large transactions this can be done reasonably cheaply on a one-for-one basis, but if many small orders are involved it is necessary to liaise very closely with the treasury part of your finance department to ensure that the risks of fluctuating exchange rates are minimized in the most practical way possible. Organizations trading and dealing with a number of different countries will have income streams and banking facilities in many different currencies. Supplies management will work closely with the finance department to ensure that individual transactions are not being optimized to the detriment of the currency management strategy for the complete organization. Simply insisting in always buying in your own currency does nothing to eliminate the risk but simply transfers it to your supplier who may be less able to deal with it than your own organization.

Purchasing from abroad accentuates some of the other problems too, particularly where carriers or shipping agents are involved. It is important to understand just precisely where property and risk responsibilities are being transferred and to take sufficient timely action to ensure that insurance cover is correctly in place. Here there are some special acronyms or incoterms to master.

Table 8.1 shows just a small sample of the most common incoterms defined by the international chamber of commerce. The buyer has the apparently easiest time with DDP, delivered duty paid, where he simply has to agree to the seller's price and await a knock at the door of his goods inwards department. However this may not necessarily bring the best value for money. If the buyer selects any of

Table 8.1 Where the risk is transferred

Incoterms	Charges paid by buyer begin with	Delivery at/to	Property and risk pass-on
DDP (delivered duty-paid)	Nil	Buyer's premises	Delivery to buyer's premises
CIF named UK port (cost, insurance and freight)	UK port dues, dock handling charges. Transport to warehouse. Duty, clearance and delivery to buyer's premises	On tender of bill of lading to buyer	Over the ship's rail at port of shipment
C&F (cost and freight)	Marine insurance	On tender of bill of lading to buyer	Over the ship's rail at port of shipment
FOB (free on board)	Shipping expenses, documentation and freight	When safely loaded	Over the ship's rail at port of shipment
FAS (free alongside)	Dock and port expenses and outwards customs formalities	Under the ship's hook	When the ship is able and ready to load
Ex-works	Loading on to road or rail vehicle	Seller's premises or other notified warehouse	Notification that the goods are at the buyer's disposal

the other options whose quoted price is likely to be lower, then additional arrangements need to be made to place orders to cover transport and insurance costs. The entries list in descending order the arrangements where more and more of the risk, which requires insurance cover, and the responsibility for transport are laid directly at the buyer's feet.

Advance payments and performance guarantees

The normal policy is to pay invoices only after the receipt of goods or services which satisfy the requirements of the purchase order. However, there are certain circumstances in which there may be an advantage in making earlier payment of all or part of the amount due. Making payments in advance puts funds at risk and there is often very little chance of recovering the money if the organization we are trading with becomes subject to receivership or liquidation. Improved protection will be provided if the following practices are used:

● **Advance payments,** e.g. 20 per cent with order. Here there is no linkage with performance or potential transfer of ownership rights so the best protection is to ask for a Banker's Guarantee to cover the requested amount. This document should 'unconditionally and irrevocably guarantee the repayment to the buyer on demand of any such sum up to the maximum of (the amount paid), on receipt from the buyer of notice in writing of the contractor's inability to fulfil all or part of the contract, such notice to constitute conclusive evidence that such sums as shall be demanded are properly due'. The guarantee will remain valid until the supply of the goods or services has been completed.

- **Progress-related payments.** Here payment is tied to the demonstrable achievement of agreed milestones. These should be truly representative of progress being made by the supplier and the amounts agreed against the milestones should be a genuine reflection of the supplier's expenditure to the relevant point in the programme.

The milestone descriptions and amounts should be agreed prior to the placement of the order, and there should always be a significant amount (e.g. 10 to 15 per cent) held until the end to maintain at least some incentive to ensure completion. Banker's Guarantees can be demanded against each payment or a 'Certificate of Vesting' can be obtained which under the official seal of the supplier vests the property in the work carried out by the supplier to the ownership of the buyer.

Hedging in commodity markets

Primary materials traded on commodity markets around the world are subject to major fluctuations in price which can expose manufacturers dependent on them to very major risks indeed. Extreme volatility in supply and demand pressures often over very short timescales can be caused by speculation as well as political uncertainty. Enormous fluctuations in the price of substances like copper and cocoa can bring the risk of catastrophic losses to the very best managed organization.

Commodity prices are quoted for both spot, or instant purchase, and futures basis with figures which can be fixed now for delivery or receipt at a specified date in the future. Futures prices are often fairly close to spot prices with a small margin upwards or downwards which points in the direction that the market traders think prices are likely to move. The real problem is the unexpected suddenness with which changes can occur. The way to gain protection against this is to organize what is known as a hedge. This consists of an equal but opposite transaction arranged at the same time as an original sale or purchase, to try to cancel the risk of an unforecast adverse price change.

The traditional textbooks for buyers contain marvellous examples of jolly millers with wheat in store, but a more relevant case these days might be an aluminium foundry which receives an order for a large batch of precision castings to be delivered in March, in six months' time with the raw aluminium content of the price, which is 91 per cent, agreed at the price then ruling in the market. The foundry buyer purchases the aluminium alloy at £1200 per tonne, and pays the resulting invoice. The job requires 200 tonnes, so the foundry is exposed to the risk of considerable loss if the market price for aluminium drops significantly in the next six months.

To provide a protective hedge against this risk, the buyer covers himself by arranging to sell 200 tonnes of aluminium for delivery in six months, to a market speculator on a March futures contract where the price is fixed now at the published futures figure of £1180 per tonne.

When March comes round aluminium has indeed fallen quite badly to a spot price of £930 per tonne for ex-stock delivery. The foundry suffers a heavy loss of 200 x (£1200 – £930) on the metal content of its castings price. However, thanks to the hedge, the buyer is able to buy another 200 tonnes on the spot market to deliver to the speculator at a profit of 200 x (£1180 – £930). This reduces the overall loss to manageable proportions.

If the market had moved the other way, and the price in March had turned out to be higher than six months earlier, the foundry would have made a profit on its sale of castings but a corresponding loss on the contract which the buyer had agreed with the speculator. The hedging process is used purely to reduce exposure to risk. The role of the speculator is important in providing a vital link in the chain. Hedging would simply not work without the presence of speculation in the market. Speculators act to smooth the natural volatility of commodity prices by trying to identify and anticipate peaks and troughs. Speculators tend to start buying when everyone else is selling and the market price is very low. Similarly when prices have been rising for some time speculators will tend to come to the market to sell products which they have been holding.

Risk associated with time

There are two traditional methods of trying to prevent or mitigate the risk of a supplier failing to meet agreed delivery dates:

- **Time is of the essence** The inclusion of the phrase 'time is of the essence' seeks to make sure that the offered and accepted date of delivery in the contract is a condition which goes to the root of the contract. Breach of such a condition by the supplier would allow the buyer to cancel the contract and go elsewhere, as well as claiming damages from the supplier. This could potentially result in a very large loss indeed for the supplier, so the presence of the phrase is presumably meant to concentrate his mind on ensuring that delivery is made on time.

- **Liquidated damages** These are nothing more than a pre-estimate of the loss likely to be suffered by the buyer if the supplier is in breach of the contract. Liquidate in this sense means to express in money terms, often as a percentage of the price. Provided they are agreed to be a fair and reasonable estimate of the actual loss, they fall due to the buyer as soon as the failure occurs. It is common practice to arrange for them to be deducted from the price on the supplier's subsequent invoice. Again it is presumed that no-one really wants to receive the damages due on failure in preference to actual delivery. So they are really a spur to help the supplier achieve what should have been agreed to, and intended anyway.

The adoption of one or other of these two devices is often seen as additional security. They are considered by some as comfort factors, to show that supply management has teeth which can be used if things go badly wrong. However, if it is presumed that the buyer's main purpose is to obtain delivery of the required goods or services at the agreed time, it is important that the main focus of effort should be to work with the supplier to ensure that this is achieved, rather than diverting too much effort to ensure meagre compensation in the unacceptable event of failure.

Environmental risk criteria

With increasing importance being put on practice and behaviour which minimizes harm to the environment, there can be real danger that a supplier who was formerly extremely sound and secure, may face a set of quite different circumstances. Key considerations listed in *Business in the Environment* (1993) include:

- Environmental effects from a product or process which become unacceptable and subject to pressure group campaigns which may temporarily or permanently interrupt operations.
- The effect of substances or processes being banned.
- The level of investment required to comply with new legislation.
- The potential costs of cleaning up contaminated sites.
- Closure of operations forced by non-compliance with legislation.

The effect of these factors can be very real indeed as major parts of the electronics and refrigeration industries found to the detriment of their bottom line with chlorinated fluorocarbons (CFCs) and other ozone depleting substances. Controls were set up under the Montreal Protocol in 1987 scheduling their withdrawal from the market by 2000. However the European Community subsequently brought this ban forward to 1995 for member states. In addition to the environmental issues which are subject to public concern on a grand scale, such as global warming, ozone depletion, and tropical deforestation, there are regional and local issues which are much more visible and tangible. These include:

- contaminated land
- air emissions
- water quality
- noise
- waste management
- vehicular exhaust
- recycling
- packaging
- energy efficiency
- visual amenity
- greenbelt land use
- preservation of sites of special scientific interest
- environmental incidents.

Environmental risk criteria include the extent to which an organization may be directly or indirectly implicated in the activities of a supplier whose processes lead to environmental damage. For instance does the purchase order specify a mix of raw materials, process materials or process methods which are not ordinarily used by the supplier? Are any of the products specified manufactured using processes which are known to produce highly toxic wastes or emissions? British Standard BS 7750 is the UK environment management standard which defines the type of management systems and procedures that have to be in place for companies to demonstrate sound environmental performance. BS 7750 reflects the European Community eco-management and audit regulation.

Procurement ethics

Pursuing the theme of business athletes competing in the great Corporate Olympics which she develops in *When Giants Learn to Dance*, Rosabeth Moss Kanter (1989b) notes a considerable expansion in the need for the best practice:

> The doing-more-with-less strategies place an even greater premium on trust than did the adversarial-protective business practices of the traditional corporation. Business collaborations, joint ventures, labor-management partnerships, and other stakeholder alliances all involve the element of trust – a commitment of strategic information or key resources to the partners. But the partners have to rely on one another not to violate or misuse their trust.

The staff of the supply management function are in the key position of driving the relationship with the providers of external resources. They must work to ensure that the necessary trust is never abused. This must extend to the confidentiality of information from innovative ideas to costing breakdowns. As the new closer relationships develop between customer and supplier with contact and interaction across a whole range of disciplines, supply management needs to set the lead by standard and example. The image of the buyer or engineer, or scientist forcing competing suppliers through the process of a Dutch auction must be eradicated.

In the same way, it is important to have a code of personal ethics in the procurement manual which applies to all staff, and not just those in the supply management function. Suppliers ought to be advised of the policy too. GEC Ferranti used to send all their suppliers a letter each year, thanking them for their support over the year, then saying (Barr 1993):

> It is also important at this time of year to remind you of our declared and documented policy that soliciting or receiving gifts and entertainment by our employees is prohibited.

The letter goes on to say to suppliers:

> We need your co-operation to make this policy effective, enabling the continuance of impartiality and mutual respect which keeps our company relationships in the highest possible order.

This is a clear and unambiguous statement of company respectability, and that the issue of ethics is a serious one. Both the National Association of Purchasing Management in the United States, and the Chartered Institute of Purchasing and Supply in the United Kingdom, publish codes and professional standards for their members. The guidance from the UK Chartered Institute's code is reproduced in Table 8.2.

Regular contract review.

When two organizations work closely together to achieve agreed objectives, problems encountered along the way become opportunities to examine and root causes to eliminate. The relationship develops awareness and understanding of each other's ability and

Table 8.2 Guidance from the Ethical Code of the Chartered Institute of Purchasing and Supply

---

1 Declaration of Interest

Any personal interest which may impinge or might reasonably be deemed by others to impinge on a member's impartiality in any matter relevant to his or her duties should be declared.

2 Confidentiality and Accuracy of Information

The confidentiality of information received in the course of duty should be respected and should never be used for personal gain; information given in the course of duty should be true and fair and never designed to mislead.

3 Competition

While bearing in mind the advantages to the member's employing organization of maintaining a continuing relationship with a supplier, any arrangement which might, in the long-term, prevent the effective operation of fair competition should be avoided.

4 Business Gifts

Business gifts, other than items of very small intrinsic value such as business diaries or calendars should not be accepted.

5 Hospitality

Modest hospitality is an accepted courtesy of a business relationship. However, the recipient should not allow him or herself to reach a position whereby he or she might be or might be deemed by others to have been influenced in making a business decision as a consequence of accepting such hospitality; the frequency and scale of hospitality accepted should not be significantly greater than the recipient's employer would be likely to provide in return.

When it is not easy to decide between what is and is not acceptable in terms of gifts or hospitality, the offer should be declined or advice sought from the member's superior.

Advice on any aspect of the guidance set out above may be obtained on written request to the Institute.

---

expectation. Ideas begin to be shared for innovation, and reduction of cost and time to market. When one party awards an order or contract to another and then eschews all communication until it becomes time to phone up to find out why nothing has been delivered, suspicion, fear and the allocation of blame become the most likely candidates for development. Contract reviews conducted regularly with openness and understanding on both sides provide a sound mechanism to manage exposure to risk throughout the duration of the project.

9 Strategic cost management

Introduction

The total cost of ownership concept is not widely understood or utilized by most buyers. In many organizations, sourcing decisions are based simply on price without any reference to, or understanding of whether the alleged cost saving translates into an actual total cost saving. Unfortunately demonstrable evidence proves that total cost can be significantly increased. This is not a new phenomenon, and provoked the following often quoted advice from nineteenth century visionary John Ruskin:

> It's unwise to pay too much. But it's worse to pay too little. When you pay too much, you lose a little money, that is all. When you pay too little, you sometimes lose everything, because the thing you bought was incapable of doing the thing it was bought to do. The common law of business balance prohibits paying a little and getting a lot. It can't be done. If you deal with the lowest bidder, it is well to add something for the risk you run. And if you do that, you will have enough to pay for something better. There is hardly anything in the world that someone can't make a little worse and sell a little cheaper, and people who consider price alone are this man's lawful prey.

For years, purchasing departments in many organizations have talked about purchasing based on total cost rather than just price. Unfortunately very few of the available information and reporting systems can provide the necessary data to support such a goal. Purchasing departments can easily find themselves pushed into watertight compartments, expected to squeeze the last penny out of suppliers by constant rounds of bidding and blinkered negotiation, while the downstream consequences of their decisions are left to others to sort out. The total cost of ownership concept examines the cost associated with purchased goods and services throughout the entire supply chain. Total cost of ownership considers costs all the way from idea inception, as in working with a supplier to develop a new part, right through to warranty liability and spares holdings associated with that part once the final product is in use by the customer.

This chapter will provide an overview of the relationship between cost and competitiveness and identify the contribution of strategic supply management to total cost management activities. It is the main argument of the chapter that the total cost of ownership is strongly linked to the management of suppliers to achieve end market cost competitiveness.

The cost challenge

Burt and Doyle (1993) are very pessimistic, but they don't pin the blame entirely on the buyer:

> Based on personal observations and interviews with dozens of executives in many industries, it is apparent that most buyers are 'price' oriented. This results largely from management evaluating buyers on their ability to get the lowest price. Often a purchase variance report is the only formal measure of purchasing performance. Unfortunately, the lowest price frequently does not result in the lowest 'all-in-cost' or total cost from the perspective of the firm's total cost of operations.

Moving forward from the traditional purchasing fixation with price as the only factor and measure of supply costs is one of the prime challenges of strategic supply management. As expertise in procurement spreads, and total quality management and the commitment to customer driven planning become a prerequisite for survival, leadership and success will come only to those organizations which not only produce breakthroughs in technology, but even more importantly to those which understand how to manage their costs efficiently. The cost of acquisition, life cycle costing, and the cost of quality are the three key areas of challenge. Supply management has a lead role to play, not just in harnessing and harvesting the very best that can be made available from external resources, but in facilitating their optimum use and influence throughout the organization and into the hands of external customers.

The challenge of cost management lies in identifying costs in the system; working out ways of measuring them; separating out the main cost drivers; and developing strategies to reduce them.

Strategic procurement and total cost management

Effective cost management by suppliers must be aligned carefully with the buyer's organization's mission goal of global competitiveness. Strategic procurement has some basic requirements that should be communicated and demanded of key suppliers to ensure that cost management is properly set up

They must have systems in place to collect all direct and indirect labour costs and there should be targets to compare these to, and quality improvement goals to optimize them further. Labour cost data should be current, not historical, accurate, and in use throughout the organization. All the supplier's personnel need to be aware of the cost impact that they have on the product, and be under active encouragement and fully trained in cost reduction methods. Rework hours should be recorded separately and labour efficiency recorded, analysed and appropriately rewarded.

All non-labour cost data should be collected, be subject to comparison with goals, and used in a process of continuous improvement and end-product cost reduction. When labour, material and overhead costs are combined the resulting total should only reflect the costs of the activities contributing to the particular product under consideration. Inventory turnover and stock holding costs should be scrutinized carefully. Overhead costs can be benchmarked by comparison to organizations in a similar business.

All personnel are aware of the importance of their job as related to the overall cost of the end-product. Employees are trained in cost reduction methods, and encouraged to find ways to eliminate unnecessary costs. Budget and pricing information is regularly communicated to employees in the project team. Cost of quality calculations are carried out and the results analysed.

The supplier's pricing structure is supported by a cost reduction policy aimed at continuously reducing its selling price. The supplier co-operates fully in furnishing current, accurate, and complete cost and pricing data. A contract review process exists and is actioned on a regular basis.

It is important to ensure that the cost analysis carried out by key suppliers and hopefully shared in general terms if not in detail, takes due account of the particular circumstances of your purchasing arrangements. The supplier must show that the figures being assessed are the costs directly relevant to your orders or contracts. In *Competitive Advantage* (1985), Michael Porter describes the need to make sure that the price being charged by a supplier is both soundly and specifically based:

> A business unit usually produces a number of different product varieties and sells them to a number of different buyers. It may also employ a number of different distribution channels. Any of these differences may give rise to segments in which the behaviour of costs in the value chain may be different. Unless the firm recognizes differences in cost behaviour among segments, there is a significant danger that incorrect or average-cost pricing will provide openings for competitors. Thus cost analysis at the segment level must often supplement analysis at the business unit level.

In *Relevance Lost*, Thomas Johnson and Robert Kaplan illustrate the importance of Porter's comments in one business which they studied:

A division thought that its product line sold to Original Equipment Manufacturers (OEM) was less profitable than product lines sold to distributors and wholesalers because the gross margins on its OEM line were much lower. Only after performing a study that broke out total distribution costs into the cost of supplying and servicing each channel did it realize that the OEM business was as profitable as all the other lines. Before doing the study, the division managers had failed to realize how inexpensive it was to sell and distribute to OEM accounts relative to all the other channels it was using. Conversely business previously thought to be quite profitable turned out to be only marginally so because the cost of reaching customers through the channel exceeded the price premium obtained from this class of customer. Therefore when products are sold to different classes of buyers – industrial, commercial, institutional, government – the costs of reaching different classes should be traced to the products. Similarly, the costs of different distribution channels – distributors, retail, wholesale, brokers, direct mail, OEM, export – need to be understood and traced to the products sold through each of these channels.

Suppliers' performance in managing cost is every bit as important a criteria for vendor assessment and rating as compliance with specification, and adherence to delivery schedule. There needs to be some quantified means of making a supplier selection which takes account of the importance of commitment to working with you on cost reduction. Hewlett Packard's supplier performance expectations for cost are world-wide price leadership and cost reductions through the following criteria:

- leads Hewlett Packard designers towards standard parts and processes;
- implements continuous process improvements and passes on savings;
- has effective cost management programmes;
- pro-active in identifying cost reduction opportunities.

Suppliers are examined and rated on how many of these criteria are being consistently met.

Total cost ownership, Life Cycle Costing, terotechnology or 'womb to tomb'

When the narrow field of focus on price is widened to include clear vision of the other costs which occur before, during and after acquisition, a much better picture appears of the true total cost of ownership of any goods or services purchased. Most well-managed organizations conduct some form of investment appraisal for major items of capital equipment but it is important that this is not left entirely in the hands of the accountants. Like so many other aspects of good supply management work, it provides an excellent opportunity to bring the functions involved together to flush out all aspects of potential expenditure. Specifiers, users, service providers and maintainers all have a valuable input to make.

Early supplier involvement can act to ensure that different options are examined for major purchases. A simple checklist for more basic items will promote awareness and reduce the costly consequences of a blinkered price-only decision. The logical analysis that most organizations apply to the running of their company car, or transport, fleet applies equally to the acquisition of more humble items like laser printers and fax machines. Chapter 3 lists the pre- and post-acquisition factors which should be taken into account. As well as ensuring that the true total cost of ownership is understood, the need to budget adequate funding for operating and service expenditure becomes clear, and there is the important early opportunity to negotiate a beneficial long-term service agreement. Access to spare parts and in some cases specialist knowledge over an extended life, may call for the handover of manufacturer's drawings and specifications either for open use or via some form of escrow agreement.

Once the emphasis is placed on the total cost of ownership or life cycle cost, the purchase price may become a much less significant factor in the overall decision. Indeed, options and alternatives which were originally ruled out of consideration because they were perceived as having too high a purchase price may now be eligible for inclusion in the selection if the superior features or better construction behind the higher price leads to lower operating, maintenance or disposal costs in the long run.

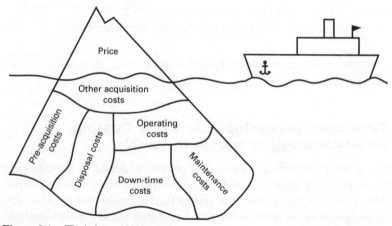

Figure 9.1 *The iceberg of hidden costs*

Costs considered over the whole life of an asset also need to be managed and reviewed over the whole life. Supply management's role does not end with the safe delivery and the clearance of a purchase invoice.

Figure 9.1 shows the dangers of concentrating on price alone. The buyer in charge feels comfortable with the costs that he can see above the water surface, but is sadly about to expose himself and his colleagues to the much more serious consequences that he has failed to take into account by not examining what lies in the cold and murky waters below.

Terotechnology is defined as 'a combination of management, financial, engineering and other practices applied to physical assets in pursuit of economic life cycle costs'. It sets out to ensure that the design of a physical asset like a piece of equipment or machinery, takes full account of requirements for reliability and maintainability, as well as ease of installation, commissioning, functional operation and eventual disposal. User specifications and selected design solutions should take full account of the complete cost spectrum from cradle to grave, or womb to tomb.

Present value calculations

Calculations of the total cost of a piece of equipment or machinery over its complete life serve to allow much better informed investment appraisal decisions to be made. However even when future costs and incoming cash flows can be predicted with reasonable accuracy, it is very difficult to form a straightforward comparison between alternative investment proposals unless all costs and earnings can be brought together to a common base. The normal way to do this is to carry out a present value analysis. Selecting a reasonable figure as a standard interest rate, all future outgoings and incomings are calculated back to what they are really worth at the present value of money.

Hence a forecast cost of £1000 for a second year's maintenance contract, to be incurred in 12 months' time, will have a present value of £909.09 negative at a standard rate of interest of 10 per cent. Similarly an inflow of earnings of £5000 expected at the end of the second year of the project's life, will have a present value of £4132.23 positive, using the same standard interest rate of 10 per cent. The sum of £909.09 is the amount which if invested now for one year at 10 per cent would produce £1000. £4132.23 is the amount of money which if invested now for two years at an interest rate of 10 per cent would result in a final value of £5000.

All the forecast cash flows on a proposed investment can be calculated back to their present values using the chosen standard interest rate. The initial purchase price of the investment is added in without adjustment, as a true present value cost. Costs are given negative signs as outflows, and earnings, including any anticipated proceeds from the final disposal transaction, are designated positive, and the whole list of present values are netted together to produce one final figure. This is called the net present value of the project. If the result is positive, the proposal is said to be viable because there are enough earnings to cover costs and interest rate payments at the rate chosen. If the net present value is negative, there are clearly insufficient earnings to cover outflows and interest rate charges, and the proposal is normally rejected as not being economically viable.

In a more sophisticated method of using the net present value concept, the actual anticipated rate of return of an investment can be calculated using a process known as the discounted cash flow yield method. The discounted cash flow yield is the rate of interest which when applied to all the cash flows on a particular project results in a net present value of zero. It seeks to quantify the true rate of return of the project and hence provides a means of comparing one proposal with another. Many organizations will set a lower limit for discounted cash flow yield for any investment, below which sanction will not be given. It used to be rather laborious to calculate, and investment appraisal sections in purchasing and accountancy textbooks were full of tables of discounted cash flow factors. However computer spread-sheet packages and programmable calculators now make light work of a very useful concept. The discounted cash flow yield calculation should be just one among a number of criteria for evaluating invest-ment proposals. It has been criticized as providing an apparently precise determinant for what are sometimes no more than a series of guesses and stabs in the dark, and as such the result can only be as good as the assumptions on which it is based.

Cost of quality

The cost of quality is one of the fundamental concepts of total quality management. It is made up of all the costs to an organization of producing products and services that do not meet customer require-ments first time around. It is made up of failure and rectification costs, checking and inspection costs, and prevention costs. Failure and rectification costs, sometimes called correction costs, are normally the highest of all. If failures are not identified until the customer tries to use the product, then the whole panoply of warranty claims, product recall, and lost repeat business comes into play. When manufacturers first became aware of the problems that poor quality could cause, the emphasis swung heavily to inspection and rectification after manufacture but before release to the customer. In *The Machine that Changed the World* (Womack, Jones and Roos 1990) there is a marvellous image of General Motors senior managers from the company's Framingham plant visiting the Toyota-GM joint venture car assembly unit (NUMMI) which used Japanese techniques: One reported that secret repair areas and secret inventories had to exist behind the NUMMI plant, because he hadn't seen enough of either for a "real" plant.'

If it is difficult to see how the cost of quality can be measured with any meaningful precision, then it is also difficult to see how, without some measurement, any meaningful resources can be redirected to address any organization's most basic problem. One popular technique which can only give a very crude indication, is to arrange for a group of staff to keep a special diary for two or three days. The idea is to find out what percentage of time is spent in checking things, in correcting their own or someone else's work, and in taking steps to prevent future problems.

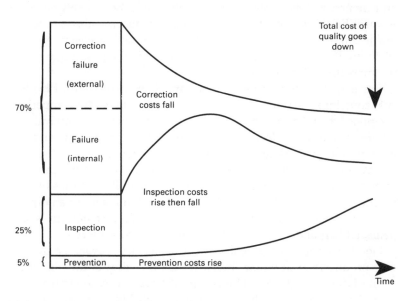

Figure 9.2 *Reducing the cost of quality*

Results vary dramatically but estimates of an average of 25 per cent are common. Within this 25 per cent, the major proportion is usually on correction of failures. Can this really mean that one-quarter of your human resources and their associated material and overhead costs are being wasted? If you are not already engaged in a quality improvement programme, it normally does. More to the point in this particular section, does your supplier measure the cost of quality? Do they have strategies and goals to reduce it? Figure 9.2 illustrates the hopeful prospects of reducing the cost of quality by working together with your suppliers to improve the quality of their processes.

Cost containment, competitiveness and strategic procurement

The management of costs through the development of strategies of containment offers major opportunities to organizations by lending support to overall corporate and business strategies through the provision of a consistent, comprehensive and continuing focus on cost as a critical competitive dimension.

The aim of a strategy of cost containment need not necessarily be to attain a position of lowest absolute cost per unit in the market. It should also ensure that there is both long-term and short-term consistency between product positioning, selling price, acceptable return and incurred costs. Volvo, for example would be unlikely to strive towards being the lowest cost automobile producer in absolute terms, but it could be seen as having targeted its strategy at ensuring a cost structure to provide good profit margins within the price segments of the market in which it competes.

Further, the effective deployment and implementation of explicit cost containment strategies can be seen as being powerful competitive weapons which can often make the difference between survival and failure in mature or declining industries, and between slow and fast growth for organizations in new markets. This recognition of the need to develop cost containment plans can help reduce the likelihood of managers and staff losing sight of costs, especially in times of high profits or expansion. It also helps to establish a mission for an organization through the creation of a shared set of cost objectives and goals, and an understanding of how these can be achieved.

Good examples of the achievement of business advantage by low-cost producers in declining industries are the cases of the mini-mills in the US steel industry. The failure of larger firms to control their costs has not been at the operational level, but in terms of costs associated with poor business decisions and corporate strategies, such as failure to invest in new process technologies. In a different scenario, for related product firms such as Hewlett Packard and Gillette, sharing experience across diverse business units can provide competitive advantage in new technology, production resources, joint marketing, and distribution. Multi-business organizations may have economies of scale not available to single product firms, arising from the breadth of their business activity (Porter 1985). Being a low cost producer also means that a corporation may be better positioned to survive cyclical downturns in markets or the whole economy, and may consequently be well placed to take advantage of any upturn when it comes (*Business Week* 1987; Bernard and Rajagopal 1992).

In developing cost containment strategies, organizations must be aware of and focus on activities that add value to the product or service. These must be distinguished from those that merely add cost. This is significant for gains in competitiveness. For example, field service is a necessary part of the computer business for which customers may be quite prepared to pay a price. However, 'fix-it' teams set up to correct poor quality construction work in the housing industry are an added cost which no customer should be expected to pay for. Well directed technical development, engineering and quality management teams may add value, whereas quality control inspectors on their own generally create little value, but rather rely on fire fighting to preserve customer relations in the short-term without necessarily addressing the prime causes of poor quality production and its attendant costly waste.

Way back in 1963, Peter Drucker realized that unless management directed costs into revenue producing activities, costs would tend to allocate themselves by drifting into activities which produced nothing. In Drucker's view, the real cost of a product,

> is the proportion of the total cost of the business that corresponds to the ratio between the number of transactions (orders, production runs, service calls, and the like) needed to obtain the products revenue, and the total number of similar transactions in the business.

In recent years mechanisms and programmes have been designed to reduce both the numbers and the costs of transactions. Examples which are often quoted include product simplification, standardized component specifications, just-in-time production systems, and reduction of engineering change orders, among many others. The essential conclusion is that the design of effective cost containment programmes is of crucial importance in the attainment of a position of competitiveness in the marketplace.

Richardson (1988) illustrated that the competitive advantage of the low cost producer may be translated into major opportunities for the firm in the marketplace. A classic example is Honda's low-cost production motorcycles. Honda initially concentrated on low-cost product with which it greatly expanded the market for its motorcycles as basic transportation in developing countries throughout the Far East. Then using its high-volume production facilities as the basis for a product higher up the market, Honda proceeded to push the traditional European and North American producers into the higher priced segments of their domestic markets. In some cases producers quit the market altogether. The Honda example illustrates two of the key opportunities available to low-cost producers: to stimulate market growth; and to destroy the competition, whether or not elimination of rivals is initially a principal objective.

Cost reduction can also be an effective strategy for late entrants to an existing market. Although the Japanese were relatively late to enter the semiconductor chip business, they were able to gain a dominant position through their ability to improve process yields, resulting in unit costs significantly below those of the competition.

These examples identify cost containment as an important competitive driver in the business machine. The ability for strategic supplies management to assess all the costs associated with purchases becomes even more important as organizations strive to achieve more of their true potential and to place more scrutiny on their overheads. This shift in focus from purchase price to all-in cost can play a major role in helping an organization achieve and maintain true cost competitiveness. All-in cost is defined as the summation of the purchase price and all the internal costs involved in receiving and converting the purchased material into finished products, including any costs resulting from field failures attributable to defects in purchased items (Burt and Doyle 1991).

The concept of zero based pricing developed by Burt, Norquist and Anklesaria (1990) focused sharply on the need for the all-in-cost approach to be adopted by the buyer's entire design and manufacturing team. The emphasis on zero based pricing stemmed from its ability to help to improve return on investment by reducing the cost of correctly specified prime materials and the costs of processing them when purchased to the required quality, and at the specified time. As procurement costs for materials and services seem to be ever rising, the design of purchasing strategy offers great opportunities to reduce costs both internally and at the supplier's facility.

Likewise, as manufacturing strategies move towards the adoption of such tools as computer-aided design, and flexible manufacturing within a just-in-time environment, close involvement with suppliers becomes even more important. Working together with suppliers can make a significant contribution to cost reduction with value engineering and value analysis throughout the design stage driving out waste and eliminating costs which add no value during manufacture. By optimizing design specifications and tolerances, the use of specialist vendors can be reduced and stock holding minimized by a just-in-time procurement strategy (Ansari and Modarress 1990).

Conclusions

Strategic cost management takes purchasing beyond the simple process of price comparison. It requires the determination of the complete cost of ownership of goods and services, and the need to understand and challenge selection and specification by analysis of the all-in-costs which are the direct consequences of them.

By adopting total quality management, organizations can reduce costs by the simplification of operations and processes. Value engineering and value analysis techniques can combine with quality improvement tools like zero defect programmes and statistical process control to work to minimize inspection and correction costs. Using strategic supplier and customer alliances, organizations can reduce costs by technological innovation as suppliers participate in new designs and product development. The integration of computer-aided design and computer-aided manufacturing systems between firms and their suppliers can compress the time to release new products into the marketplace.

By working very closely with suppliers, the strategic supply management function can make the best use of different types of contract, and strive together to identify all possible ways of reducing wasteful costs.

10 Global sourcing

Introduction

As international trade barriers ease progressively, if slowly and fitfully, economic development and business survival hinges increasingly on the ability to compete globally. This affects internal markets as well as external trade as overseas competitors target previously secure domestic markets, whilst domestic competitors increasingly search overseas not only for new markets but also for new sources of supply to serve all their markets. The motives for this new procurement strategy are varied but most commonly identify cost reduction, product and service innovation, technology acquisition and risk spreading. Increasing competitive pressures mean that growth, if not actual survival depends on an organization's awareness of market and resource centres beyond the immediate circle of existing customers and suppliers. Unquestioning adherence to long-standing relationships is no longer sufficient to guarantee future prosperity.

Some literature on the concept of globalization does exist particularly covering the relationship between marketing and procurement strategies, but it lags well behind established industrial practice. A framework is needed for the application of a global approach to procurement, linking the influence of competitive strategy directly to the development of changes to sourcing policy. This chapter addresses both these problems and sets out models for entry strategies using a relationship continuum stretching from purely domestic to true global sourcing orientation.

Global business: key elements in the literature

'Globalization', 'global products', 'global marketing', and other similar terms are buzz words and phrases which have gained increasing currency in marketing literature, at least since Levitt's influential paper of 1983. Despite their widespread use, it is not really clear that they are sufficiently well defined or understood. Everyday business usage suggests that in many instances the word 'global' is considered to be virtually synonymous with 'international', or 'multinational'. However, stricter study of the literature reveals a much stronger emphasis on the universal dimension, and the co-ordination of activities with a strategic focus independent of natural, linguistic or cultural boundaries. Authors in the areas of business strategy and marketing have devised various formulae to attempt to arrive at workable definitions which distinguish global activities from simpler forms of international operations. In doing so, certain generic elements have been identified for example by Albaum et al.; Keegan; and Young et al.; all writing in 1989:

- universality of need and of strategic approaches to markets;
- co-ordination of product ranges, and of location of production facilities;
- standardization of communication messages.

The central concept of globalization is not the production or supply of a universally standard product, such as the BMW car, nor the promotion of an international brand name such as Nestlé, Toshiba or Ford, but rather that the supplier identifies the existence of a need which is more or less universal, and the supplier is able to provide satisfaction of that need by use of a standardized business approach and product concept.

The product offering itself may be universal with a standardized promotional message, e.g. Coca-Cola; the product may be standard but with differing communications messages, e.g. IBM, Apple microcomputers; or, within a universal product concept, there may be variations of product offering to suit perceived differences of needs and tastes in individual markets, e.g. the motor car industry. The common denominator in all of these examples is not the product, the message or the source of supply, but the underlying strategic approach to doing business. It is of course equally possible to exemplify products which find application world-wide, but where the circumstances of use, the motivation for purchase, the promotional and marketing strategies are highly differentiated between cultures and national markets. One such is baby food. Whether the supplying companies have a co-ordinated overall global business strategy is open to debate, but what is clear, is that the product itself can be considered as having a world-wide application.

The results of these potentially complex and confusing scenarios, and the growing profusion of brand names and products which are becoming more nearly universal in availability and recognition are often cited as evidence of the 'shrinking world' or the 'global village'. Businesses increasingly identify and accept the need to compete, not merely in their hitherto secure domestic markets, but also in ever-widening arenas. This may be prompted by political edict as in the European Community's single market procurement directives, or by economic necessity like the case of the baseline industries of steel, oil, and electronics.

Linking models of internationalization to global sourcing

Numerous models have been postulated to demonstrate and explain the various steps in the development of internationalization strategies, and the factors which influence companies in their choice of market entry mode or operational programme. Authors include: Dunning 1973; Johansson and Wiedersheim-Paul 1984; Keegan 1989; Rugman et al. 1985; and Weisan et al. 1987. There has also been a great deal of rather sterile academic debate centred on the extent to which the existence of various identifiable categories actually predicate a sequence of development stages through which operations progress. Hamill in 1991 indicated that before adopting a truly global philosophy, companies generally consider and apply strategies of market extension and market diversification. In the former case, the existing domestic market is implicitly regarded as superior to those added later, whilst diversification treats all markets as being more or less self-contained, with individual needs, objectives and solutions. Real global sourcing is something of an amalgam of the two where the company has a single business philosophy and strategy, and an integrated portfolio of products and markets in which changes in the markets supplied are determined by overall benefit available, and interaction between supplier and customer; and products offered are designed to satisfy a range of individual market needs, taking into account external threats as well as opportunities.

This shifts the emphasis from a product offering and a marketing strategy which may be tailored to an individual set of circumstances or parameters, towards the supply of a 'satisfaction system' capable of benefiting individual customers as part of an overall business system, and the supplier on the basis of selection and operation within an optimized range of markets. A good example in the textile trade is described in the World Bank Report of 1991. Great Future Textiles Ltd of Taipei is a vertically integrated textile and garment manufacturer and exporter. The company is a key supplier of finished garments to Modern Fashions GmbH in Dusseldorf, Germany. While fashion designs are handled in the Taipei headquarters, tailoring takes place in an offshore manufacturing base in Thonuri in Thailand, just north of Bangkok. This factory imports high quality designer textiles from a weaver in Rajasthan in India, and cotton from Texas in the USA. Synthetic yarn is supplied from a chemical industry complex in Java, Indonesia. The final products are shipped by air from Bangkok to Dusseldorf. In all of this Great Future Textiles Ltd has to react quickly to the 'quick response' strategy of Modern Fashions GmbH.

As Fonfara and Bernard observed in 1989, the extension or development beyond merely exporting the means or 'system' of satisfaction, entails the existence or provision of investment expertise and facilities, and the existence, acquisition or transfer of appropriate technological knowledge and capabilities. Arnold in 1989, took the scenario a step further by using empirical data obtained in Germany to supplement extant literature, to postulate that the development of global business and marketing strategies entails the capability to rationalize product ranges, production resources and supply sources to serve the marketplace competitively. To supply globally, and therefore to produce world-class products of world-class quality and at world-class costs and prices, means that the company must have world-class technological expertise, and world-class purchasing sources and skills.

The implications of this philosophy are fundamental, and not infrequently also painful. Not only may cherished products need to be eliminated, but also long established business practices have to be challenged, examined and perhaps changed. The 1980s saw the dismantling of some of the world's predominant vertically integrated corporations, e.g. Ford, and the emergence in their place of a series of collaborative ventures. Whether or not in the long run horizontal collaboration will lead to competitive advantage (Porter 1990), expansion of external sourcing and vertical collaboration does reduce central overhead costs and increase product and technology flexibility, (Thackray 1986). Another significant reason which is becoming increasingly important for the changing outlook in global sourcing and marketing in today's marketplace is demand volatility.

Product cycles have become much shorter because consumer preferences change more rapidly than before. Consequently, manufacturers, wholesalers and retailers are modifying their procurement, production and marketing provisions to ensure sales arrangements which are in close relation with changing market demand. Order cycle times, the time which elapses between placing an order and its delivery to the customer, in countries in the Organization for Economic Co-operation and Development, reduced by up to 400 per cent in the 1980s according to the World Bank Report of 1991. More than 60 per cent of production and sales in these markets are now processed directly to order, and this practice is expected to intensify. Figure 10.1 shows the reduction in total processing time at Philips International B.V. in the electrical and electronics industries.

This order cycle time reduction is also done to avoid excessive inventories, to contain the costs of obsolescence, and to improve customer service. Businesses that institute these arrangements are highly dependent on reliable supplies in short time intervals. Market

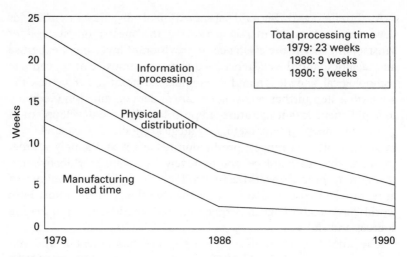

Figure 10.1 *Order cycle time development electrical/electronic industries*

research has revealed that global sourcing is expected to grow, but that those businesses with plans to continue to outsource their supply needs, will consolidate the number of suppliers to have better control over the supply lines and minimize risk. As a consequence, quick response to orders and timely delivery have become criteria for success in international trading. Throughout the world in industrial and in developing countries, business conditions are changing in two fundamental and closely related ways. Firstly, more and more activities are becoming world-wide in scope, and secondly competitive pressures are increasing nearly everywhere. This creates new opportunities as well as problems for businesses and governments alike. Global competitive capability is perhaps better illustrated in the form of vertical alliances rather than ownership, but as Arnold (1989) observes, this necessarily implies the existence of alert, proactive purchasing staff with actual authority and responsibility, and the capability to evaluate and accept risk.

Policies of global sourcing and global marketing are often closely related. In the plastic trade, Infantland Stores Inc. of Cincinnati in the USA purchases large amounts of plastic toys from Fortune 21 Ltd in Hong Kong. Fortune produces these toys in Jiangmen in China under a joint venture arrangement with a local manufacturer. Fortune buys plastic resin from Downstream Petroleum Export Sdn Bhd in Johore in Malaysia, and this is shipped via Singapore and Hong Kong to the plant in Jiangmen. Infantland buys Fortune's plastic toys loaded on to ships at the quayside in Jiangmen, and arranges for transport through Hong Kong and Long Beach to its home base in Ohio. All transactions are done on a just-in-time basis (World Bank

Report 1991). To compete effectively in global consumer markets it is virtually a prerequisite that an organization is willing and able to source in global procurement markets.

Benefits and caveats to global sourcing

Traditionally the most widely recognized benefits of global sourcing have been lower costs. Less expensive labour, less restrictive work rules, and lower land and facility costs have enticed buyers to foreign suppliers. Reduced product costs still remain the principal attraction for between one-third and one-half of all companies currently pursuing global sourcing. Tax advantages can reduce costs even further. In addition to enjoying the favourable tax treatment that a nation may use to lure foreign companies, some taxes can be avoided outright. For example, in Malaysia processing a product in a free trade zone or, 'bayanleypas', then sending it out to the world-wide market, eliminates inventory holding taxes.

However, lower costs are no longer considered to be the only benefit of global sourcing. Findings in research conducted by Monczka in 1989 indicate that a firm will source outside its home borders if it expects to achieve dramatic and immediate improvement in four critical areas. As well as cost reduction, these are quality improvement, increased exposure to world-wide technology, and delivery and reliability improvements. Similarly, research by Carter and Narasimhan in 1990 indicates that with keen international competition and the drive for lower cost, stringent quality and short product development runs are forcing firms to develop global sourcing as part of their overall competitive strategy. The whole process is self-exciting. As organizations gain more experience of global sourcing, more and more benefits are recognized and realized. Literature references here are Fagan, 1991, Davis et al. 1974, Hanafee 1984, Hefler 1988, Monczka and Guinipero 1984, listing the following positive outcomes: availability; uniqueness; quality; technical supremacy; penetration of growth markets; high speed of response; satisfying 'offset' requirements where these are a condition of export penetration.

Fagan in 1991 also identified the downside of global sourcing. There are problems with direct and indirect costs, and with business risks. Direct costs include: high cost of overseas travel and communication; fees for brokers and agents, and physical distribution expenses. Indirect costs can be made up of the following: increased and more complex paperwork; cash tied up to back letter of credit transactions; the expense for additional inventory buffers, and the difficulties in estimating their size; rework of products, due to necessary design modifications, performance changes, and methods of measurement.

Business risks centre on the cost of control over a firm's technology, as foreign countries generally provide fewer protections for products and designs. For proprietary technology, this risk may simply be too great regardless of the potential cost saving. Some nations are notorious for infringements of copyrights and patents and are generally avoided by organizations committed to global sourcing. Currency exchange rate fluctuation is another major risk unless effective ways are set in place to provide protection. The prospects for political turmoil require careful evaluation and contingency planning, as well as resolving disputes with foreign vendors and settling jurisdictional issues if claims or suits are likely to be instituted.

Development of a global sourcing strategy

One of the basic laws for the growth of any organization, is that the internal structure must change to match the new situation. In particular, the functional role of its component parts tends to become more specialized and the links between the parts more complex. Dicken, writing in 1992, observes that as the size, organizational complexity and geographical spread of multinational companies have increased, so the internal relationships between their geographically separated parts have become a highly significant element in the global economy. The precise manner in which multinational companies organize and distribute their production, or value-added chains, arises from their strategic orientation, itself influenced by history as well as geographic origins. Internationally competitive strategies can be regarded as falling along a spectrum ranging from global integration at one end to national responsiveness at the other. Although there has been a trend towards the adoption of globally integrated strategies by an increasing number of multinational companies, they must remain responsive to national and local differentiation. Both global and local perspectives need to be combined.

Writing way back in 1926, the urban economist R. M. Haig observed that: 'every business is a package of functions and within limits these functions can be separated out and located at different places'. Over time these 'limits' have become less and less restrictive. The most obvious reason has been steady development in the enabling technologies, particularly those in transport and communication. But there is more to it than this. The enabling technologies set the outer limit of what is possible, they do not determine what actually occurs.

The influence of competitive strategy on global sourcing

Porter in 1986 proposed four general types of international competitive strategy which the multinational company might pursue, in terms of their organizational or co-ordination, and geographical or configuration dimension. These are (a) export based (b) multidomestic (c) basic global, and (d) complex global strategy. Further Porter observes: 'there is no such thing as one global strategy. There are many different kinds... depending on a firm's choices about configuration and co-ordination throughout the value chain'.

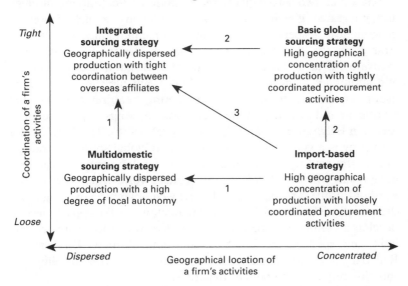

Figure 10.2 *A typology of global sourcing strategies*

Developing this argument Figure 10.2 proposes four types of international sourcing strategy which a multinational company might develop. These are shown in terms of their organizational co-ordination, and geographical configuration dimensions. The three sets of arrows suggest possible strategic development paths (numbered arrows), but it should not be assumed that only one path is inevitable. Each strategic quadrant involves different degrees of geographical concentration or dispersal of value activities. Two of the alternatives, the import-based strategy and the basic global sourcing strategy involve a high degree of geographical concentration of production activities. An interesting example of basic global sourcing approach is the relationship that Companhia Vale du Rio Doce (CVRD) in Brazil maintains with other firms both within the country and in its main external market in the processing of iron ore. CVRD, together with

Kawasaki (Japan) and private enterprises in the USA bought a steel processing plant in California which is supplied with steel plates produced in Brazil. This co-operation was expanded to include a conglomerate in Mexico which imports mineral ore from Brazil for processing into steel plates which are then supplied to the California-based plant. Since this plant is the key provider of steel products to several car and equipment manufacturers on the West Coast, most of whom have adopted just-in-time production arrangements, the supply lines for ore and steel plates have to be well co-ordinated to ensure timely and reliable deliveries (World Bank Report 1991).

The other two alternatives, the multidomestic sourcing strategy and integrated global sourcing strategy involve a high degree of geographical dispersion. An example of multidomestic sourcing strategy is the decision by Caterpillar to design small hydraulic excavators near its manufacturing plant in Belgium. Design, control and auditing remain in the United States, but the European design group can react to changing marketing requirements on the Continent and can adapt and source basic drawings to plant require-ments in Belgium more quickly (Davis et al. 1974). The Ford Motor Company is a good example for integrated global sourcing strategy. Ford's strategy involves centralizing the development of a car or a component wherever Ford has the greatest world-wide expertise. As Ford of Europe is recognized as having a comparative advantage over the rest of the firms in the small car market, it was the logical place to develop a common suspension and undercarriage for compact cars built and sold in the United States and Europe (Daniels and Radebaugh 1989). Ford of Europe also took responsibility for sourcing required component materials.

Modes of international sourcing entry strategies

In the internationalization of the procurement process, Rajagopal and McDermott (1992) state that firms regard foreign sourcing as risky, since these markets are unknown to them. In terms of the special costs of doing business across national boundaries, the firm faces import costs. To minimize the impact of the learning costs and risks, its strategy is to go abroad at a slow and cautious pace, often using the services of specialists in international trade outside the firm. Over time, familiarity with the foreign environment will reduce the information costs and help to alleviate the perceived risks of foreign involvement. Initially the firm may seek to avoid the risk of foreign involvement by sourcing locally.

If a firm decides to source outside its domestic markets, an important consideration is the choice of 'sourcing mode' (institutional arrangement). Terpstra (1978) identified five types of foreign production, based on the extent of the firm's involvement in production and marketing processes: (1) foreign assembly (2) contract manufacturing (3) licensing (4) joint venture and (5) direct investment. On a similar note, from a marketing view Rugman et al. (1988) identified a firm's market entry strategies as (1) licensing (2) export via agent or distributor (3) export through own sales representative/or sales subsidiaries (4) local packaging and/or assembly (5) foreign direct investment.

Deriving from Terpstra (1978), Yeoh and Cavusgil (1990) identified the internationalization of sourcing strategies as offshore purchasing contract, non-equity mode such as coproduction or joint product development, and direct investment modes involving either a wholly owned subsidiary or a joint venture. They propose that to select the best sourcing entry mode, a transaction cost-analysis approach can be used. They identified transaction characteristics which most strongly influence the choice of sourcing entry modes as: infrequent transaction; uncertainty due to perceived risk; uncertainty due to lack of knowledge or familiarity; high technological uncertainty; competitive behaviour and volume uncertainty; competitive behaviour and technology uncertainty; transaction-specific assets under high environmental uncertainty; global industries; multidomestic industries.

To reflect more accurately the different forms of international sourcing entry strategies, and after considering various works, we propose to use a variation of Rugman's five different market entry alternatives as modes of foreign sourcing entry strategies in the internationalization of the purchasing process as shown in Figure 10.3.

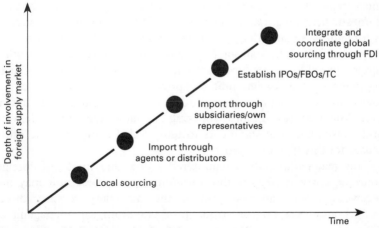

Figure 10.3 *Mode of international sourcing entry strategies*

International companies must determine the sourcing entry alternatives if they expect to maintain a global perspective to their supply market. A company may want to import directly or indirectly, or become involved in some modes of direct investment which view global sourcing as a strategic component of corporate strategy. These decisions on foreign sourcing entry modes tend to be of medium- to long-term importance, leaving little room for change once a commitment has been made. Therefore it is important to treat these decisions with the utmost care. Not only is the financial aspect of the company at stake, but also the end-market advantages to be gained depends on these decisions.

Import via agents or distributors

This form of indirect importing appears to be the simplest and least risky. Costs however can be very high with potential third-party mark-ups added to freight and duty costs as well as exchange rate cover.

Some agents are extremely professional and can fully represent the overseas manufacturer with technical knowledge and support. Others tend to be agents for a whole range of manufacturers and communication lines to the real source are difficult.

Import through subsidiaries/own representatives

Organizations can also import directly from their own subsidiaries abroad, side-stepping independent middlemen. Basically, here firms tend to use subsidiaries or other corporate units for international sourcing assistance, especially when there is an increased need for information and expanded levels of international procurement activities. Monczka and Guinipero (1983) in a study, identified that firms most frequently use resources of foreign-based subsidiaries, when the domestic firm sought assistance in locating foreign sources of supply. A foreign-based subsidiary can perform a variety of functions for the domestic firm. The reasons for using foreign subsidiaries or other foreign based locations for these tasks include (a) knowledge of local suppliers by the foreign unit (b) proximity to foreign sources (c) knowledge of foreign business practices, and (d) better communication skills with non-English speaking suppliers. Expediting delivery and consolidation of shipments to reduce air freight costs are other pluses for this type of approach.

The major difficulty encountered using this mode of foreign sourcing entry strategy is that the domestic business unit may not receive adequate attention unless the subsidiary receives direct budget authorizations or strong prodding from top management. This strategy typically becomes less effective as the volume of international procurement increases. If adequate support is not provided, the domestic firm must select a different approach that will allow it to achieve its international procurement objectives.

Establish international procurement offices

For various reasons, the needs of domestic buying units are not always satisfied through the support of foreign corporate units or local affiliates. The logical response has been the establishment of international procurement offices (IPOs) focused in function and region. Qua and Thian (1991) stated that many original equipment manufacturers (OEMs) have established IPOs in Asia due to Asia's tremendous manufacturing capacities and creditable capabilities. These IPOs buy parts, manufacturing and product development services for their plants world-wide. An interesting example is Singapore: since 1970s, Singapore has attracted IPOs, and over the past five years the number of IPOs in Singapore and their roles have increased substantially. There are now seventy-five IPOs as opposed to twelve in 1985. American and a few European companies were the first to set up IPOs in Singapore, followed by Japanese companies in the mid-1980s. Towards the late 1980s, Taiwanese and even Thai companies began to step up their IPOs in Singapore (Singapore Trade Development Board Report).

Integrate and co-ordinate global sourcing through direct investment

This strategy involves the world-wide integration and co-ordination of a firm's procurement requirements. Its main objective is to maximize the buying leverage of the firm on a global basis. In utilizing this strategy a firm can still use IPOs or the concept of comparative advantage to design, build, and source items. Firms can also go for joint production or coproduction involving the sharing of manufacturing facilities to achieve economies of scale and production cost-efficiencies. Requiring the supplier to invest in physical assets represents a form of transaction relationship. In addition, finding a partner with production efficiencies or combining production to achieve the necessary economies of scale can provide a solution to maintaining costs at a competitive level. However, corporations will be more careful in selecting partners and have fewer of them because of the amount of management time and attention they require. Typically such agreements will feature: increased sole sourcing between companies; deeper technological interchanges involving process technology in addition to access to a part; joint development of emerging technology, and commitments intended to last decades.

The shift from independence to interdependence stems from the growing understanding, 'you are not buying parts, but you are buying capacity'. Joint product development is a form of technical tie-up combining research and development production, and occasionally some marketing (Yeoh and Cavusgil 1990). This is the approach frequently taken by the Japanese in setting up a local captive supplier. They supply equipment, materials and technology and sometimes assist the local suppliers in getting financing. Marketing and particularly the distribution of the product would usually be undertaken by the supplier in the local market. Another example that typifies the formation of strategic supply alliance is the IBM Siemens agreement in telecommunications. Finally, joint ventures and the establishment of foreign subsidiaries are forms of the direct investment mode which view global sourcing as a strategic component of corporate strategy. A firm adopting this strategy accumulates common procurement requirements across world-wide business units to achieve superior procurement performance. An good example of integrated co-ordination of global sourcing strategy is a semiconductor designed by Motorola in Geneva (Switzerland), manufactured in the US, and packaged in Malaysia. It was bought by Saturn Electronics and Engineering Inc., in Michigan as a component of the control-box of a seat-belt traverse mechanism made by Bendix Corp, that was ultimately used by Hyundai for cars made in Korea and sold worldwide (*Electronics Purchasing* 1989).

Figure 10.4 *Domestic versus global sourcing orientation continuum*

The four modes of international sourcing entry strategies can best be represented as a continuum of domestic versus global sourcing orientation. This is illustrated in Figure 10.4. Where at one end the strategy focuses on local sourcing with little or no involvement with foreign suppliers, at the other end of the continuum, relational contracting for integration and co-ordination through joint ventures and direct investments are characterized by increasing complexity and a stronger focus on competitiveness. Great control needs to be exercised in such a venture due to the higher resource commitment in this institutional arrangement.

The organizational choice for most firms must involve a thorough evaluation of all the options which lie between these two extreme positions. Some firms may find that a choice to source locally or globally may optimize the ability of their purchasing department to contribute. However, the vast majority of companies will end up with a hybrid organizational choice positioned between these two extremes. Based on its specific needs, this hybrid organization must be customized by each company. This organizational choice must offer a reasonable trade-off by maximizing perceived organizational strengths with perceived organizational weaknesses.

Conclusion

Since the early 1990s firms in many industries have had to be truly global in all areas of operation. Global sourcing is not a simple or easy solution to a company's sourcing needs. But businesses aiming for future growth cannot ignore its potential. It is the belief of the authors that purchasing has a strategic role in the global environment. More organizations need to understand the nature of that role. It is essential for the procurement function in a firm to develop continuously its organizational structure, information system and global sourcing expertise in order to facilitate maximum global performance.

Firms that successfully create a system that emphasizes and views integrated global sourcing as a strategic component of corporate strategy will attain a competitive advantage that influences the success or failure of world-wide business activity.

Part Four

Supply Management Excellence

11 Making it work

Introduction

If the development of supply management as a contributor to company strategy is to succeed, a fundamental understanding of the importance of integrating change in an organization is a prerequisite. Many companies and institutions have failed to achieve the level of committed improvement planned, because they proceeded to implement change on a functional basis only. They assumed incorrectly that all the other functions and senior management would understand what the game plan was, why they were doing it, and that they would naturally provide the necessary support.

Good results and progress will only come if the purpose of each new direction is clearly linked and aligned to the vision and goals of the overall organization. People are the key. They will strive equally hard against change as for it if the raison d'être is badly put across. Individuals have their own agenda and their own strategic plan, even if it is badly thought out. As we have seen in Chapter 3, the vision and umbrella goals must include the people in the organization. As well as aligning the efforts and hearts of the workforce to the aims and objectives of the organization, the organization must align its aims and objectives to match the goals and personal vision of its people if it is to truly harness their best efforts.

This chapter provides guidelines to avoid the dangers and pitfalls associated with the upgrading of the supply management process, and the conversion to cross-functional teamwork to bring in the very best harvest possible from the supply chain.

The change elements

Change brings uncertainty and insecurity to everyone. Though few will admit it, human beings often seem to crave nothing else but the same old boring routine. The love for tradition and the memories of the long, hot days of summers past with happy, healthy, barefoot children, betray not just the use of rose-tinted spectacles, but the fear that changes since then have not always been positive. Since the mid-1980s most major organizations have embraced some form of change process, often involving a variant of a quality improvement programme. Much of this has been market-driven with ever increasing pressure from global competition. Once change begins there is no remaining control sample or placebo against which improved performance can be judged. Change resistors can point to many examples where change has seemingly made things worse, without acknowledging that the surrounding circumstances might have wreaked even more havoc if the former circumstances had been left to prevail.

Professor Daniel Jones of Cardiff Business School, in a keynote address entitled 'Architects of the value stream' (1994) declared two fundamental movements of change, one focused on changing relationships, and one on rethinking the process flow. The relationship movements are both internal and external. Internal relationships need to be changed to increase the humanization of work, with autonomous groupings, and increased motivation and teamwork. Externally these go beyond normal negotiation into relationship building and partnership sourcing. The process flow will become an integrated one with no buffers, and no waiting, handling, or checking, etc. One piece will be pulled through the system to order with flow and capacity balanced to demand, and all sources of interruption and random variability removed. This lean supply chain will be organized as one process, where the product flows towards the customer down an uninterrupted value stream, where all activities not adding value or slowing down the flow are eliminated, and the supply chain is optimized regardless of functional or corporate boundaries.

As the value stream needs dedication, skills and involvement of its people, the individual needs a job, an identity and a sense of pride and of going somewhere. At the University of Edinburgh, there are regular tours of Old College for visiting summer tourists. One of the servitors whose principal job was to collect and distribute internal mail told me of the amazing job satisfaction he experienced when he took the usual party of mainly American tourists to see the Playfair Library, designed and built in the early years of the nineteenth century. After climbing the beautiful staircase past the original Raeburn paintings, he would ceremoniously open the library doors and immediately look into the faces of the visitors to observe and absorb their wonder and astonishment. 'When you think' he confided, 'that we Scots did this before they were even properly established'. People need to have pride in their organization and in what they as individuals can contribute to it. The strategy of change must include generous provision for equipping people to move forward with the organization. New skills must be taught and old forgotten ones polished up. Employee development courses will aid improved distribution of business information.

Initial decisions

The very first decision is simple in the extreme. Either develop supply management to play a full strategic role in your organization, or step aside and let someone better get on with it. There is no ambiguity about the importance of external resource management. The first two chapters of this book should have made that very clear. The real question is whether the incumbent in the key functional role has the strength and the crusading zeal to make a proper job of it.

There is some encouragement from one of the very earliest of all the management gurus, Samuel Smiles in his 1859 book *Self help*: 'Energy achieves much more than genius.' Sheer hard work and careful attention to detail can produce amazing results. The vision and crusading zeal is all important, but torch bearers sometimes have to roast the rear ends of reluctant movers, as well as lighting up the way ahead.

There are some people in every organization who resent change, and fight hard to retain the status quo. The ones who do it actively can at least be tackled face-to-face. They will openly discuss their concerns and will often have important points to be listened to and taken into account as plans develop. People who resist actively are at least showing that they care what happens. They can often be converted to strong lieutenants and powerful advocates of the new ideas. Those who resist passively are the biggest problem. They seem to go along with you, and may even express verbal commitment. However all the time they cling to the old ways and subtly take every opportunity to cast doubt on and frustrate the moves towards a new direction. They need to be handled patiently, and very fairly. Some of the best people are late developers. But at the end of the day, it may be that they would be better in another role or in another organization.

The way you act, and are seen by others has such a big effect. Chuck Harwood of the Quality Improvement company stresses the importance of the manager's 'Apparent Interest Index':

The Apparent Interest Index is stable, predictable, and reliable. It is based on observation – what people see their bosses do. The Apparent Interest Index is much more reliable than any short-term change in management's verbal or speechmaking behaviours. Establishing commitment to quality, therefore, becomes a matter of creating changes in the actual behaviours of the managers and leaders of the organization. Saying one is committed to quality is easy. But acting regularly and consistently in ways that reflect a strong commitment to quality only happens when people truly believe what they say. Then, belief becomes a basis for regular and consistent action and decision making.

Before launching forth into sorting out top management and the other functions with all your energies, it is important to make sure that you have done as much as possible to put your own supplies management house sufficiently in order. Do the forces under your command, however humble in status, provide the best possible service? Do they understand that they are building the cathedral of their organization's published strategic goals and mission statement, or do they think that they just come in each morning to raise purchase orders and chase up queries? Do you coach and encourage them to spread the contribution that good supply management can bring? Do they achieve this by their actions as well as their words? It is much better to do it by inspiration and encouragement, rather than by command from on high. They do work for you but they will achieve much more once they buy into the idea for themselves.

As part of their winning submission to the 1994 Quality Scotland Forum awards, the team from OKI (UK) Ltd included a slide of one of their regular staff quality meetings entitled 'Management involvement discouraged'. It is very much a case of explaining and aligning objectives, providing a working mechanism as described in Chapter 3, and allowing the team to get on with it. In the early stages you will need to kick ideas like soccer balls into the team, and be ready for them to be kicked straight back out towards you. After a while however, balls kicked in by you will start to be passed around between team members, each one adding ideas and value. This time when the ball finally emerges it will be a well-thought-out solution to the problem, not a reason why they can't do it. Confidence will steadily build and the supplies management organization will begin to see itself, and be seen by others in a much better light. It is very much a process of making sure that you have all your own buttons neatly and firmly done up before going out to strive for major changes in the organization at large.

Staff in peer management positions outside the immediate supplies function are bound to be concerned and even to feel threatened. In many cases they will have been doing what they consider to be the important aspects of external resource management themselves. Supplies management will have been acknowledged as a useful, hopefully important function, with a role to play and a contribution to make in its central role of overseeing suppliers. The trouble is that the purchasing function can never really understand or appreciate the nitty-gritty needs of production department or the design office or the laboratory superintendent. It is really too specialized for non-experts. There is a major danger that they will think that you want to muscle-in on their territory and try to pull back what they see as purchasing tasks but ones which are too vital to them to release to you. They must be quickly disabused.

In fact you want to release even more of their day-to-day specialist requirements to their control, but in a managed way. You want to supply more of your resources to help them build better and closer relationships with their partner suppliers, but with supplies management supporting more efforts to make sure that these become the very best suppliers by working together to expose and solve problems and clear up mistaken assumptions.

It is really an application for strategic negotiation and the culture of the common purpose. Peer managers will react in the best fashion and most quickly when they see that your efforts and direction are helping them with their agenda, and not seeking to put their eye out or expose them. Nevertheless there is bound to be some resistance and jealousy. Procrastination and apparent acceptance of everything you suggest followed by absolutely no change at all, are very much more frustrating than outright opposition. The changes being made in supplies management need to be introduced slowly and carefully to other functions, because leverage works best if balanced with co-operation.

Design and implementation of training programmes

Teaching is by far the best way of developing learning in the teacher as well as the pupils. Even before you make any changes, there will be many people throughout any organization who regularly or occasionally get involved in purchasing activities, in addition to the people working specifically as full-time buyers. These people should be given access to training in basic purchasing skills so that they too can achieve the best value possible for the organization's money. Topics like preparing a basic statement of needs; simple cost of ownership analysis; the influence of supplier brands and sales representatives; some of the legal implications of purchasing transactions; awareness of suppliers' negotiation tactics; and if relevant, the practical aspects of store keeping and stock control, should be included.

Organizing training sessions for the 'part-time buyers' in other functions to provide them with skills to better understand and improve the relationship with outside suppliers will not give away the vital secrets that keep you and the other supplies management staff in a job. Instead it will communicate probably for the first time just what an important role you actually play, and at the same time reveal some of the potential treasures available if the functions can all work a little more closely together. Depending on the size and complexity of the organization, it can either be done by your own team or with the help of external specialist training consultants. The case study on

SmithKline Beecham illustrates the sort of impact that can be made by a comprehensive structured training programme.

Full-time supplies management staff need training and development too. It should go without saying that professional purchasing certification is the way forward, but is not the end of the road. Ongoing professional development through interaction and exchange with colleagues, participation in seminars and conferences, and publishing papers on experience and new ideas on supplies management issues, helps a great deal to keep the function up-to-date and on the right track. It also keeps enthusiasm refreshed and makes sure that the 'Apparent Interest Index' remains in good shape.

Case study: SmithKline Beecham – transforming the purchasing process (Ralph and Hughes 1994).

When SmithKline French and the Beecham Group plc merged in 1989, the resulting corporation SmithKline Beecham (SB), became one of the world's largest health-care companies. The cost of purchases in SmithKline Beecham is over £3 billion, and represents approximately 55 per cent of sales revenue.

At the time of the merger, however, purchasing was very much an undervalued business process. There was only patchy evidence of a well managed and professionally focused function capable of implementing best practice in cost management, sourcing strategy and supplier management. It is true to say that Purchasing lacked identity; it was positioned at a low level in the organization; staff had received little or no training; there were few measurement systems in place; and there were few examples of collaboration, either across the function or with staff in other service areas.

To change this, SB launched a three-year, world-wide programme – Simply Better Purchasing – and targeted purchasing savings in excess of £100 million. From 1991, the purchasing change programme was introduced across the corporation world-wide. It signalled the launch of an aggressive savings and value initiative, at the heart of which was a concerted drive to boost purchasing competence. Such development was targeted not only at the purchasing community, but also at other staff in functions such as Marketing, Research and Development, Information Resources, Engineering, Quality and Technical, and Human Resources. Indeed it was

---

recognized at an early stage that more expenditure is often controlled by these groups than by the full-time Purchasing Department.

SB also recognized that there was a lack of expertise within the company to develop and deliver the competence development programmes that were necessary if the Simply Better Purchasing initiative was to succeed. Therefore they decided to introduce ADR International Purchasing Consultants as their preferred provider of training and consulting support. ADR's brief, acting in partnership with SB, was to develop and deliver a programme targeted at introducing core purchasing tools and techniques in year one; to support SB personnel in the design of a programme of more advanced techniques and processes in year two; and then to broaden the initiative into strategic sourcing and cross-functional teamwork in years three and four.

Few organizations have had the necessary support and commitment of executive management to resource a change programme of this magnitude. But it is typical of the endorsement of the approach when the Chief Executive Designate, Jan Leschly, comments: 'The SB world is changing dramatically. In response, we must strengthen the business processes which drive this company. Purchasing and the supply chain is one such process.'

The success of the programme has been widely recognized throughout the Corporation, but it was a real pleasure for both SB and ADR when the excellence of the initiative was recognized by David Hunt, MP, Secretary of State for Employment, in his presentation of a National Training Award to ADR in December 1993.

Mobilizing executive management support

This is where the crusading zeal really comes in. Executive management likes nothing better than articulate enthusiasm, but there needs to be some carefully-planned communication and teaching in this area also, just so that they understand roughly what you are trying to do. Numbers are important too, especially if they have pound or dollar signs in front of them and if they represent cost reductions and improvements in value for money. This is where good results from your own little patch are so important. If you cannot produce improved results from the people that you control directly, it is unlikely that you will be able to deliver very much elsewhere. It is even better still if some good comments are coming in from some of your peers. A colleague in the production planning office of an early employer would each year produce an unsolicited 'April rise project'. It seemed to work practically every time the annual increments were handed out. Executive management can only judge and support things that they know about.

All change programmes need an encouraging boost on a regular basis to keep them going. One of the best ways of achieving this is to organise a celebration and involve executive management. Rather than wait for a particular success, it works well to celebrate the anniversary of starting the campaign, or the holding of the fiftieth weekly quality improvement meeting. It can be on a grand company-wide scale, or confined to the members of a small team of less than half a dozen. In *Commit to Quality*, Patrick Townsend describes the results from a huge event held by The Paul Revere Insurance Group in Worcester, Massachusetts:

> As 1985 unfolded, many team leaders pointed to the Quality Celebration as the reason why their particular team, and the quality process in general, accelerated going into its second year. They knew success was possible, that they were not alone in their efforts to improve quality, and that the company would say thank you in a way that they understood.

Be sure to invite a senior executive along even when it is just a small affair. Choose a significantly numbered weekly meeting of a small team involved in change for the better. An expensive gateaux and some percolated coffee are ideal to mark say, the fiftieth meeting. Make sure you give them enough notice to ensure that it gets a slot in their diaries, and also gives the team enough time to prepare some charts to show off what they have been doing. It is sort of 'management by wandering about' in reverse. You arrange for them to come to you, and once you have got them, let the enthusiasm of the team do the rest.

Expediting and progress chasing

It would have been nice to have left this section out and presume that with the culture of the common purpose well established, no-one would ever need to be chased for anything. Good selection of suppliers, early involvement in the specification, and a well-managed close relationship with regular reviews, is the strategic supply management means of ensuring that across-the-board expediting becomes a thing of the past. Problems and their consequent delays should be flagged up by suppliers at the first opportunity. In the traditional adversarial approach, suppliers would be reluctant to share this information at an early stage. Fearing criticism and retribution of a bad vendor rating with loss of future business, they might do all they could to keep this information away from the customer for as long as possible in the hope that some miracle might happen, keeping the kimono tightly closed.

However, even with the best arrangements, there will remain a need to expedite and even to micro-manage suppliers in some circumstances. The important issue is that these circumstances should be flagged up as a problem, as a defect to be analysed. Instead of the punitive approach, the quality improvement view is that a defect discovered is a golden treasure, a seed of opportunity for uncovering something in the relationship on which we can work together to secure a permanent fix. The most common reasons for having to expedite stem from one of the following five:

- Lack of commitment by the supplier.
- Supplier lacks the capability.
- A change by the buyer.
- Delay in material or information from the buyer.
- Misunderstanding of order requirements.

Expediting can easily become habit-forming, and lose its impact just like calling 'wolf' too often. Unfortunately in industries where aggressive expediting is common, staff of a supplier may react by taking the route of least discomfort by delivering first to those who shout loudest and chase most forcefully. Hence the problem of lack of commitment by a supplier can be caused by third-party forces not directly under supply management control. The commitment to the culture of the common purpose must be resilient. It must also be communicated throughout the supplier's organization. The four other common reasons cited above are direct relationship problems, and can be flagged up and solved by working more closely together.

Introducing cross-functional teams

In many organizations other functions are so used to supplies management seeking to exclude them from contact and negotiation with suppliers, that they may find it quite a shock to be encouraged to participate. They will probably agree that it is a good and right thing for them to do, but, unless there is a clearly defined meaningful task with the motivation of authority for decision making and some recognition for participation and successful performance, it may be seen as some sort of token effort and be only given the commitment of any other add-on task.

The report on cross-functional sourcing team effectiveness (Monczka and Trent 1993) suggests some conditions for team assignments to avoid overstretching organization resource levels:

> While no rules exist about what qualifies as a legitimate sourcing team assignment, there are certain criteria that can help clarify when to use sourcing teams. Sourcing team assignments should satisfy one or more of the following conditions:
>
> - Business unit faces a complex or large-scale sourcing decision. Assignment directly affects a firm's competitive position.
> - No single function has the resources or expertise to accomplish the assignment adequately.
> - An organization must make a sourcing decision that requires or can benefit from the 'buy-in' of different functional groups.
> - Cross-functional sourcing team interaction will likely yield a better solution or decision than individual decision making.

Case study: Defence contracting – better castings, better received

The vision of the company's materials management of the future includes a high portion of bought in parts flowing directly from vendor to production line with the minimum of checking at Goods Inwards, and the optimum level of built-in quality.

A survey of incoming inspection activity quickly revealed that 215 man days in the last twelve months had been spent inspecting production castings and raising over fifty requests for concessions to accept non-conforming parts. This was plainly not a problem that could be solved by Goods Inwards and Supplier Quality Assurance staff alone, so a decision was taken by the materials management quality improvement team to charter a cross-functional corrective action team (CAT) involving Design, Drawing Office, Machine Shop and Purchasing as well.

Twenty-six problems were identified by initial brainstorming and the most significant twelve of these were taken through impact and trend ranking and cause and effect analysis routines. In most cases the problems were seen to be occurring simply from a lack of clearly defined requirements.

The Design representative came from the mechanical design team in Display Systems Division, and he obtained agreement to use his division to test drive a pilot design guidelines document. This provided a controllable test

---

bed before going forward with a proposal for a new company-wide standard. The CAT meetings promoted great awareness among participants of the interrelated needs of each other and of the castings manufacturer. In the past the drawings submitted to foundries to quote against and subsequently manufacture to, often showed only finished machined dimensions and tolerances. The foundry had to interpret these into cast dimensions with machining allowances left where necessary. The resulting castings cannot be readily inspected against the machining dimensions on the drawing.

The new guidelines bring the attention of designers to recognizing that dimensioning and datum position selection for castings require special techniques. In the same way, blinkered checking of every single dimension on repeated batches of production castings, and subsequent repeated concession applications do nothing to improve incoming quality. With the CAT recommendations, casting drawings will in future be prepared in such a way that the Goods Inwards inspector can see clearly what the critical dimensions are. For existing castings where a full redraw could not be justified, an inspection plan can be drawn up with the co-operation of Design.

The CAT recommendations were finally published in the form of a new Drawing Office Standard. The scale of the benefits can be judged from the example of one missile support ring casting. The time taken at Goods Inwards inspection by the old method was eight hours. With the new drawing incorporating the CAT proposals this comes down to thirty-five minutes. This is not just a saving in inspection time. Real problems can now be identified more quickly and communicated directly to the manufacturer. The dense fog of checking, recording apparent deviations, and obtaining repeated concessions from Design for countless irrelevant dimensions, has been lifted to allow the real work of improving the supplier's performance to be tackled. Figures 11.1 and 11.2 show some of the analysis work done by the CAT.

One of the amazing things that happens is the reciprocal invitation from other functions to Supplies to participate in areas of their work where you had always wanted the opportunity to take part, but had considered it to be so unlikely as to be not worth the bother asking.

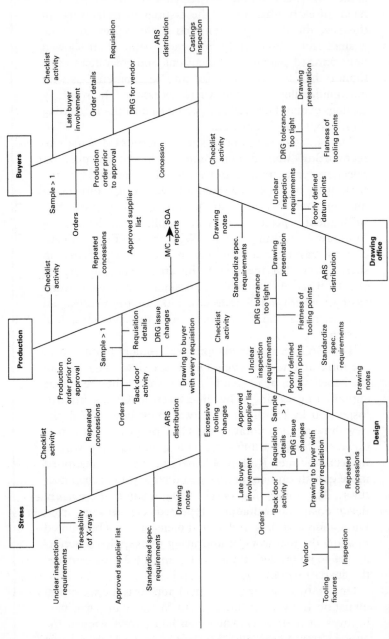

Figure 11.1 *Ishikawa diagram: ARS – alteration request sheet; DRG – drawing; M/C – machine shop; SQA – supplier quality assurance*

DEFECT/BARRIER	Impact + Trend = Priority		
Checklist	0	1	1
Review supplier list → design manual	2	2	4
Drawing presentation	0	1	1
Drawing distribution	2	2	4
Back door activity	0	1	1
Repeated concessions	0	1	1
Tooling fixtures 'vendor & SQA'	1	1	2
Traceability of X-rays	2	2	4
Abort inspection when justified	1	2	3
Adequacy of 'req' details	1	1	2
Approval of tooling (Samples ≥ 10FF) (To include History sheet/M/C feedback)	0	1	1

Impact scores
0 = High
1 = Medium
2 = Low

Trend scores
1 = Getting worse
2 = Little or no change
3 = Getting better

Figure 11.2 *Purchasing organization – impact and trend ranking*

Conclusions

Making it work is the hardest, but easily the best part of all. It depends to a large extent on how much energy and commitment that you are prepared to put in yourself. Are you and the supplies management team really serious about playing a senior and strategic role in the organization, or would you rather just carry on processing the purchasing requisitions and expediting the suppliers as before?

In a paper 'Purchasing's role in corporate management', presented to the 1994 International Purchasing and Supply Education and Research Conference, Dr Shreekant Joag of St John's University, New York, concludes:

> The corporate management function has undergone a major revolution during the past five decades. Today, its effectiveness critically depends

on its success in integrating various functions toward a common goal of establishing mutually beneficial exchange relationships with its target customers. The purchasing function too has undergone a major change in its capabilities during this period.

It is important for the purchasing function to become proactive, assess its own expertise, define its contribution potential to various management tasks, and create and use opportunities to define and achieve its proper role in the management of the organization.

People are the key. They can't be expected to go along with change for change's sake. In your own supplies management organization, there must be a clear vision and plans and goals that the whole team has been involved in and is prepared to go along with. Peer management co-operation, cross-functional involvement, executive management support, thanks and celebrations, training and staff development, that is all it takes. Nothing that an ambitious supplies management head shouldn't be capable of on his way, with his team, to the top of the executive ladder.

12 Control, performance evaluation and feedback

Introduction

As a strategic function the only real measure of success can be in direct improvements that the purchasing department makes in the overall performance of the business or organization. To contend that supplies management is crucial to the 'bottom line' of the enterprise, and then fail to link procurement performance with this ultimate measure of success or failure, would be to undermine much of the content of this book. This would also strike a serious blow at the professional status of the function, and perpetrate the problem of lack of proper recognition that many purchasing staff still suffer from.

Having made this fundamental declaration however, it must now be qualified by some cautionary notes. Management of external resources has proved notoriously difficult to measure in quantified terms. For one reason, it is far from simple to draw boundaries around responsibility for poor performance. Price increases or late delivery may stem from design changes or purchase order amendments initiated by the customer without due regard to the supplier's plans and scheduled workload. Poor quality of freely issued material and inadequate customer-supplied tooling can thwart all efforts to source good product.

In *Reinventing Government* by David Osborne and Ted Gaebler (1992), the problems of performance measurement, particularly in the public sector, are stressed:

> There is a vast difference between measuring efficiency and measuring effectiveness. Efficiency is a measure of how much each unit of output costs. Effectiveness is a measure of the quality of that output: how well did it achieve the desired outcome? When we measure efficiency, we know how much it is costing us to achieve a specified output. When we measure effectiveness, we know whether our investment is worthwhile. There is nothing so foolish as to do more efficiently something that should no longer be done.

Procter and Gamble Ltd's Total Quality Management programme extends this further with a neat two-by-two matrix with 'how we do it' along the horizontal, and 'what we do' up the vertical axis, shown in Figure 12.1. Communism collapsed very quickly in the former Eastern Bloc, largely because the wrong things were being done

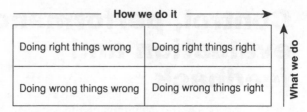

Figure 12.1 *What we do/how we do it alignment matrix*

badly. However as anyone who visited the 'self-management' run manufacturing units in the former Yugoslavia would testify, there was no shortage of measures in position.

Procter and Gamble's 'What's right check list' sets the whole business of performance evaluation in a very clear context:

- In what ways am I moving in the direction of the total organization's overall values, vision, mission, and strategies by the work I am doing?
- What would happen if I did not do it? Who would care?
- How am I using my capabilities to meet my customers' requirements?
- Would my boss agree that what I'm doing is consistent with his or her expectation of where our work group is going? In what ways?
- How is what I'm doing contributing in an important way to the Division's values and vision?
- How are my efforts meeting the needs of our external customers and ultimate consumers?

Not only must there be strategic alignment to the common purpose of the overall organization, there must also be sensitivity to the external surrounding environment. How would Supplies' performance be rated in an organization going through severe cash flow problems, where the real contribution is to achieve as near a continuous stream of incoming material and support from suppliers who ought to be more concerned about when, or even whether, their invoices might be eventually paid? Partnership sourcing takes on a whole new meaning, and the buyer requires all his negotiating and team building skills to sell his demands in a very difficult marketplace.

Performance assessment can only be truly effective when the circumstances and environment surrounding an organization are taken into account, and when measurement is used closely together with the means of improving performance.

Procurement performance evaluation

- How much does the supplies management operation actually cost?
- How much value does it deliver to the overall organization?
- Is the function targeted on goals that align with the strategic plan of the overall organization? What progress is being made towards meeting these goals?

- Is supplies management accountable for the basic procurement load of the organization?
- Is the procurement infrastructure being developed to meet the needs of the organization, by optimizing administration and inventory management?
- How effective is the staff development plan at increasing the professional competence and standing of the supplies management function?
- What percentage of business is being placed with suppliers rated as exhibiting 'class A' excellent performance?

In many ways the supplies function lends itself too easily to quantifiable measures. Leonard (1986) lists no fewer than thirty-eight. These include all the usual indices:

- Purchasing operating costs as a percentage of turnover.
- Purchasing operating costs as a percentage of total trading costs.
- Purchasing operating costs as a percentage of purchases.
- Cost of purchases as a percentage of turnover.
- Cost of purchases as a percentage of total trading costs.
- Value of total savings.
- Variance of actual to targeted savings.
- Number of purchase orders per year.
- Average value of purchase orders.
- Percentage of orders under £200.
- Cost per order.
- Number of purchasing employees.
- Purchasing employees as a percentage of total employees.
- Purchasing employee costs as a percentage of total purchasing costs.
- Value of purchases per purchasing employee per week.
- Number of purchase orders per purchasing employee per week.

Leonard observes that:

> These measures are not an absolute measure of performance, but nor are they intended as such. It must be remembered that these indicators will be used in conjunction with what the purchasing and supply director knows of his organization. His knowledge in conjunction with the information provided by the indicators will produce an accurate impression of performance.'

In his article, Leonard displays the indices changing over a number of years, and it is really this movement, hopefully in the right direction which is the indicator of good performance. Like the criteria for assessing 'world class' status in manufacturing companies, the key ratios must be improving steadily, rather than reaching any predetermined value.

Used in isolation individual measures can be very contentious and sometimes they can even become positively dangerous. How many times are supply managers asked how much it costs to place an order? What on earth does that mean, and is the questioner looking for a high or low number? Conventionally the calculation involves dividing the total annual cost of the purchasing department by the total number of orders placed in a year. Will supplies management gain a higher status if we place hundreds more orders instead of a few annual agreements, and hence increase the denominator so much in the ratio that the final answer is low? No sane person would see that as sensible development.

Effective performance evaluation

Performance monitoring can only work properly as part of a shared process of working towards agreed objectives. Measures should be as comprehensive as possible, but work best when the people whose work is being assessed see the exercise very positively, and not imposed from above or outside. Almost everyone wants to work more effectively, but progress towards the achievement of realistic agreed targets is much more motivating than marks against some arbitrary imposed standard. Tables 12.1 and 12.2 illustrate the sort of goals that a typical supplies management organization might adopt. The

Table 12.1 Purchasing organization quality improvement goals strategic level

1 Value analysis. At least twelve Key Part Analysis meetings to be held with suppliers per annum.

2 At least four Bidders' Conferences to be held per annum.

3 Participate in all new major proposals undertaken (close the gap between our involvement figures and Estimating data).

4 Bar coding/despatch. Target all item labels to be bar-coded for MoD contract item deliveries.

5 EDI. Target six suppliers to gain access to.

6 Storage systems. Acquire an automatic storage system and fully evaluate benefits.

7 Presentations. Each member of management staff to make at least two formal presentations per year to a group of our customers.

8 How did we do? Forms. Forms to be introduced and a target of one per month to be filled in by a customer of each meeting unit.

Table 12.2 Purchasing organization quality improvement goals, detailed level

---

1 Review organization strategy

2 Reduce overdue commitment on Purchase Order file to 15%.
Reduce overdue item count to 15%.

3 Reduce errors on incoming documentation by 75%.

4 Reduce vendors by 10% measured on Purchase Ledger.

5 Increase proportion of incoming goods on monitor inspection by 15%.
Work with suppliers on the supplementary list to convert them to full approval.

6 Review documented procedures for each area.

7 Process Purchase Requisitions in one week maximum.

8 Reduce amendments per order by 50% in one year.

9 Record savings of £1 million in one year.

10 Reduce discrepancy reports by 25% (measured as a proportion of GRNs).

11 Process Goods Received Notes through to destination in one week maximum.

12 Reduce shipments quarantined for lack of Good Certification by 50%.

13 Increase stock turns in general stores to 6 for call-off items (4 overall).

14 Reduce shortages on stock file to 50.

15 Reduce call-off overdues to 5%.

16 Reduce order requests from stock control to 50 per month.

17 Reduce kitting errors in stores to 0.4%.

18 Reduce floor area occupied by stores by 25%.

19 Improve process time in despatch to 3 days maximum.

20 Reduce errors and omissions on requests for new code numbers to 5%.

21 Throughput of specifications within electronic standards: CTD to final issue
within 4 months.

---

example is taken from a manufacturing company producing complex electromechanical products in small- to medium-sized batches with a high involvement in research and development. Objectives are listed on two levels, strategic (at the supply management level), and at detailed working unit level. The case study illustrates how progress could be monitored against one of the detail goals.

Case study: Measuring performance in the issue of kits of parts from stores

Having all the correct parts available at the right time and in the right quantity is clearly essential if assembly work is to be carried out smoothly and effectively. The staff in stores had always tried to do their best but required the tools and techniques to examine just how well they were meeting their customers' needs.

Using improvement techniques from a total quality management programme, consultation with the various production units led to a detailed survey of problems with the kits. Brainstorming by the stores team quickly identified three different faults with items coming from stores: wrong item being issued, and too large a quantity being issued, and too small a quantity being issued. A monitor was set up to gather details of defect levels, and an impact and trend analysis was done. Initial measures revealed that 2.35 per cent of assembly kits contained errors. Impact on customers was highest where wrong components were issued. These might not be spotted on initial assembly and could be very costly to replace if they became deeply embedded in a complex piece of production equipment. Even if found and corrected at an early stage, there could be a serious effect on work-in-progress stocks as a component which had been issued incorrectly for one assembly, quickly became a shortage holding up the build of the unit that it had originally been provisioned for.

The increased awareness that the investigation generated among the stores staff had an immediately beneficial effect, which addressed one root cause of the problem. Other ideas were examined using cause and effect analysis. Improved lighting was required and installed in some areas. Much better bin box labelling was specified, with identities and brief descriptions in large and clear printed type. Adjacent contracts were given different colours, and check digits were added to help to distinguish items with similar code numbers located in boxes next to each other.

Monitoring and analysis continued, and in six months defect levels were below 1 per cent and heading lower. Occurrences of the wrong item being issued became the least frequent, and in several months were eliminated

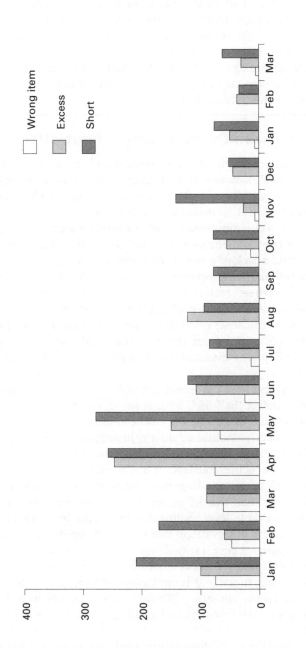

Figure 12.2 *Errors in kitting in stores*

completely. Attention now focused on excess and short quantity defects. Particular types of items were identified where counting problems occurred frequently and the boxes containing these were marked clearly so that extra care could be taken with these parts. Figure 12.2 shows that errors in kitting were reduced by a factor of more than four to under one half of 1 per cent in just over a year since performance monitoring began.

Setting goals with the minimum of frustration

Goals and targets are inevitably controversial and most often quite frustrating as well. W. Edwards Deming cautioned that they can often have effects which are the opposite to the ones being sought. Even when there has been full consultation, and the goals have emerged naturally from a well-empowered, and positively motivated team, there can be disappointment and potential for grief. This problem usually arises from a lack of a measured sense of getting somewhere, and a missing feeling of appreciation. It is not so evident at the start of a new project where real improvement can be impressive and glaringly obvious. Later on, the payback from the brainstorming and searching for problem causes often shows signs of apparently wilting, and the frustration comes from this seemingly reducing return on investment. Total quality management was good, but we've done it now, haven't we?

Art Schneiderman (1988) proposes a simple solution to this using the concept of a defect 'half-life'. This is something akin to the rate of radio isotope decay. Once a defect has been identified and is being addressed by a properly established quality improvement process, the observed defect level can be expected to progressively reduce by half towards its minimum achievable level. The time taken to produce the initial halving, will be required again to bring this newly observed defect level down by half the difference between the new value and the minimum achievable level. Schneiderman backs his hypothesis with a wide range of observations from many different industries. Where the problems being tackled are entirely within a single function he predicts half-life expectations in the zero to six months range. Where several functional boundaries are crossed, the period becomes six to twelve months. Where other organizations like suppliers play a role, the half-life can be as high as twelve to twenty-four months.

By using Schneiderman's figures initially, and then developing observed half-life values for different categories of work within our own organization, the concept does provide a means of not only monitoring progress, but of ensuring that reasonable goals are set in the first place. It also provides that feedback and reassurance to the participants which is so necessary for their comfort and appreciation. Schneiderman sums up on a cautionary note:

> I have proposed a means for arriving at reasonable goals. The potential for abuse lies with the manager who, using this approach, establishes the goals but withholds the means that people need to achieve them. Exhortation, threat, or blame are not legitimate quality improvement process activities. In fact, they are more likely to result in negative than positive half-lives. We constantly should remember that goal setting is easy; it is achieving goals that is hard.

Procurement as a profit centre

Procurement has to be paid for somehow. In most organizations this comes from overheads, either as part of a overall top slice to pay for general management and administration, or as a specific allocation to material expenditure, sometimes known rather oppressively as the material burden. An alternative approach is to make procurement run as a business in its own right, buying at least overall cost, and selling internally with a small margin to cover its running costs. This alternative should work even better in theory, if individual users are free to act fully as the customers they really are, and only use internal procurement where it provides the best deal. This provides very clear incentives to perform and generate budgets for advancement as well as maintenance of the department, while protecting the internal customer by the freedom to have direct access to the market.

One problem of the profit centre approach is that the strategy tends to bring responsibility for nearly all aspects of purchasing under one manager, who to optimize the performance of the profit centre, may seek to limit the much wider interrelationships with suppliers that we have seen to be so vital for product understanding and access to innovation. On the other hand, too much freedom for internal customers can backfire unless they have fully understood and accepted the overall strategy. Inexperienced part-time buyers may question the benefits of long-term preferred supplier relationships, if they can buy seemingly more cheaply on a one-off basis, and if the principal advocate of the official arrangement is known to be making an internal profit out of it. The profit centre approach is probably best left to discreet areas of supply, say a unit providing stationery and computer consumables, but with the overriding health warning that optimizing the particular can be to the detriment of the organization in general.

Financial savings as a performance measure

Measures of savings are also controversial in the extreme. Some buyers would argue that savings are a consequence of good purchasing rather than its principal objective. Others are more than adept at filing claims for the difference between highest and lowest quotation, or price reductions won against targets with the minimum of challenge. The UK Government Treasury Department issued some interesting guidelines on how purchasing savings could be defined for goods or services purchased on a repeat basis:

- *Price saving:* the amount by which the last price paid is reduced.
- *Price avoidance:* the amount by which a supplier's price increase request is reduced aiming towards a zero increase.
- *Equivalent financial saving:* a saving which is not based on a movement in price. The monetary benefit can be estimated but by its nature will normally be less tangible than a price benefit and may be difficult to audit. Examples would include the savings which result from elimination of, or change in the requirements stated by end-users; change in specifications; substitution of lower cost items including refurbished items or items surplus elsewhere; extended payment terms; extended warranty; consignment stock; improved operational efficiency; lower administration costs.

A practical example of good equivalent financial savings was the result of negotiation with BOC Gases to audit the large number of gas cylinders on a multisite organization with laboratories dispersed over a wide area. Of a total of 1244 cylinders, almost 300 were no longer in active use and could be returned to the supplier. For the remainder, the monthly rental invoices were converted into annual agreements. This in itself achieved a small discount, but more importantly eliminated over 1100 invoices per annum across the fifty cost centres involved, without prejudice to the pro rata reduction arrangement for cylinders returned during the year. BOC Gases were very pleased to have the return of much-needed cylinders, and to share in the elimination of unnecessary administration costs. Clearly a case of improved supplies management, but difficult to quantify easily.

There will be many similar examples in any organization. The real question is was anything done to prevent the same situation recurring in a few years time, perhaps with a different gas buyer and different staff at BOC Gases. This is the performance criteria to be measured, ensuring that the situation does not deteriorate again, wasting valuable resources but providing the opportunity for another savings claim in a year or two. The solution is to develop a new procedure and implement it across the organization. Even better is to address the real root cause, and to develop a procedure which ensures that procedures are developed whenever such problems emerge and good solutions are found. If we can measure the benefits at the same time, we will truly be on the path to evaluating supplies management performance. A ready answer to this conundrum is to use a Problem/solution/benefit form. The one in Figure 12.3 has been developed from a form in Making Quality Happen, the total quality management programme from The Quality Improvement Company of Cupertino in California.

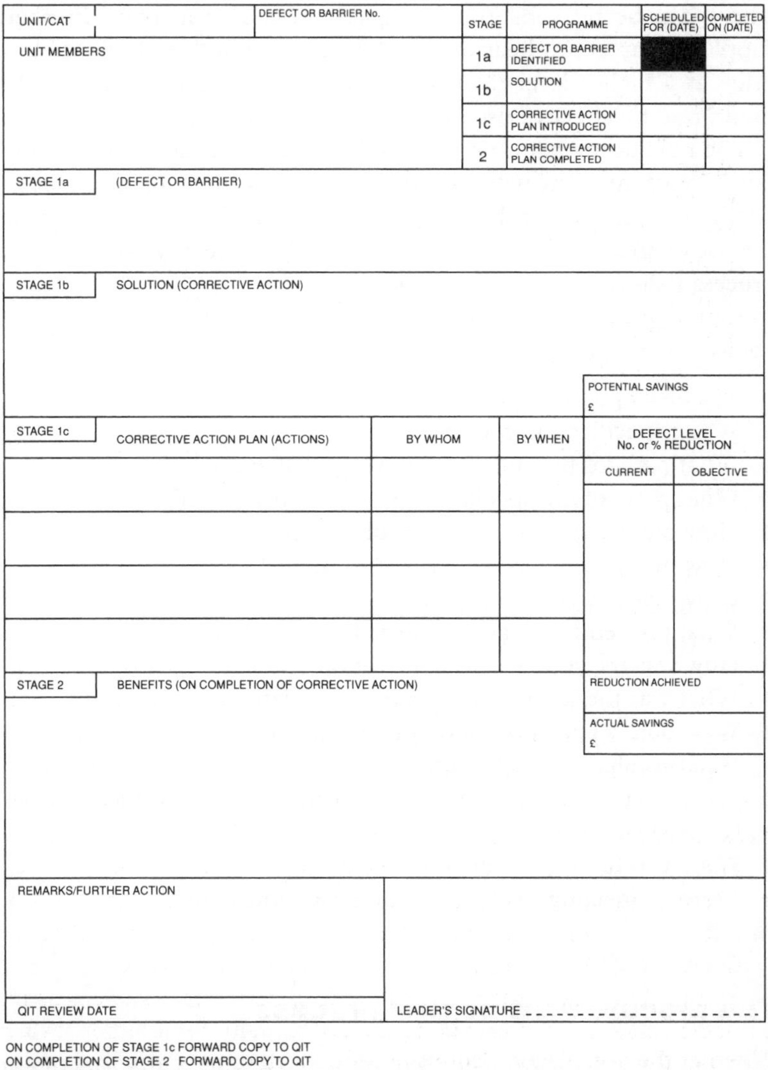

UNIT/CAT		DEFECT OR BARRIER No.	STAGE	PROGRAMME	SCHEDULED FOR (DATE)	COMPLETED ON (DATE)
UNIT MEMBERS			1a	DEFECT OR BARRIER IDENTIFIED		
			1b	SOLUTION		
			1c	CORRECTIVE ACTION PLAN INTRODUCED		
			2	CORRECTIVE ACTION PLAN COMPLETED		

STAGE 1a	(DEFECT OR BARRIER)

STAGE 1b	SOLUTION (CORRECTIVE ACTION)

POTENTIAL SAVINGS
£

STAGE 1c	CORRECTIVE ACTION PLAN (ACTIONS)	BY WHOM	BY WHEN	DEFECT LEVEL No. or % REDUCTION	
				CURRENT	OBJECTIVE

STAGE 2	BENEFITS (ON COMPLETION OF CORRECTIVE ACTION)	REDUCTION ACHIEVED
		ACTUAL SAVINGS £

REMARKS/FURTHER ACTION	

QIT REVIEW DATE	LEADER'S SIGNATURE _

ON COMPLETION OF STAGE 1c FORWARD COPY TO QIT
ON COMPLETION OF STAGE 2 FORWARD COPY TO QIT

Figure 12.3 *Problem solution benefit document*

The UK Treasury guidance also has some useful suggestions on capital equipment purchases or similar instances of non-recurring expenditure of major value. Here cost avoidance is the quantitative measure of good procurement performance:

The purchasing manager will normally set the avoidance target as a percentage of the quoted price and measure actual avoidance against this target.

In setting the target the purchasing manager should recognize that the better the pre-tender work, the less the post tender opportunity. There can be no substitute for good pre-tender activity. Further, suppliers may get to hear of the buyer's target and set their starting price at a higher level than they would otherwise do. This can be minimized by effective use of competitive tendering.

The purchasing manager's best safeguard is to back up the quantitative price measure with a qualitative assessment of the process adopted in purchasing the equipment. This can be achieved through the use of an accountability statement in which the buyer sets out the process followed and the results achieved.

Some typical questions which should be answered in an accountability statement are:

- Was a specification prepared?
- What parts of the specification were challenged?
- What parts of the specification were then changed?
- How many suppliers could supply the equipment?
- How many suppliers were asked to quote?
- How many suppliers quoted?
- What pre-tender work was carried out?
- How was the source selection made?
- What was the level of post tender negotiation?
- Was there a pre-negotiation plan?
- What results were achieved?
- Were commercial or technical shortcomings identified on the selected supplier?
- What was done to overcome them?
- Were all meetings and negotiations documented?'

The procurement control process

Whether the organization adopts a centralized or decentralized policy for purchasing, there should be some agreed rules to ensure that the process is under control. In its most basic form a high level management document should exist providing answers to the following questions:

- Where does authority for procurement actions lie?
- Is there a properly managed, up-to-date, list of authorized signatories for purchase requisitions and purchase orders?
- Are fully approved and agreed procedures in place for all activities governing procurement transactions with suppliers?
- Is a formal procedure in place for maintenance of the supplier database, both for existing and new suppliers?
- Are all suppliers measured for their performance in meeting purchase order requirements, and is due account taken of their rating before new or repeat business is placed with them?

Broadening the scope of procurement control

In a modern organization, there will be much contact with suppliers by staff outside the supplies management function. It is very important that this contact is maintained within the guidelines and disciplines laid out by the procurement function, as overall architect of the relationship. As part of the procurement process takes place outside the direct line management control of the supplies management organization, there is an important requirement to ensure that no opportunity for initiative is being missed. Regular reviews with principal suppliers should take place typically at three monthly intervals. These can address openings and opportunities as well as the more normal analysis of recent performance levels.

Major suppliers should be asked to arrange that their sales representatives copy to the supplies office the reports that they do each month or so for their own sales or marketing managers. Supplies management needs to be aware of dealings, leads and opportunities, and work with suppliers to see that leads and initiatives are being followed up and not missed.

Good communication is vital to promulgate best practice and the feelings of teamwork that fully devolved procurement requires. Control only comes after knowledge, understanding, and acceptance of correctly aligned plans. As well as a centre of support and professional development, the central core of procurement must be able to collect and disseminate the information required by the people involved in the day-to-day dealings with suppliers to ensure that they themselves can control the process along the lines that they have fully bought into.

Procurement audit

As well as the normal processes carried out by internal and external financial auditors, the supplies management function can expect to be included in any quality appraisals carried out by customers or national accreditation bodies. Audits should always be welcomed as helpful, rather than unwelcome intrusions. No one wants to do a bad job, but rather to take any opportunity to start an improvement process. Sometimes it is only an outsider looking in who can ask the silly question, and highlight an obvious but hidden inefficiency.

Audits often concentrate on checking compliance with approved procedures and work instructions. This immediately begs the question as to whether there are any approved procedures and if so, how up-to-date they are. Simple procedures and flow charts are worth writing for all activities. They are complied with best by the people who understand enough about the process to write them. So as well as timetabling formal reviews, the best results occur when the people who regularly do the work are involved in writing and reviewing the words.

In large organizations it may be possible to arrange for procurement staff from another division or site to carry out a procurement audit, concentrating on the technical issues that only experts can really identify.

Benchmarking the performance of supply management

The Centre for Advanced Purchasing at Arizona State University produces benchmarking reports across 24 industry sectors, from aerospace through electronics, food and textiles to transportation. These are available for a small fee to support the ongoing work. A summary of the benchmarks for the higher education sector is included as Figure 12.4.

In the UK the John Major Government's White Paper *Competitiveness, helping business to win* (1994) declared benchmarking to be among its new initiatives for public purchasing:

> The Government believes that its purchasing practices should be tested against world-class standards. In collaboration with the professional institutions and universities, it will further develop effective benchmarking systems. It will seek views from suppliers and other interested parties on existing performance, and provide for appropriate independent comparisons with best private sector practice.

The benchmarks are based on data supplied by 53 colleges and universities. Average institution revenue was $534 million. Twenty-six purchasing benchmarks were calculated. More complete data on each of the benchmarks follow under the same number. In summary:

1 Total purchases (the dollars spent with suppliers) accounted for 22% of revenue.

2 The purchasing department processed 71% of total institution purchase dollars.

3 Goods purchases accounted for 12% of revenue; services purchases accounted for 7% of revenue; construction accounted for 5% of revenue.

4 The per cent of institution purchase dollars processed by the purchasing department for goods purchases was 71%; for services purchases was 53%; for construction was 44%.

5 The expense of operating the purchasing function (the purchasing budget) was 13/100 of a cent per dollar of revenue.

6 It cost 59/100 of one cent to purchase a dollar of goods or services.

7 There was one purchasing employee for every 329 institution employees.

8 There was one purchasing employee for every $30 million of revenue.

9 There were $6.5 million purchases per purchasing employee.

10 Each professional purchasing employee handled $12 million of purchases.

11 There were 580 active suppliers per purchasing employee.

12 Each professional purchasing employee managed 1040 active suppliers.

13 On average, each institution had two purchasing employees with a professional purchasing certification.

14 Each active supplier received $11 255 of institution purchases.

15 For each active supplier, it cost $67 to operate the purchasing function.

16 During the one year reporting period, the number of active suppliers that account for 90% of total purchase dollars decreased by 0.7%.

17 Of all active suppliers, 21% received 90% of total purchase dollars.

18 Minority-owned suppliers received 3% of total purchase dollars.

19 Women-owned suppliers received 3.4% of total purchase dollars.

20 Small business suppliers received 25% of total purchase dollars.

21 During the one year reporting period, the number of active suppliers that account for 90% of total purchase transactions increased by 0.77%.

22 Of all active suppliers, 35% received 90% of total purchase transactions.

23 The average purchase order cycle time was 5 days; the average purchase order cycle time for transactions requiring formal bids was 22 days; the average purchase order cycle time for informal transactions was 4 days.

24 Electronic data interchange (EDI) was used to process 3% of total purchase dollars.

25 Small order systems that allow departments to purchase independently were present in 83% of all institutions; the dollar limit per small order transaction was $535; 7% of purchase dollars were processed through the small order system; 43% of purchase transactions were processed through the small order system.

26 The average mandatory dollar threshold required for formal sealed bids was $11 126.

Figure 12.4   *CAPS summary of higher education benchmarks*

One response to this has been the Benchmarker service devised by Purchasing Index (UK) Ltd in association with the Chartered Institute of Purchasing and Supply. In addition to the more usual quantitative measures of activities and transactions, this attempts to provide a means of comparison at a more strategic level. Questions are raised on organizational aspects, purchasing strategies, use of manuals and procedures, and management perspective of procurement's contribution, as well as performance measurement. It sets out to provide answers for top management on:

● What does procurement really cost?
● What value does the procurement unit add to the supply chain?

- Are there alternatives to an in-house procurement unit?
- How do other organizations manage procurement?
- If more is spent on procurement, will input prices be reduced?
- How can the procurement unit's performance be measured?

Supply managers with access to a consortium or structured buying group have some opportunities to share and compare information if there is an open working relationship between partners. Conferences and professional meetings can bring access to comparisons for others. Visits to the supply management function in customers and suppliers, and working together on bidders' conferences and the like will steadily develop and spread best practice. However without some form of objective third-party overview, there will always be the danger of the 'angler's school of benchmarking' (Hewitt 1995):

> Buyers talking about price, of course, is a bit like fishermen bragging about the one that got away – always entertaining but rarely true.

13 Final conclusions

A career in the supply management function will never be other than demanding with the tremendous challenge of playing a full role in the strategic planning of the organization. Supply management has come a long way from simply buying low-value raw materials and basic services. Managing external resources requires another dimension to the normal general management skills. Techniques like managing by walking around are just not possible, other than with a very few key suppliers. Indeed the job of strategic supply management has even gone beyond the need to provide a means of managing the complex and vital range of external resources on which today's successful organization depends so heavily. Daniel Jones and Richard Lamming (1993) have described it as 'relationship management'. All aspects of the buying organization need to learn how to couple up with its supplier base across the whole range of functions. In many cases the supplier community needs to be taught how best to sell their products and open up their capability, to the long-term advantage of both organizations.

There is first and foremost a requirement to realize and accept the increasing importance of strategic supply management. Changes in the business environment, rapidly accelerating technological breakthroughs, and the crumbling of national trade barriers are all combining to force organizations to become more efficient and innovative to survive and succeed in global markets. These revolutionary changes should force top management to re-examine its expectations of supply management. No longer can products be launched which are viable throughout their life cycle, without careful regard to the supply aspects of the materials and components which go into them. The structure of the organization will be changed to reflect this realignment of strategic awareness. Supply management will move from negotiating and processing purchase orders and contracts, through the enlarged responsibilities of supply chain management, towards the really key role of designing and developing the value stream itself.

The new supply management function must call on a broad range of power tools to implement its strategic role. These are used in a context of the culture of the common purpose, with strategic negotiation focused sharply on the longer term. The traditional adversarial approach with its complete lack of trust and focus on the winning of as many tactical skirmishes as possible, can never achieve the sort of relationship with suppliers that brings maximum advantage. Only when supply management leads the way by working with suppliers as partners can the emphasis be firmly put on working together to meet requirements and develop new advantages. Supply management can only make a recognized, and measurably cost effective contribution to the success of the overall organization when the relationship with suppliers is properly managed.

We should no longer fear interference from designers, production engineers or scientists, in doing our work 'dealing with outside suppliers'. In fact we should actively encourage the multiple channels of contact, so that well-informed decisions can be taken and fully supported where the best strategy is not to do or make it ourselves, but to harness the skills, expertise, and investment of a specialist in what is for us, a non-core activity. In this way we can create a supplier base of the right size with a high proportion having the top rating for quality, delivery, service, responsiveness, contribution to innovation, and value for money. Our organization will be able to provide the informed specifications, authorization, and ongoing support to ensure that the capabilities of the supplier base are fully understood, and that our requirements of them are clearly communicated and realized.

The empowerment and training of staff is vitally important. However they must be good staff who are prepared to accept change and to take on new and expanded responsibilities with enthusiasm. Those who prefer the past and work hard to resist any new ideas require patience, but they only deserve so much. The actions and attitudes of people within supply management will be a powerful signal both internally and externally as to the importance and ability of the function. Access to professional qualifications and general staff development workshops ensure that skills and knowledge are built up. Regular, formalized weekly group meetings provide the mechanism to work slowly but steadily along the continuous improvement path.

People do work better when they are happy and fulfilled, working comfortably to clear published procedures with the opportunity and the techniques to search out and correct the root causes of problems and thus prevent their recurrence. Training must go out beyond the edges of the supply management team. Instead of keeping all our expertise to ourselves, we must share it across the other functions or they will not understand their role in the new relationship with suppliers. The open kimono must be extended internally as well as with our external partners.

Time, risk, and cost are three vital elements that can either be barriers or strengths in the path ahead. As the proportion of any organization's dependence on external resources grows steadily, so the contribution from outside increases in either positive or negative sense. We can work closely with suppliers to examine and understand all the implications and opportunities contained within these three critical factors, and to exploit and develop the power tools available to do the job. These tools can be effectively adopted either as a toolkit deployed by a well established strategic supply management function, or one at a time by a knowledgeable buyer working to establish a higher level role for the purchasing department. Steady, gradual, successful application even if seemingly piecemeal at first, builds confidence and awareness both in the external supplier base and among the other internal functions. Before long the transition from clerical to strategic will begin to take shape.

The influence and impact of global marketing can no longer be avoided. The retail shops in the high street, the vehicles on the roads, the facilities management service providers, come from all over the earth. There is no protected home market anymore, and there probably never will be again. Supply management must lift its search above the horizon, and demand world-class standards from all its suppliers, whether small and local or huge and far distant.

Making it work means making the time and commitment necessary. The old adage of the woodcutter who had so many trees to cut down that he could not spare the time to sharpen his axe, can be applied to many supply management departments. Flying by the seat of your pants is all very well if someone else is paying for the fuel, but if you want and feel the responsibility to contribute to your organization's future, there needs to be time set aside to make a plan and set up the controls, performance evaluation and feedback necessary to make it work effectively and to maximum advantage. The key requirements of time allocation, training, preparation and commitment can still let you down unless one crucial element is missing. Above all else you need to enjoy it. The 'Apparent Interest Index' will soon betray role play. Your own supply management team, the suppliers, and the other functions in the organization will be much more convinced and won-over by a relaxed smile, than any amount of strategic dogma.

Working in supply management is a very important career, with a clear strategic role, but it is also great fun. Use the toolkit at every opportunity, but most of all enjoy it!

Bibliography

Ackoff, R. L., (1970) *A Concept of Corporate Planning*, John Wiley.

Adamson J., (1980) Corporate long range planning must include procurement, *Journal of Purchasing and Materials Management*, Spring, pp. 25–32.

Aggarwal S. C., (1982) Thinking ahead: Prepare for continual material shortages, *Harvard Business Review*, May–June, pp. 6–10.

Albaum, G., Strandskov, J., Duerr, E. and Dowd, L., (1989) *International Marketing and Export Management*, Addison Wesley.

Ansari, A. and Modarress, B., (1990) *Just-In-Time Purchasing*, The Free Press.

Argenti, J., (1974) *Systematic corporate planning*, Van Nostrand Reinhold.

Arnold, U., (1989) Global Sourcing: An Indispensable Element in Worldwide Competition, *Management International Review*, **29**, No. 4, April.

Baily, P. and Farmer, D., (1990) *Purchasing Principles and Management*, Chapman and Hall, 6th edn.

Baker, E. L., (1980) Managing organizational culture, *Management Review*, July, pp. 52–70.

Barr C., (1993) A code of ethics: good bad or indifferent, *Proceedings of the 2nd PSERG conference*, pp. 19–26.

Batchelor, J., Donnelly, T. and Morris, D., (1994) A Lean Future for SME Suppliers and Sub-contractors?, *Proceedings of 3rd IPSERA Conference*, University of Glamorgan, pp. 11–39.

Belasco J., (1990) *Teaching the Elephant to Dance*, Hutchison Business Books.

Bernard, K. N. and Rajagopal, S., (1992) Integrated Marketing and Procurement: A conceptual approach for profitability', in Grunert, K. and Fuglede, D. (eds), *Proceedings of the 21st annual conference of the European Marketing Academy*, Aarhus: Denmark, pp. 1229–32.

Briggs, P., (1994) Vendor Assessment for Partners in Supply, *European Journal of Purchasing and Supply Management*, **1**, March, pp. 49–59, Oxford: Butterworth-Heinemann.

Burt, D. N. and Doyle, M. F., (1991) Strategic supply management: prerequisite to world-class manufacturing, *Industry Forum*, American Management Association, October, pp. 1–3.

Burt, D. N. and Doyle, M. F., (1993) *The American Keiretsu*, BusinessOne/Irwin.

Burt, D. N., Norquist, W. E. and Anklesaria, J., (1990) *Zero based* pricing^{TM}: *Achieving world class competitiveness through reduced all-in-costs'*, Probus Publishing Company.

Business Week, (1987a) The meaner and leaner sit down to just desserts, *International Business Week*, McGraw-Hill, 9 February, pp. 28–29.

Business Week, (1987b) 'Xerox rethinks itself: And this could be the last time', 13 February, pp. 90–93.

Business Week, (1991) Whirlpool goes off on a world tour, 3 June, pp. 99–100.

Business Week, (1991) Honeywell is finally tasting the sweet life, 3 June, p. 34.

Business Week, (1991) IBM and Apple: Can two loners learn to say teamwork? 22 July, p. 25, commentary by Depke, D.

Business Week, (1992) Compaq: The making of a comeback, 2 November, pp. 66–73.

Cardozo, R. N. and Cagley J. W., (1971) Experimental Study of Industrial Buyer Behaviour, *Journal of Marketing Research*, **8**, August, pp. 329–334.

Carlisle, J. A. and Parker R. C., (1989) *Beyond Negotiation, Redeeming Customer–Supplier Relationships*. John Wiley.

Carroll, P., (1993) *Big Blues: The Unmaking of IBM*, Crown Publishers.

Carter, J. R. and Narasimhan, R., (1990) Purchasing in the International Market Place: Implications for Operations, *Journal of Purchasing and Materials Management*, Summer, pp. 2–11.

Cavinato J., (1987) Purchasing performance: What makes the magic?, *Journal of Purchasing and Materials Management*, Fall, pp.10–15.

Chadwick, T. D., (1993) Bidders' conferences – bringing suppliers into the fold to reduce costs and to win new business, *Purchasing and Supply Management*, November, pp. 34–36.

Chadwick, T. D., (1994) Partnerships and preferred supplier arrangements - do they just happen or are they created to order?, *Proceedings of the 3rd International Purchasing and Supply Education and Research Association conference*, pp. 75–83.

Copley T. P. and Callom F. L., (1971) Industrial Search Behaviour and Perceived Risk, *Proceedings of 2nd Annual Conference Association for Consumer Research*, Gardner D. M. (ed.), College Park: University of Maryland, pp. 208–31.

Cousins, P. D., (1993) A framework for the selection, implementation, measurement and management of partnership sourcing strategies: a multiple criteria objective modelling approach, Working Paper, School of Management, University of Bath. Reported in Briggs, P., (1994).

Crosby L. A. and Stephens N. J., (1987) Effects of Relationship

Marketing on Satisfaction, Retention, and Prices in the Life Insurance Industry, *Journal of Marketing Research*, **24**, November, pp. 404–411.

Crow, L. E., Olshavsky, R. W. and Summers J. O., (1980) Industrial Buyers' Choice Strategies: A Protocol Analysis, *Journal of Marketing Research*.

Daniels, J. P. and Radebaugh L. H., (1989) Ford in Europe – The Early Years, *International Business*, Addison Wesley.

Davies, J., (1994) A comparative investigation into the supplier selection criteria adopted by business organisations based in the UK and the traditionally based British firm, *Proceedings of the 3rd International Purchasing and Supply Education and Research Conference*, pp. 85–90.

Davis, H. L., Eppen, G. D., and Mattson, L. G., (1974) Critical factors in worldwide purchasing, *Harvard Business Review*, Nov./Dec., pp. 81–90.

Dicken, P., (1992) *Global Shift: The Internationalism of Economic Activity*, Paul Chapman, 2nd edn.

Dickson, G., (1966) An Analysis of Vendor Selection Systems and Decisions, *Journal of Purchasing*, **2**, pp. 5–17.

Doyle, M., (1989) Strategic purchasing can make or break an arm, Strategic Purchasing Executive Viewpoint, *Electronic Business*, March, Cahners.

Drucker, P. F., (1955) *The Practice of Management*, William Heinemann.

Drucker, P. F., (1963) Managing for business effectiveness, *Harvard Business Review*, May/June, p. 563.

Drucker, P.F., (1992) *Managing the Future*, Oxford: Butterworth-Heinemann.

Dunning, J. H. (1973) The determinants of international production, *Oxford Economic Papers*, **25**, no. 3.

Dwyer F. R., Schurr, P. and Oh, S., (1987) Developing Buyer–Seller Relationships, *Journal of Marketing*, **51**, April, pp. 11–22.

Edwardes, M., (1983) *Back from the Brink*, William Collins.

Electronics Purchasing, (1989) Global sourcing grows more complex, *Gardner*, F. (ed.) February.

Ellrom L. M., (1991) A managerial guideline for the development and implementation of purchasing partnerships, *International Journal of Purchasing and Materials Management*, **27**, No. 3, Summer, pp. 2–8.

Ernst & Young, (1993) Good Management of Purchasing – A report for the committee of Vice-Chancellors and Principals and the Standing Conference of Principals, The Higher Education Funding Council for England.

Erridge, A. and Perry, S., (1993) Closing the skills gap: the National Standards Development Programme and purchasing competence', *Management Education and Development*, 24, Part 4, pp. 368–387.

Fagan, M. L., (1991) A guide to global sourcing, *The Journal of Business Strategy*, March/April, pp. 21–25.

Farmer, D. H., (1970) *The impact upon traditional construction of packaging methods and the use of components*, UMIST.

Farmer, D. H., (1972) The impact of supply markets on corporate planning, *Long Range Planning*, March, pp. 10–15.

Farmer, D.H., (1974) Purchasing Myopia, *Journal of General Management*, Winter, pp. 15–25.

Farmer, D., (1992) Conference Dinner Address, *Proceedings of the 1st Purchasing and Supply Education and Research Group conference*, University of Strathclyde.

Fombrun C. J., (1992) *Turning Points Creating Strategic Change in Corporations*, McGraw-Hill.

Fonfara, K. and Bernard, K. N., (1989) Cooperative development and commercial internationalisation: An appraisal of recent transfers of technology between Poland and developed industrialised countries, *Proceedings of the 18th conference of the European Marketing Academy*, Athens.

Furlong, P., Lamont, F. and Cox, A., (1993) Competition or Partnership: CCT and EC Public Procurement Rules in the Single Market, *Proceedings of the second PSERG Conference*, Bath, pp. 61–73.

Galbraith, J. and Kazanjian, R., (1986) *Strategy Implementation*, West Publishing Co.

Gersick, C. J. C., (1991) Revolutionary change theories: A multilevel exploration of the punctuated equilibrium paradigm, *Academy of Management Review*, 16, pp. 10–36.

Ginsberg, A., (1988) Measuring and modelling changes in strategy: Theoretical foundations and empirical directions, *Strategic Management Journal*, 9, pp. 559-75.

Greiner, L. L. and Bhambri, A., (1989) New CEO intervention and dynamics of deliberate strategic change, *Strategic Management Journal*, 10, pp. 67–86.

Gronhaug, K., (1977) Exploring a complex organisational buying decision, *Industrial Marketing Management*, 6, December, pp. 439–444.

Haig, R. M., (1926) Towards an understanding of the metropolis, *Quarterly Journal of Economics*, 40, pp. 421–433.

Hakan, H. and Wootz, B., (1975) Supplier selection in an international environment: An experimental study, *Journal of Marketing Research*, 12, February, pp. 46–51.

Hakansson, H., (ed.) (1983) *International marketing and purchasing of industrial goods, an interaction approach*, Wiley.

Hamel, G. and Prahaled, C., (1989) Strategic intent, *Harvard Business Review*, May–June, pp. 63–76.

Hamill, J., (1991) Global Marketing, MSc in International Marketing by Open Learning, University of Strathclyde Press.

Hanafee, P. L., (1984) The role of purchasing and materials management in international trade, *Journal of Purchasing and Materials Management*, Summer, pp. 7-13.

Handscombe, R. and Norman, P., (1989) *Strategic Leadership: The Missing Links*, McGraw-Hill.

Handy, C., (1994) *The Empty Raincoat – Making Sense of the Future*, Hutchinson.

Hefler, D., (1988) Global Sourcing, *Journal of Business Strategy*, Summer, **24**, pp. 7–12.

Hewitt, D., (1995) The consortium option, *Purchasing and Supply Management*, January, pp. 32–3.

Higgins, J. C. (1980) *Strategic and Operational Planning Systems: Principles and Practice*, Prentice Hall.

Hines, P., (1994) *Creating World Class Suppliers*, Pitman Publishing.

H.M. Department of the Environment, (1993) Buying into the environment: guidelines for integrating the environment into purchasing and supply, HMSO.

H.M. Government, (1994) *Competitiveness Helping Business to Win*, HMSO.

H.M. Treasury, (1989) Central Unit on Purchasing Guidance No.14 Measuring Performance in Purchasing, HMSO.

H.M. Treasury, (1992) PURSUIT, HMSO.

Hofer, C. and Schendell, D., (1978) *Strategy Formulation: Analytical Concepts*, West.

Hussey D. E., (1982) *Corporate Planning: Theory and Practice*, Pergamon Press, 2nd edn.

Hutt, M. D. and Spell T. W., (1992) *Business Marketing Management*, Dryden Press, 4th edn.

Jackson, B., (1985) *Winning and Keeping Industrial Customers*, Lexington Books.

Jackson, T., (1994) Corporate camps divide and prosper, *Financial Times*, 9 March, p. 18.

Jauch, L. R. and Glueck, W. F., (1988), *Business Policy and Strategic Management*, McGraw-Hill International Editions, 5th edn.

Joag S. G., (1994) Purchasing's role in corporate management, *Proceedings of the 3rd International Purchasing and Supply Education and Research Conference*, pp. 259–274.

Joag, S. G., Scheuing, E. E. and Hagstrand, A., (1992) Transforming supplier relationships from transactions to partnerships, *Proceedings of the National Purchasing and Materials Management Research Symposium*, pp. 295–312.

Johansson, J. and Wiedersheim-Paul F., (1984) The internationalisation of the firm: 4 Swedish case studies, *Journal of Management Studies*, 2, No. 3.

Johnson, H. T. and Kaplan, R. S., (1987) *Relevance Lost – The Rise and Fall of Management Accounting*, Harvard Business School Press.

Kanter R. M., (1989a) The new managerial work, *Harvard Business Review*, November-December, pp. 85-92.

Kanter R. M., (1989b) *When Giants Learn to Dance*, Simon and Schuster.

Keegan W. J., (1989) *Global marketing management*, 4th edn., Prentice Hall.

Kirkland R. J., (1988) The great rebound: Britain is back, *Fortune*, May 9.

Knox, S. O. and Denison, T. J., (1989) Innovation and inter-company technology transfer: an alternative research paradigm, *Proceedings of the annual MEG conference*.

Lamming R., (1993) *Beyond Partnership - Strategies for Innovation and Lean Supply*, Prentice Hall International (UK).

Lee-Mortimer A., (1993) A Dynamic Collaboration, *The TQM Magazine*, February, 1993 pp. 31–34.

Leonard, R., (1986) Ratios and Indices for measuring overall performance, *Purchasing and Supply Management*, March, pp. 28–32.

Levitt, T., (1983) *The Marketing Imagination*, The Free Press.

Macbeth, D. K., (1994) The role of purchasing in a partnering relationship, *European Journal of Purchasing and Supply Management*, 1, March, pp. 19–25, Oxford: Butterworth-Heinemann.

McGrath, M. and Hoole, R., (1992) Manufacturing's new economics of scale, *Harvard Business Review*, May–June, pp. 94–102.

Machiavelli, N., 1469–1527, *The Prince*.

Miles, L. D., (1972) *Techniques of Value Analysis and Engineering*, McGraw-Hill.

Miles, R., (1989) Adopting to technology and competition: a new industrial relations system for the 21st century, *California Management Review*, Winter, pp. 9–28.

Monczka, R. M., (1989) Are you aggressive enough for the 1990s?, *Purchasing*, Morgan J. P. (ed.), 16 April, pp. 50–56.

Monczka, R. M. and Guinipero L., (1984) Purchasing internationally: Managing worldwide procurement, Research paper series, Graduate School of Business Administration, Michigan State University, p. 64.

Monczka, R. M. and Trent R. J., (1993) *Cross-functional Sourcing Team Effectiveness*, Center for Advanced Purchasing Studies.

Nelson, D., (1992) Building Strategic Long-Term Supplier Relationships, Strategic Supply Management Forum VII, University of San Diego.

Nock, O. S., (1958) *Railway Race to the North*, Ian Allan.

Osborne, D., and Gaebler, T., (1992) *Reinventing Government*, Addison Wesley.

Peters, T., (1988) Creating the fleet-footed organisation', *Industry Week*, April 18, pp. 18-22.

Peters, T. and Austin, N., (1985) *A Passion for Excellence – The Leadership Difference*, Random House.

Peters, T., (1991) The Boundaries of Business: Partners – The Rhetoric and Reality, *Harvard Business Review*, September–October, pp. 97–9.

Porter, M. E., (1985) *Competitive Advantage*, The Free Press.

Porter, M. E., (ed.) (1986) *Competition in Global Industries*, Harvard Business School Press.

Porter, M. E., (1990) *Competitive Advantage of Nations*, Macmillan.

Procter and Gamble Ltd, (undated) Total Quality Management, a development programme for the University of Edinburgh, The University of Edinburgh, Personnel Office.

Qua, C. F. and Thain, T.C., (1991) Procurement from Asia: Emerging sources in S.E. Asia', *76th international purchasing conference proceedings*, NAPM, pp. 219–22.

Rajagopal S. and Bernard K.N., (1992) 'Integrated marketing and procurement: A conceptual approach for profitability', *Proceedings of the 21st annual conference of the European marketing academy*, Aarhus, Denmark, p. 1229.

Rajagopal, S. and Bernard K. N., (1993) Cost containment strategies: Challenges for strategic purchasing in the 1990s, *International Journal of Purchasing and Materials Management*, Winter, **29**, No. 1, pp. 17–24.

Rajagopal, S. and McDermott, M., (1992) Internationalisation of the purchasing process: A conceptual view, *Proceedings of the first purchasing and supply education and research group conference*, **2**.

Ralf, M. and Hughes J., (1994) 'Transforming the purchasing process', *Purchasing and Supply Management*, March.

Richardson, P. C., (1988) *Cost Containment: The Ultimate Advantage*, The Free Press.

Rugman, A. M., Lecraw, D. J. and Booth L., (1985) *The International Business Firm and the Environment*, McGraw-Hill.

Rugman, A. M., Lecraw, D. J. and Booth L., (1988) *International Business: Firm and Environment*, McGraw-Hill International Editions, 3rd edn.

Scheuing E. E., (1989) *Purchasing Management*, Englewood Cliffs, Prentice Hall, 7th ed.

Schneiderman A. M., (1988) Setting quality goals, *Quality Progress*, April, pp. 51–7.

Schonberger, R. (1986) *World Class Manufacturing: The Lessons of Simplicity Applied*, The Free Press.

Shapiro B., (1985) Towards effective supplier management: International comparisons', Harvard University Working Paper Series.

Singapore Trade Development Report, (1991).

Smiles S., (1985) *Self Help*, reprinted by Penguin Books (1986).

Speckman, R. and Johnston, W., (1986) Relationship management: Managing the selling and buying interface, *Journal of Business Research*, **14**, December, pp. 519–33.

Terpstra, V., (1978) *International Marketing*, Hinsdale, Illinois: The Dryden Press.

Thackray, J., (1986) American vertical cutback, *Management Today*, June.

The Quality Improvement Company, (1989) *Making Quality Happen*, Quality Improvement Team Reference Manual.

Tichy, N. and Devanna, M., (1986) *The Transformational Leader*, Wiley.

Townsend, P. L. and Gebhart, J. E., (1990) *Commit to Quality*, John Wiley.

Townsend, R., (1970) *Up the Organisation*, Michael Joseph.

Tulip, S., (1991) FM - all the hits!, *Purchasing and Supply Management*, September, pp. 22–3.

Webster, F. and Wind, Y., (1972) *Organizational Buying Behaviour*, Prentice Hall.

Weir, D., (1992) Organisation in the year 2000: Strategy, skill, space and timing, *6th annual conference of the British Academy of Management*.

Weisan, S., Hampton J. J., Yang, W. L. Y., and Wagner, C. L., (1987) China's foreign trade marketing strategy: Problems and prospects, *Journal of Marketing Management*, **2**, no. 3.

Westing, J., Fine, I. V. and Zenz, C. J., (1969) *Purchasing Management*, John Wiley.

Wheelen, T. L. and Hunger, J. D., (1989) *Strategic Management and Business Policy*, 3rd Edn, Addison Wesley.

White, F. M. and Locke, E. A., (1981) Perceived detriments of high and low productivity in three occupational groups: A critical incident study, *Journal of Management Studies*, **18**, (4) pp. 375–87.

Williams, I. and Alderson, R., (1992) Partnership Sourcing - a Healthy Marriage?, *Proceedings of the 1st Conference Purchasing & Supply Education & Research Group*, **2**, University of Strathclyde.

Womack, J. P. and Jones, D. T., (1994) From Lean Production to the Lean Enterprise, *Harvard Business Review*, March–April, pp. 93–103.

Womack, J. P., Jones, D. T. and Roos, D., (1990) *The Machine that Changed the World*, Rawson Associates, New York.

World Bank Report, (1991) Trade and industry logistics in developing countries, Peter, H. J.

Wriston, W. B., (1990) The state of American management, *Harvard Business Review*, January–February, pp. 78–83.

Yeoh, P. L. and Cavusgil, S. T. (1990) Global sourcing entry strategies: A contingency approach based on transaction cost analysis, *Proceedings of the Summer American Marketing Association conference*, pp. 350–354.

Young, S., Hamill, J., Wheeler, C. N. and Davies, J. R., (1989) *International Market Entry and Development: Strategies and Management*, Harvester Wheat Sheaf.

Index